Materials and Techniques
of Twentieth-Century Music

Stefan Kostka
University of Texas at Austin

PRENTICE HALL, *Englewood Cliffs, New Jersey 07632*

Library of Congress Cataloging-in-Publication Data

Kostka, Stefan M.
    Materials and techniques of twentieth-century music / Stefan
Kostka.
      p.   cm.
    Bibliography: p.
    Includes index.
    ISBN 0-13-560830-9
    1. Composition (Music)   I. Title.
MT40.K8 1989
781.3'09'04--dc20   89-3982
                                                       CIP
                                                       MN

Editorial/production supervision
  and interior design: *Carole Brown
  and Patricia V. Amoroso*
Cover design: *20/20 Services*
Manufacturing buyer: *Raymond Keating*

© 1990 by Prentice-Hall, Inc.
A Division of Simon & Schuster
Englewood Cliffs, New Jersey 07632

Printed in the United States of America

10 9 8 7 6 5 4 3 2 1

ISBN 0-13-560830-9

Prentice-Hall International (UK) Limited, *London*
Prentice-Hall of Australia Pty. Limited, *Sydney*
Prentice-Hall Canada Inc., *Toronto*
Prentice-Hall Hispanoamericana, S.A., *Mexico*
Prentice-Hall of India Private Limited, *New Delhi*
Prentice-Hall of Japan, Inc., *Tokyo*
Simon & Schuster Asia Pte. Ltd., *Singapore*
Editora Prentice-Hall do Brasil, Ltda., *Rio de Janeiro*

For my mother and father

Contents

7 Form in Twentieth-Century Music   144

8 Influences from the Past, the Present, the Exotic   164

9 Nonserial Atonality 183

10 Classical Serialism 206

11 Timbre and Texture: Acoustic 231

12 Timbre and Texture: Electronic 256

Preface

Instruction in music theory at the college level has for many years been concerned primarily with the music of the tonal era, spanning roughly some 300 years and including the Baroque, Classical, and Romantic periods. The reasons for this are not hard to imagine. After all, the masterworks that are our steady diet as concertgoers and performers almost invariably were composed during that time, some significant exceptions such as concert-band music notwithstanding. And probably no one who has studied the tonal system in depth has failed to be impressed with what must surely rank as one of the greatest of mankind's artistic achievements.

But the achievements of the twentieth century have also been of great significance, and theorists in recent years have shown interest in devoting more instructional time to the music of this century. One problem, however, has been the lack of appropriate instructional materials. While there are several fine books available on twentieth-century music, none of them deals with the topic in a way that seems appropriate for the general music student, and it is this need that the present text is intended to meet.

Materials and Techniques of Twentieth-Century Music is organized primarily by compositional technique and only partly chronologically. Most chapters deal with some aspect of music (rhythm, for instance) throughout the twentieth century, but there is a quasi-chronological method in the ordering of the chapters. No attempt is made in the text to teach music history per se or to explore in detail the styles of individual composers. Instead, the emphasis is on musical materials and compositional techniques. Each chapter includes an introduction, several subheaded sections, and a summary. The discussions are illustrated by a large number of musical examples drawn from the music literature of this century. With few exceptions, all of the examples are currently available on recording, and as many of them as possible should be listened to. The last part of each chapter consists of exercise material that in most cases is divided into four subsections: Fundamentals, Analysis, Composition, and Further Reading. (See the Bibliography for complete bibliographical references for notes and Further Reading assignments.) Most teachers will find that there are more exercises than they can make use of profitably.

Materials and Techniques of Twentieth-Century Music is appropriate for a twentieth-century unit as short as several weeks or as long as a year. In the former case, the author suggests omitting some of the chapters that are less vital for a short overview—perhaps Chapters 1, 7, 8, 11, 13, and 15, for example, depending on the interests of the instructor and students. A short course would also have to omit most of the exercise material, but the usefulness of these exercises for class drills and discussion should not be overlooked. Few teaching situations would allow the thorough study of every chapter and the completion of all of the exercises. Some of the Further Reading exercises, in particular, are appropriate only for the more advanced and highly motivated student. Another point to keep in mind is that some chapters (9 and 10, for instance) require more time than the average to complete successfully, while others (such as 8 and 15) require less.

I benefited substantially in the development of this book from the critiques provided by my students at the University of Texas at Austin, and I am grateful for their sympathetic and helpful evaluations. David Rains was generous in sharing his expertise in the area of electronic music, while Mary Blackman applied her considerable organizational skills to the task of obtaining permissions. Thanks go as well to the staff of the Fine Arts Library of the University of Texas, and especially to Olga Buth and Karl Miller, for their expertise and assistance. Finally, it would have been much less easy to persevere to the completion of this project without the love and encouragement of my friend and companion, Mary Robertson.

STEFAN KOSTKA   *University of Texas at Austin*

1

The Twilight
of the Tonal System

INTRODUCTION

Before beginning our study of the materials of twentieth-century music, we should first look back at what happened to the system of triadic tonality, the primary organizing force in the music of the preceding three centuries. Tonal music and the principles that govern it did not develop overnight, of course, nor did they decline overnight. In fact, tonal music still abounds today in music for television and film, commercials, jazz, popular music, and so forth. But it is safe to say that by around 1900 the tonal system had been so strained by chromaticism and by the desire for originality that further development of the system seemed impossible. The situation was not unlike the one that prevailed around 1600, when the intervallic modal system of the Renaissance had run its course and was giving way to a new emphasis on harmony and what eventually emerged as triadic major/minor tonality. At both points in music history lively debates occurred in print and in person, and at both times there were composers who faithfully held to the older style while others rushed to develop the new. The cause of this crisis at the beginning of the modern era—the decline of the tonal system as an organizing force—is the subject of this chapter.

DIATONIC TONAL MUSIC

Almost all of the music of the seventeenth and eighteenth centuries is essentially diatonic on all levels.[1] Diatonic tonal music does not, of course, lack accidentals or altered tones; after all, there exists hardly any tonal music of any length that does not contain altered tones. But in diatonic tonal music the difference between diatonic and altered tones is always clear, and seldom do we lose our tonal bearings, our sense of key and scale, and our immediate understanding of the function of the altered tones.

Diatonic relationships also prevail at the background levels of a diatonic tonal composition. Think of the keys that Bach is apt to reach in the course of a fugue, or the traditional key schemes for sonata forms and rondos. All represent diatonic relationships because in all cases the secondary tonalities are closely related to the primary tonality of the movement. Remember that the keys closely related to some primary key are those keys represented by the *diatonic* major and minor triads in the primary key. In a major key, ii, iii, IV, V, and vi are closely related tonics; in a minor key, III, iv, v, VI, and VII are closely related tonics.

Even at the highest level—key relationships between movements—diatonicism prevails. For example, all of the movements of a Baroque suite will be in a single key (the ultimate in diatonicism). More interesting in terms of the present discussion are the key relationships found in multimovement works of the Classical period. In such works, the first and last movements are *always* in the same tonality (although sometimes in a different mode), and this is considered to be the key of the piece. This is a fundamental characteristic of any multimovement tonal composition. In the music of the Classical period, the tendency is for one (and only one) of the inner movements to be in some contrasting but closely related key. Some examples are shown in the list on page 3.

Only two of these works, the first of the Haydn symphonies and the third of the Beethoven quartets, exhibit a nondiatonic relationship between the key of an inner movement and the key of the piece. Both of the exceptions involve a chromatic mediant relationship (to be discussed later).

Mozart: 8 Piano Sonatas K. 330–333, 457, 545 570, 576 (1778–89)	Haydn: 6 Symphonies, Nos. 99–104 (1793–95)	Beethoven: 6 String Quartets, Op. 18 (1800)
I–IV–I	I–III–I–I	I–vi–I–I
I–I–I	I–IV–I–I	I–IV–I–I
I–IV–I	I–IV–I–I	I–♭VI–I–I
I–IV–I	I–V–I–I	i–I–i–i
i–III–i	I–vi–I–I	I–I–IV–I
I–V–I	I–IV–I–I	I–IV–I–I
I–IV–I		
I–V–I		

CHROMATIC TONAL MUSIC

The point at which tonal music becomes chromatic instead of diatonic is not an absolute one. Much of the harmony of chromatic tonal music can be analyzed by using the same vocabulary for altered chords, modulations, chromatic nonchord tones, and so forth, that we use in the analysis of diatonic music. It is partly a matter of emphasis. Instead of a texture with diatonic tones predominating over nondiatonic tones, both in number and in significance, we are dealing here with music that is so saturated with chromaticism that the diatonic basis of the music is no longer apparent to the listener. One writer refers to this style as "ultrachromaticism," which "results from the prevalent use—-both harmonically and melodically—of the twelve tones of the chromatic scale."[2] Another puts it this way: "The critical distinction between the two styles lies in the transformation of the diatonic scalar material of the classical tonal system into the equally-tempered twelve note chromatic complex of the chromatic tonal system."[3] Using these broad definitions as a starting point, we will examine some of the details of nineteenth-century chromatic harmony. In one chapter our discussion cannot be as detailed as those found in several admirable books on this subject,[4] but it should be sufficient to suggest some analytical approaches to the style.

CHROMATIC HARMONY

Two fundamental root movements in diatonic tonal harmony involve (1) the circle-of-5ths progression, particularly vi–ii–V–I; and (2) the diatonic mediant progression, particularly I–vi–IV–ii. Though these progressions by no means disappear in chromatic harmony, another relationship, the *chromatic mediant relationship*, finds a popularity that it did not have in earlier styles. Two triads or keys are in a chromatic mediant relationship if they are of the same quality (major or minor) and their roots are a major 3rd or minor 3rd apart. These relationships are illustrated in Example 1–1 (lowercase indicates minor). For some reason, the major-mode chromatic mediants (top staff of Example 1–1) seem to have been used more often than the minor-mode versions. Notice that in each case the two triads share exactly one pitch class.[5] Third-related triads of opposite quality (major and minor) sharing no pitch classes at all are said to be in a *doubly chromatic mediant relationship* (e.g., C major and E♭ minor).

EXAMPLE 1–1   Chromatic mediant relationships

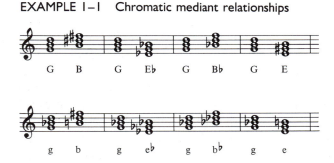

Two examples from Liszt's *Les Préludes* illustrate the effective use of chromatic mediants. In the first (Example 1–2), the relationship is not between chords, but between the keys of C major and E major. Notice that this is a *direct modulation* (one that does not make use of a common chord between the two keys), but the modulation is smoothed over by the common tone (A♭/G♯) between the F minor and E major triads at the double bar.

EXAMPLE 1–2   Liszt: *Les Préludes* (1854), mm. 51–54

Chromatic mediant relationships between triads in a nonmodulating passage contribute to the color and excitement of Example 1–3. The excerpt is clearly in C major, and it uses the following progression:

C–a–F–d–B♭–G–C–A♭–F–C

EXAMPLE 1–3   Liszt: *Les Préludes* (1854), mm. 35–42 (simplified texture)

Certainly both the circle-of-5ths and diatonic mediant progressions are important here, but the three chromatic mediant relationships (B♭–G, C–A♭, and A♭–F) add a certain freshness and unpredictability to the harmony of the passage. Incidentally, this simplified piano reduction gives only a hint of what this music is really like; try to listen to a recording with the full score.

Example 1–4 provides a further illustration of chromatic mediants, and several other things besides. Chord roots, inversions, and qualities are indicated below the sample. The progression contains two circle-of-5ths progressions (D–G and C–f and three chromatic mediants (C–A♭, G–B♭, and B♭–G♭). It also contains two *tritone relationships* (A♭–D and G♭–C), a root movement commonly found in earlier music in only a few progressions (IV– vii° in major, VI–ii° in minor, and N6–V). A listener could interpret Example 1–4 as a IV6–N6–V–I6 progression in G, followed by an identical progression in F, ending on a minor tonic. Except for the last chord, the excerpt illustrates a *real sequence*, a sequence in which the pattern is transposed exactly, as opposed to a diatonic sequence, where only the notes of a single diatonic scale are used; thus the pattern is reproduced only approximately. A real sequence has the effect of quickly throwing the music out of one key and into another, even if only for the duration of a few chords. Real sequences contribute a good deal to the *brief tonicizations* that are typical of much chromatic harmony.

EXAMPLE 1–4   Wagner: *Siegfried* (1871), Act II, Scene 1

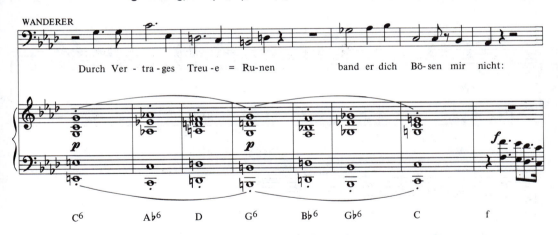

A real sequence begins Example 1–5 (mm. 1–4), using only dominant 7th chords (the last one enharmonically spelled) from the keys of D♭, B♭, E, and D♭ again. The root movements involve two chromatic mediant relationships (A♭7– F7 and B7–A♭7) and one tritone (F7–B7). Notice that in each case the dominant 7th chords share exactly two pitch classes. This is true only of dominant 7ths whose roots are separated by a minor 3rd or a tritone. Example 1–5 illustrates two more characteristics of chromatic harmony—*suspended tonality* and *enharmonicism*. The first term is used to refer to passages that are tonally ambiguous. The dominant 7th chords in Example 1–5 do little to establish any key, because they are both unexpected and unresolved, and the Ab7–C–Ab progression that ends the excerpt is of little help. Presumably Liszt had the tonality of Ab in mind, since the piece ends similarly to mm. 5–6. Play through the example, and see what you think. The enharmonicism involves the chord in m. 4. We hear all of the chords in mm. 1–4 as dominant 7th chords, but the chord in m. 4 is spelled as a German augmented-6th chord in C, resolving to a I6 instead of to the conventional tonic $^6_4$.

EXAMPLE 1–5 Liszt: "Blume und Duft" ("Flower and Fragrance") (1862), mm. 1–6

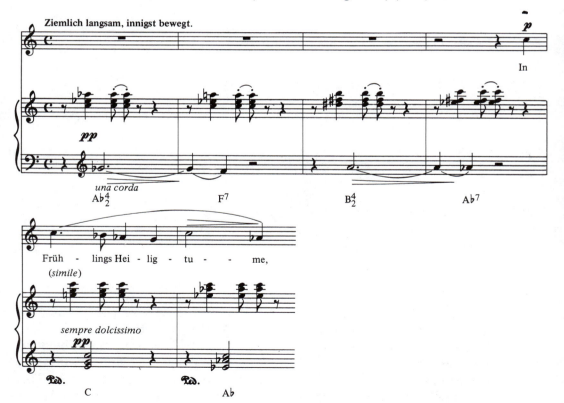

Parallel voice leading, keeping the chord type constant, is seldom found in diatonic tonal music, but it is a favored device of chromaticism. Probably the first sonority to be used in this fashion was the *diminished-7th chord*, as in Example 1–6. Here, in a passage modulating from C minor to E♭ major, four diminished 7th chords move in parallel motion down by half-steps in mm. 40–45. Notice that the spelling of the diminished-7th chords suggests that Beethoven was thinking of a circle-of-5ths progression, even though the listener might not perceive it that way:

Circle of 5ths, Using
Dominant 7th Chords

D7–G7–C7–F7

Circle of 5ths, Substituting
Diminished-7th Chords

f♯°7–b°7–e°7–a°7

EXAMPLE 1–6 Beethoven: *Coriolan Overture*, Op. 62 (1807), mm. 36–46 (simplified texture)

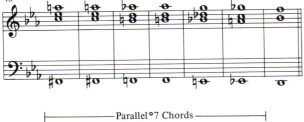

But no such functional analysis is possible in the next example. Here Wagner portrays ravens in flight by means of parallel half-diminished-7th chords, some of them enharmonically spelled. The effect is not one of a progression of chords toward a harmonic goal, but more like a line painted with a broad brush instead of drawn with a pen. Obviously, none of these chords function in the ways that half-diminished-7th chords do in diatonic

EXAMPLE 1–7   Wagner: *Götterdämmerung* (1874), Act III, Scene 2

harmony. The chords in Example 1–7 form a *nonfunctional chord succession*, which does not imply that it is useless, but rather that the chords do not "progress" in any of the ways found in diatonic tonal harmony. Such successions are often the result of what we shall call *voice-leading chords*. Such chords are the result of goal-directed motion in the various voices, rather than an attempt to express some traditional harmonic progression. This goal-directed motion is usually stepwise, often chromatic, sometimes in similar motion and sometimes not. The resulting verticalities are usually tertian (triads and 7th chords), but the chords form nonfunctional successions or brief tonicizations. For instance, play through Example 1–8. The essential elements are a chromatic descent from B4 to E4 in the top voice and B2 to E2 in the bass to make a convincing cadence.[6] The soprano is shadowed in parallel major 3rds by the alto, stopping its descent upon reaching the leading tone, which eventually resolves. The tenor enters on a C4 and moves in parallel with the upper voices for three beats, stops momentarily on Bb/A♯3, and then moves to the 7th of the dominant chord before resolving to G3. The bass enters last, doubling the soprano momentarily before moving into its cadential figure. On a higher level, the progression in this excerpt is simply tonic–dominant–tonic, beginning with the incomplete tonic triad at the opening of the phrase. But on the surface, the

EXAMPLE 1–8   Grieg: "Gone," Op. 71, No. 6 (1901), mm. 1–2   *(From Edition Peters. Used by permission.)*

chords created by the various voices, beginning with beat 2 of the first measure, are as follows (the c°7 and the F7 are enharmonically spelled):

F–E–Eb–c°7–F7–B7(b5)–e

Although there is a IV6–ii°7–V$_3^4$ progression in Bb here, it is doubtful that anyone would hear it that way. The only traditional harmonic progression in the excerpt is the final authentic cadence (with a lowered 5th in the dominant 7th creating a French 6th sonority). The music preceding the cadence makes use of voice-leading chords and creates a nonfunctional chord succession.

The voice-leading chords in Example 1–8 were created primarily by parallel or similar motion. Three independent gestures combine to produce the voice-leading chords in Example 1–9. The first is a chromatic ascent in

EXAMPLE 1–9 Liszt: "Gray Clouds" ("Nuages gris") (1881), mm. 33–48

the melody from F#4 to G5 (doubled at the octave above). The second element is an augmented triad in the inner voices (beginning in the third measure of the excerpt), which moves, more slowly than the soprano, chromatically downward through a minor 3rd. The final element is the neighbor motion in the bass, swaying back and forth from Bb2 to A2, finally settling on A. The voice-leading chords created by the combination of these three gestures are sometimes tertian and sometimes not; some of them are highly dissonant (mm. 38–39, for example). Suspended tonality is the result, even at the end, where the final sonority does little to confirm the presumed tonality of G.

Unresolved dissonances, as in the Liszt example, are typical of some late nineteenth-century music. In many cases they come about through the juxtaposition of apparently independent musical ideas (melodies, sequences, and so on) with no attempt being made to put those dissonances into any traditional context, and they often contribute to a feeling of suspended tonality.

Augmented triads and diminished-7th chords are both examples of *equal division of the octave*. Real sequences also frequently divide the octave into equal parts, usually by transposing the pattern by a minor 3rd or a major 3rd. Traditional division of the octave had been asymmetrical, as in the perfect 5th and perfect 4th of the tonic-dominant relationship and the major and minor 2nds that make up the major scale.

The music of Example 1–10 is less radical tonally than the previous example, but the voice leading is much more complex. All of the voices of the predominantly four-part texture in the piano tend to move by step, often chromatically, but there is no preconceived pattern to be discovered. The *nonfunctional bass line* does little to help us get our tonal bearings, except at the end, where a V7–I cadence in G major is apparent. Often in the excerpt the distinction between chord tones and embellishments is unclear, making chord labeling difficult. Nevertheless, if you play through the example slowly, you will notice the following:

D major tonic (m. 7)
Tonicization of A minor (E7–F in mm. 7–8)
Tonicization of Bb major (F7–Bb in m. 9)
Tonicization of C minor (G7–c in m. 10)
Modulation to G major (iv6–Ger + 6–I $^6_4$–V7–I in mm. 10–12)

A truly thorough analysis would have to consider the function, harmonic or otherwise, of all of the notes in the passage, but it will often serve the purposes of the performer or student just as well to identify the broader harmonic motions, as we have done in this case.

EXAMPLE 1-10 Hugo Wolf: "Anacreon's Grave" ("Anakreons Grab") (1888), mm. 7–12

CHROMATICISM AND MUSICAL FORM

The diatonic tonal relationships typically found within single movements in the Classical period (typically I–V or i–III) are gradually replaced in the nineteenth century with chromatic tonal relationships. While there are still many works from the nineteenth century that employ the traditional key schemes, a good number of others explore other relationships. A famous early example is the first movement of Beethoven's "Waldstein" Sonata, Op. 53, where the two keys of the exposition are C major and E major.

More destructive to the tonal system is the notion of beginning a movement in one key and ending it in another.[7] "Wrong key" beginnings, in which the listener is deliberately led astray for a few bars, constituted the first step. Examples include Beethoven's Symphony No. 1 (1799), beginning with a V7/IV, and the last movement of Mendelssohn's Piano Concerto No. 1 (1831), which begins with a short section in the supertonic key.

Still more experimental are the numerous works that seem to be in two keys. Two types can be identified. In the first, the piece contains two distinct parts, each in its own key. Examples include Schubert's Waltzes, Op. 50, Nos. 7, 24, and 31 (1825), and Chopin's Ballade No. 2, Op. 38 (1839). In the second type, the tonality of the work alternates more than once between a major key and its relative minor. Examples include Schubert's German Dance, Op. 33, No. 15, and Schumann's Davidsbündlertanz, Op. 6, No. 11 (1837).

The final stage is reached with those works that proceed through several keys, with none of them seeming to govern the tonality of the piece as a whole. Such works simply cannot be considered "tonal" in the traditional sense of the term. Examples include Liszt's symphonic poem *Orpheus* (1854) and the first movement of Saint-Saëns's Symphony No. 3 (1886).

There was also experimentation in the nineteenth century with unusual key schemes among the various movements of multimovement works. The greatest challenge to the tonal tradition came from those works in which the first and last movements are not in the same key. For instance, the three movements of Mendelssohn's Symphony No. 2 (1840) are in B♭ major, G minor, and D major. With Mahler the practice is almost a mannerism: Symphonies Nos. 2, 3, 4, 5, 7, and 9 (1894–1909) all belong to this category.

SUSPENDED TONALITY AND ATONALITY

Earlier in this chapter we used the term *suspended tonality* to describe a passage with a momentarily unclear or ambiguous tonality. This term is appropriate only when used in the context of a tonal composition. It is not the same as *atonality*, a term that will appear frequently in this text, and which needs to be defined at this point.[8]

In a very general way, atonality means music without a tonal center. More specifically, it refers to the systematic avoidance of most of those musical materials and devices that traditionally have been used to define a tonal center. Those materials and devices would include, among others, the following:

Diatonic pitch material

Tertian harmonies

Dominant–tonic harmonic progressions

Dominant–tonic bass lines

Resolution of leading tone to tonic

Resolution of dissonances to more consonant sonorities

Pedal points

Though chromaticism led historically to atonality, chromatic tonal music is not the same as atonal music. A more thorough study of atonality will have to be postponed until later chapters, although the term will come up from time to time throughout this text.

SUMMARY

The decline of the tonal system as the primary organizing force in music coincided with and was largely due to the ascendancy of chromaticism. Diatonic tonal music is essentially diatonic on all levels, whereas chromatic tonal music is based to a much greater extent on the chromatic scale. Some of the characteristics of chromatic tonal harmony are the following (listed in the order in which they are introduced in the chapter):

Chromatic mediant relationships

Direct modulations

Tritone relationships

Real sequences

Brief tonicizations

Suspended tonality

Enharmonicism

Parallel voice leading

> Diminished-7th chords
> Nonfunctional chord successions
> Voice-leading chords
> Augmented triads
> Unresolved dissonances
> Equal division of the octave
> Nonfunctional bass lines
> Unclear distinction between chord tones and embellishments

Chromaticism is also a factor in musical forms in the nineteenth century, both within and between movements. At times, tonality lost its control over the tonal structure of individual movements and multimovement works as well.

Atonality is not a characteristic of music of the nineteenth century. Atonal music avoids the use of most of those musical materials and devices that traditionally have been used to define a tonal center.

NOTES

1. "Diatonic" here simply means "in a given key." The notes and chords diatonic to C major are all drawn from the scale C–D–E–F–G–A–B–C.
2. Paul O. Harder, *Bridge to 20th Century Music*, p. 74.
3. Gregory Proctor, "Technical Bases of Nineteenth-Century Chromatic Harmony: A Study in Chromaticism," p. 131.
4. See, for example, notes 2 and 3.
5. The term "pitch class" is used to group together all pitches that have an identical sound or that are identical except for the octave or octaves that separate them. For example, all B♯'s, C's, and D♭♭'s belong to the same pitch class, no matter in what octave they are found.
6. Octave registers in this book follow the convention that names the octave starting with middle C as octave no. 4, the one below it as octave no. 3, and so on.
7. Much of the discussion that follows is based on: Sarah Reid, "Tonality's Changing Role: A Survey of Non-Concentric Instrumental Works of the Nineteenth Century" (Ph.D. diss., University of Texas, 1980).
8. There are various well-founded objections to this term. Nevertheless, it has by now attained a permanent place in our theoretical vocabulary, whereas possible improvements, such as "pantonality," have not. Also, though "atonal" is used by some writers only in reference to the preserial works of the second Viennese school, it is used in this book in its broader meaning of "not tonal."

EXERCISES

Part A: Fundamentals

1. For each triad below, list the four triads that are in a chromatic mediant relationship to it.

   B♭ major   C minor   F major   D minor   E major

2. Name several traditional chord progressions in tonal harmony that make use of chromatic mediant relationships. Use Roman numerals.

3. Which of the following progressions involves dominant 7th chords that share two pitch classes?

   V7–V7/vi   V7/ii–V7/V   V7/IV–V7/V

4. For each dominant 7th chord below, list the three dominant 7th chords that share two pitch classes with it.

   E♭7   G7   F7   C♯7

Part B: Analysis

1. Fauré: Barcarolle No. 6, Op. 70 (1896), mm. 24–28.

a. This passage begins and ends in B major, but chords 4 and 5 imply some other key, although one of them is spelled enharmonically. What key is it, and what is its relationship to B major?

b. The raised 5th in chord 6 results in how many common pitch classes between chords 5 and 6?

c. Provide Roman numerals for all of the chords.

2. Berlioz: *Requiem* (1837), mm. 66–78.

This passage modulates from B♭ major to G minor.

a. Are the keys of B♭ major and G minor in a chromatic mediant relationship?

b. Still another tonality is implied in mm. 71–74. What is it, and what is the relationship between that key and G minor?

c. Explain the construction of mm. 66–68.

d. Provide a Roman-numeral analysis in G minor of mm. 68–70 and mm. 75–78.

3. Grieg: "Summer's Eve," Op. 71, No. 2 (1901), mm. 9–19.

(From Edition Peters. Used by permission.)

    a. Label the root and chord type of each of the numbered chords (e.g., "G7," "f♯," etc.).

    b. List the tonalities implied by these chords.

    c. Which of those tonalities is confirmed by a tonic triad?

    d. The sixteenth-note figures use pitches from what tonalities?

    e. What single tonality is the most important in this passage?

    f. How many pitch classes are shared by chords 9 and 11? chords 12 and 14? chords 15 and 16?

    g. Do these shared pitch classes appear in the same register?

    h. Discuss the use of sequence in this passage.

4. Brahms: "Der Tod, das ist die kühle Nacht," Op. 96, No. 1 (1884), mm. 7–10.

    a. Analyze the first and last chords in the key of C.

    b. Label the roots and qualities of all of the other chords.

c. Assuming that second-inversion triads tend to be heard as tonic $^6_4$ chords, list all of the keys implied by dominant 7th chords or $^6_4$ chords.

d. The tonalities other than C are weakly implied, at best. Explain in your own words what is really going on in this passage.

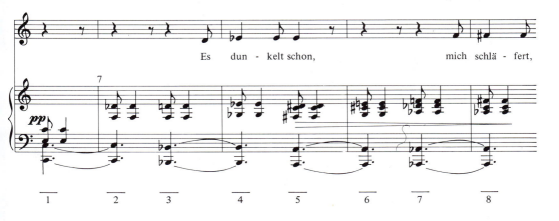

5. Wagner: *Siegfried* Act I, Scene 1.

a. Explain this passage as best you can in your own words, following the approaches used in the previous exercises and in the chapter text. Incidentally, would there be any justification for hearing the B♭ in chord no. 7 as an A♯?

Part C: Composition

1. Continue this example, using chromatic mediants above the asterisks and employing conventional voice leading.

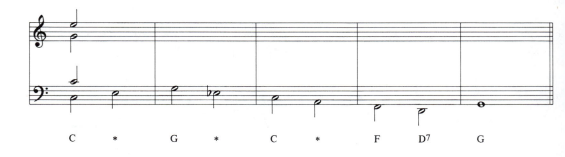

2. Wagner: *Siegfried*, Act I, Scene 2.

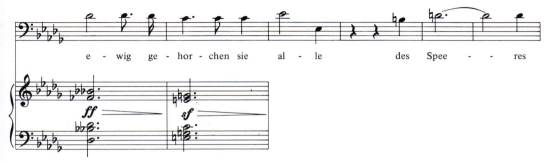

e - wig ge - hor - chen sie   al - le   des Spee - - res

Use the first two measures of this accompaniment as the first part of a three-part real sequence, moving down a minor 2nd each time. Place an asterisk between each pair of chords in a chromatic mediant relationship.

3. Using only augmented triads in a four-voice texture, see if you can combine a chromatically ascending soprano line with a circle-of-5ths sequence in the bass. Continue for several chords.

4. Compose a passage similar to Example 1–9, using a chromatically descending melody with chromatically ascending half-diminished-7th chords as an accompaniment. The accompaniment chords should be in second inversion and should ascend faster than the melody descends. Let the dissonances fall where they may.

5. Compose an example in four-part texture using a conventional harmonic progression and employing mostly stepwise motion in all of the voices. Then elaborate with a generous application of stepwise nonchord tones, especially chromatic passing tones, neighbors, and suspensions. The added tones in most cases should not create sharp dissonances (minor 2nds, major 7ths) with the chord tones or with each other. Be sure to do this work at a piano! The excerpt below can serve as an example.

Part D: Further Reading

The suggested reading assignments are intended to help you get a broader exposure to the subject of this chapter. The approach and terminology used in the texts will probably differ from each other as well as from this text. Complete bibliographical information is provided in the Bibliography at the end of this book.

ALDWELL, EDWARD, AND CARL SCHACHTER. *Harmony and Voice Leading*, Vol. 2. See Chapter 31, "Chromatic Voice-Leading Techniques," and Chapter 32, "Chromaticism in Larger Contexts."

BENWARD, BRUCE. *Music in Theory and Practice*, Vol. 2, See Chapter 14, "Chromatic Mediants."

CHRIST, WILLIAM, AND OTHERS. *Materials and Structure of Music*, Vol. 2. See Chapter 13, "Enriched Tonal Resources."

GROUT, DONALD JAY. *A History of Western Music*. See Chapter 16, "The Nineteenth Century: Romanticism; Vocal Music," Chapter 17, "The Nineteenth Century: Instrumental Music," and Chapter 18, "The Nineteenth Century: Opera and Music Drama."

HARDER, PAUL O. *Bridge to 20th Century Music*. See Chapter 4, "Expanded Tonality," Chapter 5, "Ultrachromaticism (I)," Chapter 6, "Ultrachromaticism (II)," and Chapter 7, "Denial of Harmonic Function."

KOSTKA, STEFAN, AND DOROTHY PAYNE. *Tonal Harmony*. See Chapter 27, "Tonal Harmony in the Late Nineteenth Century."

SAMSON, JIM. *Music in Transition*. See Chapter 1, "The Nineteenth-Century Background."

SHIR-CLIFF, JUSTINE, AND OTHERS. *Chromatic Harmony*. See Chapter 18, "Parallelism," Chapter 19, "Mediant Relationships," Chapter 20, "Tritone Root Relationships," and Chapter 23, "Harmonic Sequence."

SIMMS, BRYAN R. *Music of the Twentieth Century*. See Chapter 1, "Tonality in Transition."

ULEHLA, LUDMILA. *Contemporary Harmony*. See Chapter 3, "Harmonic Growth."

2

Scale Formations
in Twentieth-Century Music

INTRODUCTION

The music of the Baroque, Classical, and Romantic periods was based almost exclusively on the major and minor scales with which we are all familiar. Though these scales have not been discarded altogether, composers in this century have also made use of a large number of other scale formations. Not all of these scale formations are new—in fact, some of them had first been used centuries earlier and had since fallen out of fashion. But new or old, these scales were all unfamiliar to audiences accustomed to major/minor tonality, and so they helped the composer to distance himself from the older style.

It is unusual in the twentieth century to find an entire piece that uses only a single scale (with the exception of chromatic and microtonal scales). Instead, one typically finds that only a few measures will use a particular scale, or the melody may conform to the scale while the accompaniment does not, or the music may include only a few notes that seem to imply the scale.

The organization of this chapter is based on the number of notes in the scale; that is, five-note scales first, then six-note, and so on. (In counting the number of notes, we do not include the octave, so the major scale, for instance, is a seven-note scale.) Examples have been chosen to illustrate clearly the scales being discussed, but the reader should be aware that in much music it would be difficult to say with certainty what scale formation is the basis of a given passage.

FIVE-NOTE SCALES

"Pentatonic" is a generic term for all five-note scales, but when one refers to *the* pentatonic scale, the scale in Example 2–1 is usually the one that is meant. Notice that it uses only major seconds and minor thirds. Because this version of the pentatonic scale contains no half steps, it is sometimes called the *anhemitonic pentatonic scale*. The pentatonic scale is often used to give an oriental flavor to a passage, but it certainly occurs often enough outside of the Orient, particularly in folk melodies and children's songs.

EXAMPLE 2–1 The Pentatonic Scale

Any member of the pentatonic scale can serve as tonic; thus, five "modes," or rotations, are available.

EXAMPLE 2–2 Modes of the Pentatonic Scale

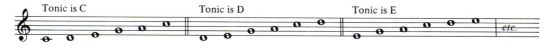

And, of course, the pentatonic scale can be transposed.

EXAMPLE 2–3 Transpositions of the Pentatonic Scale

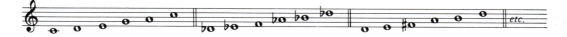

The pentatonic scale is obviously a limited source of melodic pitch material, and it is also limited in its tertian harmonies. The only tertian chords that could be constructed from Example 2–1 are triads on C and A and a minor 7th chord on A. This means that the accompaniment to a pentatonic melody will probably be either nontertian or nonpentatonic or both. In Example 2–4 Bartók harmonizes a pentatonic melody (top line in the example) with major triads, using the melody note as the root of the triad in each case. The accompaniment here uses no particular scale, although the tonality is certainly C. A few measures later, the same melody is harmonized again with major triads, but this time each melody note is the 5th of its triad. The last melody note is changed to a D, resulting in a "half-cadence" on a G chord.

EXAMPLE 2–4   Bartók: *Bluebeard's Castle* (1911) (piano reduction)   (© *Copyright 1921 by Universal Edition; Copyright Renewed. Copyright and Renewal assigned to Boosey & Hawkes, Inc. for USA only. Reprinted by permission.*)

Other versions of the pentatonic scale are possible—versions employing minor 2nds and major 3rds—but they occur less often in Western music. One example is the scale Eb–F–Gb–Bb–C, used by Ralph Vaughan Williams for the opening theme of his Concerto for Bass Tuba (1954). Another is the closing section of George Rochberg's *Slow Fires of Autumn* (1979) for flute and harp, which is based largely on the scale F–G–Ab–C–Db, presumably in this case to suggest an exotic image.

SIX-NOTE SCALES

The only six-note scale to see much use in the twentieth century is the *whole-tone scale.* It is constructed entirely from major 2nds (and a diminished 3rd, which sounds like a major 2nd). In terms of pitch-class content, only two whole-tone scales are possible; any other transposition or "mode" will simply duplicate the pitch-class content of one of the scales in Example

2–5. The actual spelling of the scale is usually irrelevant; for instance, the first scale in the example could have used G♭–A♭–B♭ instead of F♯–G♯–A♯.

EXAMPLE 2–5 Whole-Tone Scales

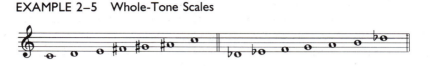

The whole-tone scale is often associated with Impressionism, and especially Debussy, but it is also found in the music of other composers. Interestingly, it is more limited both melodically and harmonically than the pentatonic scale. No major or minor triads are possible, and the only 7th chords available are the dominant 7th with the 5th lowered (the traditional French augmented-6th sonority) or raised.

Example 2–6 begins with three measures using the whole-tone scale spelled "on" B♯, followed by two measures using the whole-tone scale spelled "on" F. The listener cannot tell how the scale is spelled, of course,

EXAMPLE 2–6 Paul Dukas: *Ariadne and Bluebeard* (1906), Act III

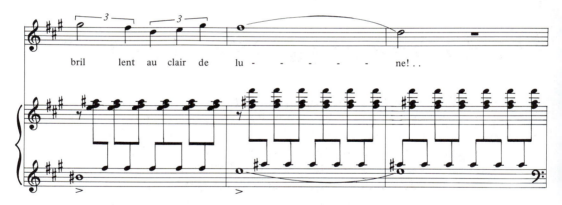

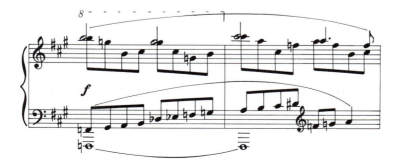

and the tonality or tonalities of the passage would be open to some interpretation.

A more recent use of the whole-tone scale is seen in Example 2–7. Here the whole-tone scale is in the vocal duet, except for the A at the end

EXAMPLE 2–7   Hans Werner Henze: *Elegy for Young Lovers* (1961), Act I, Scene 12, mm. 984–986

of Toni's melody. Notice that the pitch class G♯/A♭ is spelled one way in Hilda's part in m. 984 and another way in m. 986. The tonal center of this excerpt, if there is one, would be difficult to determine. The accompaniment will be discussed in more detail later in this chapter.

SEVEN-NOTE SCALES: THE DIATONIC MODES

Modal scales had been largely out of favor with composers since the beginning of the Baroque, although interesting exceptions, such as the Phrygian opening of Chopin's Mazurka in C♯ minor, Op. 41, No. 1 (1839), do occur. But modality was enthusiastically rediscovered by a number of early twentieth-century composers. Though the modal theory of the Renaissance recognized both authentic and plagal modes, the distinction is not important in modern usage. One way to present the modes is to notate them using the pitches of the C major scale.

EXAMPLE 2–8   The Diatonic Modes

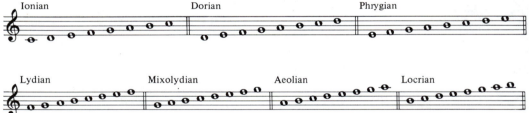

For practical purposes, we can eliminate the Ionian, since it is the equivalent of the major scale. The Locrian mode has rarely been used, probably because it lacks a consonant tonic triad. But an unusually clear use of the Locrian mode occurs in the opening of Shostakovich's String Quartet No. 10, Op. 118 (1964), second movement.

It is most efficient to learn the modes in relation to the major and natural-minor scale patterns. The following information should be memorized:

Major Modal Patterns

Lydian: same as major with raised $\hat{4}$.*
Mixolydian: same as major with lowered $\hat{7}$.

*The carat over a number indicates scale degree.

Minor Modal Patterns

Aeolian: same as natural minor.

Dorian: same as natural minor with raised $\hat{6}$.

Phrygian: same as natural minor with lowered $\hat{2}$.

Locrian: same as natural minor with lowered $\hat{2}$ and lowered $\hat{5}$.

You will not always be able to identify the scale being used just by determining the tonic and looking at the key signature, because not all composers use modal key signatures. Instead, a composer might use the conventional major or minor key signature and add the accidentals necessary to produce the modal scale desired. This is the case in Example 2–9, where we see a G minor key signature used for a G Phrygian theme. Notice the leading-tone F♯ in the viola. Such nonscale tones are as common in modal music as they are in major/minor music, and we should not let them confuse us in our analysis.

EXAMPLE 2–9   Debussy: String Quartet, Op. 10 (1893), I, mm. 1–3

EXAMPLE 2–10   Bartók: *Music for String Instruments, Percussion, and Celesta* (1936), IV, mm. 5–9
(melody only)   *(© Copyright 1937 by Universal Edition; Copyright Renewed. Copyright and Renewal assigned to Boosey & Hawkes, Inc. for USA only. Reprinted by permission.)*

There is no key signature at all for Example 2–10, the opening theme of a movement in A. The accompaniment to this Lydian tune consists only of A major triads in second inversion.

In Example 2–11 the music drifts easily from D Aeolian (mm. 1–4) into D Dorian (mm. 5–8). A change in modal flavor such as we find here is a frequently encountered device. Note that this is *not* a modulation, because the tonal center is unchanged.

EXAMPLE 2–11 Debussy: Preludes, Book I (1910), No. 6, "Footprints in the Snow" ("Des pas sur la neige") mm. 1–7

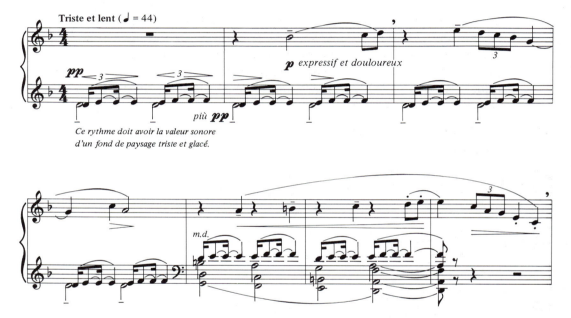

OTHER SEVEN-NOTE SCALES

Many other seven-note scales are possible, although none of them have been used as frequently as the diatonic modes. Fourteen modes can be derived from the scales shown in Example 2–12. All of them use major and minor 2nds exclusively, yet none of them is identical to any of the diatonic modes. These two scale systems, along with our familiar diatonic modal system, exhaust the possibilities for seven-note scales using only major and minor 2nds.

EXAMPLE 2–12   Two Seven-Note Scale Systems

You may expect to encounter these scale formations occasionally in twentieth-century music. The first scale in Example 2–12 was used several times by Bartók, and it has acquired the name "Lydian-Mixolydian" because of its combination of raised 4th and lowered 7th scale degrees. Debussy makes momentary use of this scale on C in the first three measures of Example 2–13. Then the G and A are replaced by A♭ in the fourth measure, resulting in a whole-tone scale.

Some seven-note scales make use of one or more augmented seconds. A familiar example is the harmonic minor scale. Example 2–14 would seem to be constructed from a G Aeolian scale with a raised fourth scale degree.

EXAMPLE 2–13   Debussy: *The Joyous Isle (L'isle joyeuse)* (1904), mm. 45–51

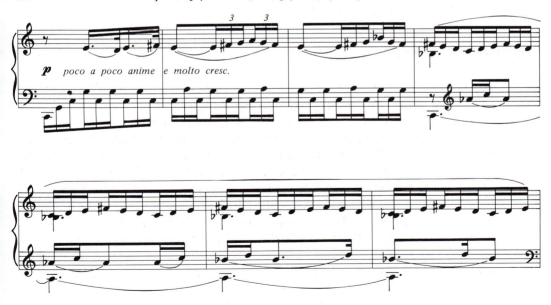

EXAMPLE 2–14   Grieg: "Shepherd Boy," Op. 54, No. 1 (1891), mm. 1–8   *(From Edition Peters. Used by permission.)*

To list all of the possibilities would be impractical.[1] It is enough to be aware that a particular passage must be approached on its own terms, not with the assumption that only certain scales are allowed.

EIGHT-NOTE SCALES

Octatonic, like *pentatonic*, is a generic term that has nevertheless come to refer to a specific scale. This scale, illustrated in Example 2–15, consists of alternating major and minor seconds, so another name for this scale is the *whole-step–half-step scale.* Yet another name is the *diminished scale*, which refers to the fact that any two nonenharmonic diminished-7th chords combined will produce an octatonic scale (in Example 2–15 they are f♯°7 and g♯°7). There are only two modes to this scale—one begins with a major 2nd, the other with a minor 2nd—and only three transpositions: the one shown, one containing C♯ and D♯, and one containing D and E. Any other transposition or mode will simply duplicate the pitch-class content of one of these three octatonic scales. The actual spelling of an octatonic scale is optional; for instance, the F♯ and G♯ in Example 2–15 could have been written as G♭ and A♭.

The octatonic scale is a rich source of melodic and harmonic material. It contains all of the intervals, from minor 2nd up to major 7th. All of the

EXAMPLE 2–15 The Octatonic Scale

tertian triads except for the augmented triad can be extracted from this scale, as can four of the five common 7th-chord types (the major-7th chord cannot). If it has a weakness, it is its symmetrical construction, a characteristic it shares with the whole-tone scale, which can make establishment of a tonal center more difficult.

Certain nineteenth-century Russian composers, notably Rimsky-Korsakov, were among the first to make use of the octatonic scale. An excerpt from a twentieth-century Russian work appears as Example 2–16. In this passage Scriabin uses the octatonic scale formed by diminished-7th chords on A and A♯ (or C and C♯, etc.—the spellings are arbitrary). The tonality here, if there is one, would seem to be E♭.

EXAMPLE 2–16 Alexander Scriabin: Prelude, Op. 74, No. 5 (1914), mm. 14–17
(Excerpted from the International Music Co. edition, New York, NY 10018.)

EXAMPLE 2–17 Stravinsky: *Oedipus Rex* (1927), rehearsal no. 158 *(© Copyright 1927 by Edition Russe de Musique; Copyright Renewed. Copyright and Renewal assigned to Boosey & Hawkes, Inc. Revised version © Copyright 1949, 1950 by Boosey & Hawkes, Inc. Copyright Renewed. Reprinted by permission.)*

Another Russian-born composer whose name is associated with the octatonic scale is Stravinsky.[2] Diminished-7th chords on B and C♯ account for all of the pitch material in the first 6½ measures of Example 2–17. The C♮ in the bassoon begins a transition back to a diatonic pitch material. The horns are in F in this excerpt.

The octatonic scale has also found a home in contemporary jazz, where it is especially useful in improvisation over diminished-7th chords and altered dominants.

THE CHROMATIC SCALE

Many musical passages in the twentieth century avail themselves of all or nearly all of the tones of the chromatic scale. In some cases it is only the harmony or only the melody that is chromatic, while in other cases both are. In Example 2–18 Hindemith omits only the pitch class D in the course of an eighteen-note melody. Hindemith's melody is obviously a tonal one, beginning strongly on F and ending with a convincing melodic cadence on A. We could even "explain" the chromaticism in terms of diatonic scales—F major (notes 1–6), G♭ major (notes 7–14), and A minor (notes 14–18)—but such explanations of chromatic passages are not always helpful. Turn back to Example 2–7 and consider the accompaniment. The voices, you will recall, are confined almost entirely to a whole-tone scale, but the accompaniment uses the chromatic scale as its pitch source. All twelve notes of the chromatic scale are used in the first 1½ measures of the accompaniment, and though there are some conventional sonorities (an A major triad in m. 984 and a D♭ major triad in m. 986), it makes no sense to attempt to discuss the accompaniment in terms of any scale other than the chromatic.

EXAMPLE 2–18   Paul Hindemith: Sonata for Trombone and Piano (1941), I, mm. 1–5
(trombone only)   *©Schott & Co., Ltd., London, 1942. Copyright renewed 1970. Assigned to B. Schott's Soehne, Mainz. All rights reserved. Used by permission of European American Music Distributors Corporation, sole U.S. agent for B. Schott's Soehne.)*

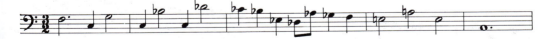

MICROTONAL SCALES

In modern usage, *microtone* means any interval smaller than a minor second. While we might assume that microtones are a very recent discovery, they actually were used in the music of ancient Greece and were mathematically defined by the theorists of that time. Nevertheless, microtones, like the diatonic modes, were rediscovered in the twentieth century by composers who have used them in new and varied ways.[3] Though in most cases the microtones employed have been quarter-tones—that is, an interval half the size of a minor 2nd—other microtonal intervals have been used as well.

A number of methods have been derived for specifying microtones in musical notation. In his Chamber Concerto (1925), Alban Berg notated quarter-tones by placing a "Z" (for "Zwischenton") on the stem. The "Z" means the performer must raise the tone if the musical line is ascending chromatically, and lower it if it is descending. Julián Carrillo, in his *Bosquejos for String Quartet* (1926), used a slanted line after the notehead to indicate a quarter-tone alteration up or down, while Bartók used ascending and descending arrows above the notes in his Violin Concerto No. 2 (1937).

Other methods have typically involved variants of the traditional system of accidentals. György Ligeti uses microtones of various sizes in his String Quartet No. 2 (1968). In his system, an arrow is attached to a flat, sharp, or natural sign, pointing up or down. The resulting intervals are no larger than quarter-tones and may be smaller, the precise size being determined partly by context and partly by the choice of the performer. Krzysztof Penderecki in several works uses variants of the traditional sharp sign to indicate tones a quarter-tone and three quarter-tones higher, and variants of the flat for a quarter-tone and three quarter-tones lower. Traditional accidentals are used for half-step intervals.

Alois Hába's method of notation is illustrated in Example 2–19. He developed four new accidentals, two of which appear in the example. One resembles an accent with a stem (before the first G in the example), meaning to raise the tone by a quarter-tone, and the other looks like an incomplete reversed flat (before the second G), meaning to lower the tone by a quarter-tone. (The letters above the staff indicate which strings should be used.)

EXAMPLE 2–19   Alois Hába: Fantasy for Solo Violin, Op. 9a (1921)   *(Used by permission of Filmkunst-Musikverlag GmbH & Co.)*

Microtones smaller than a quarter-tone have been used on occasion. One example by Ligeti was mentioned above; another is Ben Johnston's String Quartet No. 2 (1964), employing a scale with 53 tones to the octave. Harry Partch advocated microtones of various sizes, especially a 43-tone scale using unequal intervals, and he designed instruments to play them.[4] Julián Carrillo founded an ensemble, the Orquesta Sonida 13, that specialized in playing in microtones. In his own music, Carrillo experimented with intervals as small as sixteenth-tones—one-eighth of a minor 2nd.

Stringed instruments would seem to be the most suited of all traditional instruments for playing microtones, pianos and organs the least. Nevertheless, microtonal works for specially tuned pianos have been composed. Examples include *Three Quarter-Tone Pieces for Two Pianos* (1923–24) by Charles Ives, Henri Pousseur's *Prospections* (1952) for three pianos, using sixth-tones, and Johnston's *Sonata for Microtonal Piano* (1965). The most natural environment of all for microtones is the electronic medium, where the entire pitch spectrum can be precisely partitioned into intervals of any size or combination of sizes; however, a discussion of electronic music will have to be postponed until a later chapter.

OTHER POSSIBILITIES

It would not be correct to assume that everything there is to know about scales in twentieth-century music has been discussed in this chapter. There are always other possibilities, Olivier Messiaen, for example, has been interested in what he calls "modes of limited transposition." These are scales of from six to ten notes that have fewer than twelve transpositions without duplication of pitch-class content.[5] He has identified seven such scales, including the whole-tone and diminished (octatonic) scales, and used them in various compositions.

EXAMPLE 2–20   Bartók: *Mikrokosmos* (1926–37), No. 148, Six Dances in Bulgarian Rhythm, No. 1, mm. 4–8   *(© Copyright 1940 by Hawkes & Son, Ltd. Copyright Renewed. Reprinted by permission of Boosey & Hawkes, Inc.)*

Another possibility is the simultaneous use of more than one scale type. We have already seen this in connection with Example 2–7, where a whole-tone vocal duet was provided with a chromatic accompaniment. In Example 2–20 an E Phrygian melody is set over an E major ostinato.

Be sure not to confuse the simultaneous use of different scales with "polytonality," a term for the simultaneous use of different tonal centers. This will be discussed in a later chapter.

SUMMARY

Though the major and minor scales of the tonal era have by no means become extinct in the twentieth century, they have to some extent been supplanted by a variety of other scales, some of them quite old, others recently devised, using from five to dozens of notes within the octave. The scales most often encountered in twentieth-century music are included in this chapter, but you should not be surprised to encounter still others, some of which may not even have names.[6] The scales discussed in this chapter include the following:

Pentatonic scale (with modes and variants)

Whole-tone scale

Diatonic modes

Other seven-note scales using only major and minor 2nds

Seven-note scales using augmented 2nds

Octatonic (diminished) scale

Chromatic scale

Microtonal scales

Modes of limited transposition

The distinctive character of a particular phrase or melodic figure may often be explained by reference to some scale type that is only hinted at. For instance, Example 2–11 was seen to conform entirely to the Aeolian and Dorian modes. But Debussy chose to begin the melody in a manner that reminds us of yet another scale, the whole-tone scale: B♭–C–D–E–D–C–B♭.

NOTES

1. Vincent Persichetti illustrates and names several on p. 44 of his *Twentieth-Century Harmony*.
2. Pieter C. van den Toorn, in *The Music of Igor Stravinsky*, finds the octatonic "collection" in much of Stravinsky's music.
3. Joseph Yasser, in *A Theory of Evolving Tonality*, attempted to show that a nineteen-tone scale would be the logical historical successor to the chromatic scale.
4. Harry Partch, *Genesis of a Music*.
5. Olivier Messiaen, *The Technique of My Musical Language*, pp. 58–62.
6. Several dozen scales are named and defined by Robert Fink and Robert Ricci in *The Language of Contemporary Music*; see especially the list on p. 114.

EXERCISES

Part A: Fundamentals

1. Taking the pattern C–D–E–G–A as the model, notate pentatonic scales starting on the following notes:

   G   F♯   B   E♭

2. Notate whole-tone scales starting on the following notes:

   E   C♯   A♭   F

3. Notate the following modal scales:

   a. Dorian on F   e. Phrygian on A   i. Lydian on D♭
   b. Mixolydian on E   f. Aeolian on A♭   j. Dorian on C
   c. Lydian on E♭   g. Aeolian on G   k. Phrygian on B
   d. Mixolydian on D   h. Locrian on F♯   l. Ionian on B♭

4. Notate the following octatonic (diminished) scales:

    a. One beginning F♯–G   d. One combining a°7 with b°7

    b. One beginning A♭–B♭   e. One combining d♯°7 with e°7

    c. One beginning D–E♭   f. One combining a♯°7 with e♯°7

5. Notate and label every major, minor, augmented, or diminished triad available in the following scales:

    a. Pentatonic on A   d. Mixolydian on A♭

    b. Whole-tone on B   e. Octatonic beginning E–F

    c. Phrygian on C♯

Part B: Analysis

1. Respighi: *The Pines of Rome* (1924), "Pines near a Catacomb," mm. 6–9 (piano reduction).

    a. The tonal center in this excerpt is E♭. Name the scale.

2. Debussy: *Six Antique Epigraphs* (1914), I, mm. 4–7.

a. Name the scale found in the melody.

b. The melody at the beginning of the excerpt suggests G as a tonal center. If so, the melody combined with its accompaniment uses what G scale?

c. The cadence at the end of the excerpt suggests C as a tonal center. In that case, the melody combined with its accompaniment uses what C scale?

3. Anton Webern: Symphony, Op. 21 (1928), I, mm. 1–14.

a. This is a "concert score"—all of the instruments sound as notated. What scale is being used?

*) Klingt wie notiert

4. Alfredo Casella: *Eleven Children's Pieces* (1920), "Siciliana," mm. 1–19.

This excerpt suggests several scales, all with D as a tonal center. Be sure to consider the accompaniment when answering the following questions.

a. Which scale is used in mm. 1–9?

b. And in mm. 9–11?

c. What scale is hinted at in m. 12?

d. And what scale is used in mm. 13–17?

e. There are eight pitch-classes in mm. 18–19. Do they form a diminished scale?

5. Rimsky-Korsakov: *Sadko* (1896), Act II, rehearsal no. 76.

(© Copyright 1937 by Boosey & Hawkes, Inc. Copyright Renewed. Reprinted by permission.)

   a. The tonal center of this passage is difficult to identify, but perhaps it is C♯. What scale is being used?

6. Debussy: Preludes, Book I, "Sails" ("Voiles"), mm. 38–44.

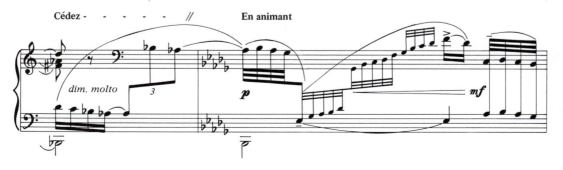

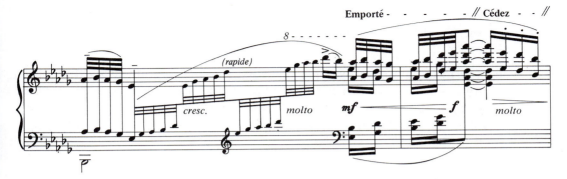

a. Two scales are used in this excerpt. The first is in mm. 38–41. What is it?

b. The second scale is found in mm. 42–44. Name it.

Part C: Composition

1. Compose short melodies illustrating the pentatonic, whole-tone, octatonic, and chromatic scales.

2. Compose short melodies illustrating the Dorian, Phrygian, Lydian, Mixolydian, and Aeolian modes. In each melody, try to emphasize the tonic note as well as those notes that are especially characteristic of that scale.

3. Continue this example, using the G Mixolydian mode.

4. Continue this example, using the F Dorian mode.

5. Compose an example that makes use of several different scales, using the Casella excerpt (Example 2–B–4) as a model. Label each scale you use.

6. Try to compose an example of two-voice counterpoint using the octatonic scale. Start with a slow, rather simple tune, unaccompanied, and bring in the second voice after a measure or two. Continue to a cadence on an octave. Compose for instruments in your class, or be able to play it at the piano.

Part D: Further Reading

DALLIN, LEON. *Techniques of Twentieth Century Composition.* See Chapter 3, "Modal Melodic Resources," the section titled "Additional Scale Resources" in Chapter 4, and Chapter 16, "Microtones."

HARDER, PAUL O. *Bridge to 20th Century Music.* See Chapters 9 and 10, "Enlarged Scale Resources I" and "II."

KOSTKA, STEFAN, AND DOROTHY PAYNE. *Tonal Harmony.* See the section titled "Scales" in Chapter 28.

PERSICHETTI, VINCENT. *Twentieth-Century Harmony.* See Chapter 2, "Scale Materials."

PISTON, WALTER. *Harmony.* See the section titled "Modal Scales and Modal Harmony" in Chapter 30 and the sections titled "The Pentatonic Scale," "The Whole-Tone Scale," and "Artificial Scales" in Chapter 31.

ULEHLA, LUDMILA. *Contemporary Harmony.* See Chapter 8, "Modal Influence," and Chapter 9, "Influence of Modes on Harmony."

VINCENT, JOHN. *The Diatonic Modes in Modern Music.* See Chapter 30, "The Modes in the Contemporary Period."

3

The Vertical Dimension: Chords and Simultaneities

INTRODUCTION

The music of the tonal era is almost exclusively tertian in its harmonic orientation. That is, its harmonies can generally be thought of as being constructed of stacked 3rds, the only exceptions being "voice-leading chords" such as the family of augmented-6th chords and the chords produced by the so-called "omnibus progression."[1] That tonal music used tertian harmony was not the result of a conscious decision on anyone's part, but instead was the result of classifications of consonance and dissonance and the development over centuries of various voice-leading procedures. The fact that the underlying harmonies in the tonal style are known to be tertian makes the labeling of chords and the identification of nonchord tones in tonal music a relatively simple task.

Much of the music of the twentieth century is also basically tertian, but there is in addition a good deal of music using chords built from 2nds, from 4ths, and from combinations of various intervals. Even the tertian music frequently uses new kinds of tertian sonorities, as we shall see. One result of this unlimited array of harmonic material is that the distinction between chord tones and nonchord tones is often difficult or impossible to make. Also, chords sometimes seem to result more or less accidentally from the combination of harmonically independent lines. For these reasons, many writers prefer at times to use terms such as "verticality," "simultaneity," "sonority," or "note complex" instead of "chord." In this text, however, "chord" will be used freely along with the other terms to refer to any vertical collection of pitches, no matter how it originates.

The present chapter surveys in an organized way the chords found in twentieth-century music. The *contexts* in which these chords are used is a subject that involves both voice leading and harmonic progression. These topics will be taken up in Chapters 4 and 5.

CONVENTIONAL TERTIAN SONORITIES

Tertian triads and 7th chords are an important, if less preponderant, part of the harmonic vocabulary of twentieth-century music. Certain composers make more use of these sounds than others do. Some of the works by composers such as Sergei Rachmaninoff, Gian-Carlo Menotti, and Aaron Copland, for example, might be expected to contain a high proportion of triads and 7th chords, whereas other composers, such as Paul Hindemith, tend to reserve the pure sound of a triad for important cadences or even for the end of a movement. Still other composers rarely make use of these more traditional sounds. Examples of the use of triads and 7th chords will be found in later chapters, where voice leading and harmonic progression are discussed.

Tertian sonorities "taller" than the 7th chord—9th chords, 11th chords, and 13th chords—are not an important part of the harmonic vocabulary before the late nineteenth or early twentieth century. In theory, any diatonic triad can be extended to a 13th chord before its root is duplicated (see Example 3–1). In practice, however, it is the dominant and secondary dominant chords, and to a lesser extent the supertonic and submediant chords, that tend to be singled out for this treatment. Chromatic alterations, especially of chords with a dominant function, are often used. Example 3–2 illustrates some of the possibilities.

EXAMPLE 3–1   Diatonic 13th chords

C: I13   ii13   iii13 *(etc.)*

EXAMPLE 3–2 Altered Dominants

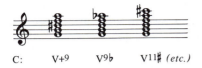

C: V+9   V9♭   V11♯ *(etc.)*

Chords taller than a 7th are frequently incomplete, posing certain problems in analysis. In Example 3–3, for instance, the first chord would certainly seem to be an incomplete supertonic 11th chord in the key of A♭, even though the 9th (C) is missing. But is the second chord an incomplete dominant 9th or an incomplete dominant 13th? The answer depends on whether one hears the C5 in the melody as a chord tone or as an appoggiatura, and either reading is defensible. The final chord is a tonic triad, the F3 in the tenor being an ornamented suspension.

EXAMPLE 3–3 Debussy: Preludes, Book II (1913), "Heaths" ("Bruyères"), mm. 1–5

A♭:   ii11   V9?   I

Ninths and other tall chords can be inverted, of course, but inversions can be problematical in analysis. For instance, referring back to Example 3–1, notice that the pitch-class content of every diatonic 13th chord is identical, meaning that every diatonic 13th chord could be analyzed as an inversion of every other diatonic 13th chord. The situation is only slightly less ambiguous with 9th and 11th chords, as Example 3–4 illustrates.

EXAMPLE 3–4 Inverted 9th and 11th chords

C13?   C13?
F9?   D11?

A typically ambiguous example is seen in Example 3–5. The excerpt begins with a tonic triad in D major, but the next chord is open to some interpretation (remember to include the soloist in your analysis). The pitch classes, in alphabetical order, are A, C, D, E♭, F♯, G. Bass notes usually want to be roots, if they can, and the high D in the flute on the fourth beat reinforces the notion that this might be some sort of G chord. On the other hand, the G could be the 11th of a complete D 11th chord: D–F♯–A–C–E♭–G, and the A5 to D6 in the flute seems to support that. Or perhaps it should be analyzed as a D 9th chord presented simultaneously with G, its note of resolution. The uncertainty is not resolved by the major 7th chord that follows, since neither G–B♭ nor D–B♭ seems particularly compelling as a progression. The remainder of the excerpt is more straightforward: A minor 7th to D minor 7th in m. 3, both slightly ornamented, to a more lavishly ornamented G major triad in m. 4.

EXAMPLE 3–5   Prokofiev: Sonata for Flute and Piano, Op. 94 (1943), I, mm. 1–4   *(Music by Sergei Prokofiev. Edited by Jean-Pierre Rampal. Copyright © 1986 International Music Co. Copyright Renewed. International copyright secured. All rights reserved. Used by permission.)*

TERTIAN CHORDS WITH ADDED NOTES

Though the possibility of a triad's having a note added a 6th above the root was recognized by theorists as early as the eighteenth century, chords with added notes (sometimes called *chords of addition*) did not become an accepted part of the harmonic vocabulary until the twentieth century. The basic chords are usually triads, and the added notes are usually 2nds or 6ths, less frequently 4ths (always figured above the root). Any triad with an added 6th could also be analyzed as a 7th chord, but the context will usually settle the issue, as Example 3–6 illustrates. Similarly, a triad with an added 2nd or 4th could be interpreted as an incomplete 9th or 11th chord, especially if voiced with the added note above the triad. Since the root is the

EXAMPLE 3-6   Added 6th and Inverted 7th Chords

$$C:\quad V9\qquad \text{I add 6}\qquad G:\ \ \text{ii}\,{}^6_5\qquad V7\qquad\qquad I$$

same in either case, the distinction is not a crucial one. For all practical purposes, a chord with an added 2nd or 4th can be considered the same as one with an added 9th or 11th. See Example 3–7.

EXAMPLE 3-7   Chords with Added 2nds and 4ths

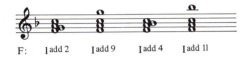

$$F:\quad \text{I add 2}\qquad \text{I add 9}\qquad \text{I add 4}\qquad \text{I add 11}$$

The situation is unambiguous in Example 3–8, where the cadential chords are the dominant 7th and the tonic with added 6th in G♭ Major. And in Example 3–9, the final chord is clearly a C triad with an added 9th. But Example 3–10 is more involved. In the first phrase (mm. 1–2) a double pedal point on G4 and B4 (in the middle of the texture) adds bite to a conventional progression. Though several of the sonorities could be analyzed as added-note chords, the pedal-point analysis is just as good, ex-

EXAMPLE 3-8   Debussy: Preludes, Book I (1910), "The Girl with the Flaxen Hair" ("La fille aux cheveux de lin"), m. 23–24

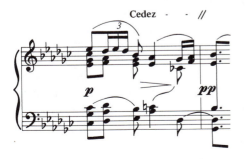

plaining all the dissonances except the added 4th in the passing tonic $^6_4$. The second phrase (mm. 3–4) keeps the B as a pedal point, shifting it down an octave in m. 4. Again, the pedal point accounts for most of the dissonances.

EXAMPLE 3–9   Debussy: Preludes, Book II (1913), "Canope," mm. 29–33

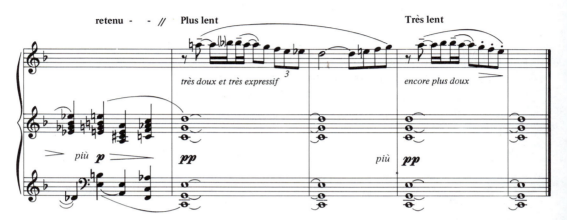

EXAMPLE 3–10   Stravinsky: Suite Italienne (1932), "Introduction," mm. 1–4 (*© Copyright 1934 by Boosey & Hawkes, Inc. Copyright Renewed. Reprinted by permission.*)

Added notes are a feature of what is sometimes called "wrong-note style," in which the listener's conventional expectations are almost met, but not quite. The result is often humorous, as in Example 3–11, where the melody heads toward a G4 but lands a half-step too high (m. 41), then a half-step too low (m. 42), before finally succeeding (m. 43).

EXAMPLE 3–11   Gian Carlo Menotti: *The Telephone* (1946), mm. 41–43
Used by permission of G. Schirmer, Inc. and Associated Music Publishers.

TERTIAN CHORDS WITH SPLIT CHORD MEMBERS

A special kind of added-note chord features one or more chord members that are "split" by adding a note a minor 2nd away. Common examples are triads and 7th chords with split 3rds, but split roots, 5ths, and 7ths also occur. Some of the possibilities are shown in Example 3–12. There is no standard analytical symbol for split chord members. In this text an exclamation point will be used, as in the example. The dominant 7th chord with split 3rd is a traditional "blues" chord, where it is analyzed as a dominant 7th with an augmented 9th. Debussy uses a Db7 (3!) in Example 3–13 to achieve a Spanish flavor. The split 3rd (Fb) is spelled here as an augmented 9th (E♮). Either analysis is acceptable.

In Example 3–14 the effect is that of an F♯ 13th chord (F♯–A♯–C♯–E–G–D♯) with a split 3rd (A♮), even though the two 3rds are never struck simultaneously. A few bars later in the same work, Ravel uses a series of major triads with split roots (Example 3–15).

A more complex example was contained in Example 2–7 (p. 29). The accompaniment in m. 984 clearly contains an A major triad on beat 3, accented. Below and above it are C♮s (a split 3rd), the higher C leaping up to an F (a split 5th), while an inner voice sustains an Eb (another split 5th). Meanwhile, the singers produce Bb (split root) and G♯ (adding a major 7th to the chord). The listener cannot follow all of this, of course; the aural effect is one of extreme dissonance competing with the sound of a pure triad.[2]

EXAMPLE 3–12   Chords with Split Chord Members

F(3!)   F(1!)   F7(7!)   F7(3!)

EXAMPLE 3–13   Debussy: Preludes, Book II, (1913), "La Puerta del Vino," mm. 9–15

EXAMPLE 3–14   Ravel: *Mirrors (Miroirs)* (1905), "Sorrowful Birds" ("Oiseaux tristes"), mm. 10–11

EXAMPLE 3–15   Ravel: *Mirrors (1905)*, "Sorrowful Birds," m. 15

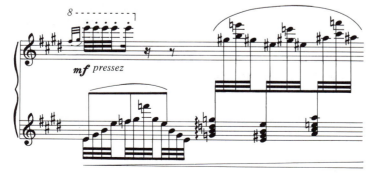

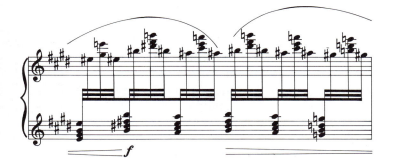

EXAMPLE 3–16 Carl Orff: *Carmina Burana* (1936), "Veris leta facies," mm. 4–6

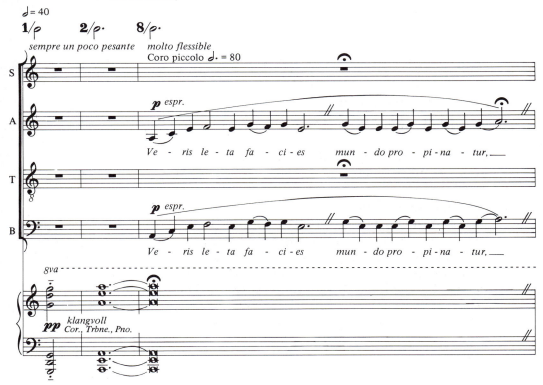

OPEN-5TH CHORDS

While a large number of added-note chords are possible, there is only one important "chord of omission"—that is, a traditional sonority that is transformed into something unusual by leaving out a note—and this is the triad without a 3rd. Omitting the root or the 5th, or omitting anything from a 7th chord, only results in yet another traditional sonority. But the sound of an open 5th had been out of style for centuries, except for its occasional use in two-part counterpoint.

The sound of open 5ths rapidly becomes tiresome, so extended passages based on this chord are rare. Typically they are used to create an impression of the Orient or of the distant past. In Example 3–16 open 5ths on G and A are used to introduce a chant melody in the chorus. The notation of the time signatures in Example 3–16 is a very practical one that a number of twentieth-century composers have adopted.

QUARTAL AND QUINTAL CHORDS

Composers of the twentieth century have not restricted themselves to tertian sonorities—that is, to chordal formations based on stacked 3rds. There are essentially only four possibilities:

Chords built from 2nds (7ths)
Chords built from 3rds (6ths)
Chords built from 4ths (5ths)
Chords built from mixed intervals

In this section we will explore quartal and quintal chords—those built from 4ths and 5ths. Later sections will deal with chords constructed from 2nds and with mixed-interval chords.

A *quartal chord* can have as few as three pitch classes (as in Example 3–17a) or it can have several (Example 3–17b). It is sometimes possible to omit a member of a quartal or quintal chord (the E4 in Example 3–17b, for instance) without losing its character. Various voicings and octave duplications are also used (as in Example 3–17c), but some arrangements could destroy the quartal character of the sonority. *Quintal chords* work the same way (as in Example 3–17d), but they have a more open and stable sound and, of course, occupy more vertical space per chord member. Surely a near-record for range must be held by the ten-note quintal chord that occurs near the end of György Ligeti's *Melodies for Orchestra* (1971), spanning a range of more than five octaves, from A♭1 to B6.

A convenient way to describe quartal and quintal chords is to use, for example, "3 × 4 on B" to mean a three-pitch-class quartal chord with B as the bottom pitch class, as in Example 3–17a. Example 3–17b would be a "7 × 4 on C♯." All of the chords in Example 3–17c would be "4 × 4 on E," and "5 × 5 on G" would describe Example 3–17d. A static 6 × 4 chord on A is the basis for Example 3–18.

EXAMPLE 3–17   Quartal and Quintal Chords

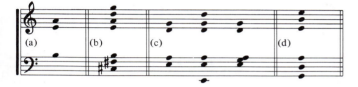

EXAMPLE 3–18   Howard Hanson: Symphony No. 2, Op. 30 (1930), I, rehearsal J (strings only)   *(Copyright © 1932 by the Eastman School of Music. Copyright renewed. Reprinted by permission of Carl Fischer, Inc., sole agent for the Eastman School of Music Publications.)*

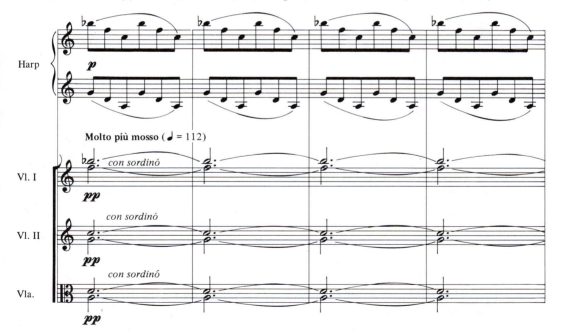

The chords in Example 3–19 are almost exclusively quartal, but the analysis is complicated by arpeggiations and voicings. One possibility is to analyze the harmony as four quartal chords, as marked on the score.

a = 5×4 on F♯

b = 3×4 on D ("inverted")

c = 5×4 on B♭

d = 4×4 on D♭

EXAMPLE 3–19 Copland: *Piano Fantasy* (1957), mm. 20–24 *(© Copyright 1957 by Aaron Copland; Copyright Renewed. Used by permission of Aaron Copland, Copyright Owner, and Boosey & Hawkes, Inc., Sole Licensee and Publisher. Reprinted by permission.)*

A second approach (and still others are possible) would be to combine a and b into a single 7×4 chord on F♯ and to combine c and d into a single 7×4 chord on B♭. Notice that the a/b chord contains all of the pitch classes of the G major scale, whereas the pitch classes from C♭ major make up the c/d chord. Notice also the oversize time signatures Copland employs here. Presumably these are seen more readily than are the traditional time signatures, certainly when used in a conductor's score, as in Example 3–20.

The last 21 measures of the movement from which Example 3–20 is taken are static harmonically, consisting for the most part of embellishments of a quintal chord on D♭. At the very end, shown here, the chord turns out to be a 5×5 chord on D♭.

Quartal and quintal chords are most often made up of perfect intervals, but augmented and diminished 4ths and 5ths may be included. In Example 3–21 each of the arpeggiated triplet chords, as well as the eighth-note chords beneath them, is a 3×4 chord, with the lower 4th augmented.

EXAMPLE 3–20 Percy Grainger: *Lincolnshire Posy* (1937), III, "Rufford Park Poachers," mm. 99–103 *Used by permission of G. Schirmer, Inc. and Associated Music Publishers.*

EXAMPLE 3–21 Debussy, Preludes, Book II (1913), "Ondine," mm. 4–7

EXAMPLE 3–22   Scriabin's Mystic Chord

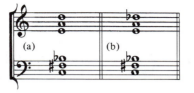

The use of diminished 4ths and augmented 5ths in quartal and quintal chords can lead to perplexing questions, since these intervals sound like 3rds and 6ths. Alexander Scriabin's "mystic chord," a sonority that flavors much of his music though it is seldom literally quoted, is an example. The "mystic chord" is found in at least the two forms shown in Example 3–22. Example 3–22a contains one °4, while Example 3–22b contains two of them. As long as the voicing is predominantly quartal, as it is here, it is probably correct to analyze both chords as altered 6×4 chords, but other voicings might lead to other analyses. The diminished scale can serve as the source for the chord in Example 3–22b. If you turn back to Example 2–16 (p. 35), you will see that this chord is strongly suggested in various transpositions and voicings in that excerpt.

SECUNDAL CHORDS

The third possibility for chord construction is the secundal chord, a sonority built from major or minor 2nds or from a combination of the two. Such chords may be voiced as 7ths rather than as 2nds, but this is the exception. More often the notes of a secundal chord are placed adjacent to each other, an arrangement sometimes referred to by the terms "cluster" and "tone cluster."

The secundal chord in the second measure of Example 3–21 is voiced as a cluster, but the arpeggiations obscure this somewhat (the chord is F♯–G–A–B–C♯). Example 3–23 provides a clearer illustration of clusters.

In some keyboard works, special notation is used to indicate whether or not the black keys are to be included in the cluster. Others require that the cluster be performed with the forearm or with a board.

EXAMPLE 3–23 Charles Ives: Piano Sonata No. 2 *(Concord)* (1915), II *(Copyright © 1951 by G. Schirmer Inc. Copyright renewed. International copyright secured. All rights reserved. Used by permission.)*

Penderecki makes effective use of clusters in many of his compositions. In Example 3–24 the tonal span of each cluster is indicated by the black rectangle. The actual pitch to be performed by each player is shown in parentheses, even, in the case of the violins, down to the level of quarter-tones.

The chords that accompany the first violin in Example 3–25 might be explained as secundal chords, the first one containing the pitch classes G♭, A♭, B♭, C, and D, and the other chords being transpositions of the first one. The voicing of the chords, however, is not as clusters, but as alternating major 3rds and tritones, resulting in the sound of an incomplete B♭ 13th chord:

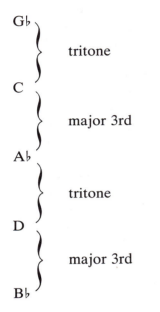

G♭ } tritone

C } major 3rd

A♭ } tritone

D } major 3rd

B♭

EXAMPLE 3–25 Paul Hindemith: String Quartet No. 3, Op. 22 (1921), V, mm. 64– 66 *(© B. Schott's Soehne, Mainz, 1923. © renewed Schott & Co., Ltd., London, 1951. Used by permission of European American Music Distributors Corporation, sole U.S. agent for Schott & Co., Ltd.)*

MIXED-INTERVAL CHORDS

A *mixed-interval chord* is one that did not originate as a series of 2nds, 3rds, or 4ths,[3] but instead combines two or more of those interval types (with their inversions and compounds, of course) to form a more complex sonority. The possibilities are numerous:

Most mixed-interval chords are subject to other interpretation— that is, they could, on closer inspection, be arranged to look like secundal, tertian, or quartal chords. Example 3–26c, for instance, might be a secundal chord (G♯–A–B♭–C–D– E) or a quartal chord (B♭–E–A–D–G♯–C), whereas the Hindemith excerpt, Example 3–25, featured chords that might have been analyzed either as secundal or as mixed-interval chords. In many cases the context will suggest the correct analytical approach. For example, if occasional secundal chords seem to be produced more or less coincidentally in an otherwise mixed-interval environment, then it might be better to analyze the entire passage in terms of mixed-interval chords.

Which brings us to the question of just how one goes about analyzing and labeling these sonorities, a complicated problem that has been tackled by various composers and theorists—notably Paul Hindemith, Howard Hanson, and Allen Forte. Because so many combinations of intervals are possible, a completely new system of chord classification had to be devised, and this system is the subject of much of Chapter 9.

EXAMPLE 3–26   Mixed-Interval Chords

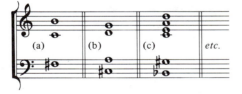

WHOLE-TONE CHORDS

Any chord whose members could be obtained from a single whole-tone scale is a *whole-tone chord*.[4] A number of such chords are possible, of course. A few of them are illustrated in Example 3–27. Such sonorities for the most part appeared rarely in classical tonal harmony, but some whole-tone chords, including those in Example 3–27, are at least reminiscent of traditional chords. Example 3–27b, for instance, is an incomplete dominant 7th chord, and Example 3–27d is a French augmented-6th chord, but Examples 3–27c and e would have to be explained as altered versions of simpler chords.

EXAMPLE 3–27   Whole-Tone Chords

    (a)   (b)   (c)   (d)   (e)

Whole-tone chords will naturally occur in any music that is based on the whole-tone scale. For an illustration, turn back to Example 2–6 (p. 28), a whole-tone excerpt by Dukas. The first measure uses a French augmented-6th sonority (B♯–E–F♯–A♯). When the B♯ moves to E in the next measure, we are left with only the notes of an incomplete dominant 7th chord (E–F♯–A♯). Neither of these chords is used in a traditional manner. The last two measures are based on a different whole-tone scale, and the whole-tone chords, though present, are more difficult to characterize.

More interesting, perhaps, is the use of whole-tone chords in passages that are not based primarily upon the whole-tone scale, because here they provide an unexpected harmonic color. Again an earlier example, Example 2–9 (p. 31), can provide an illustration. In this case the pitch environment is Phrygian, except for the last chord of the second measure (A♭–F♯–C–D). The altered tone, F♯, produces a whole-tone chord that could be explained as a French augmented-6th chord moving directly to the tonic G, or as a second-inversion dominant in G with a flatted 5th (A♭).

More whole-tone chords are seen in Example 3–28, the first phrase of a prelude that is clearly in B♭ major. Although the B♭ major orientation is never lost, the eleven chords in this first phrase include four whole-tone sonorities (indicated with an "x").

EXAMPLE 3–28   Debussy: Preludes, Book I (1910), No. 1, "Dancers of Delphi," mm. 1–4

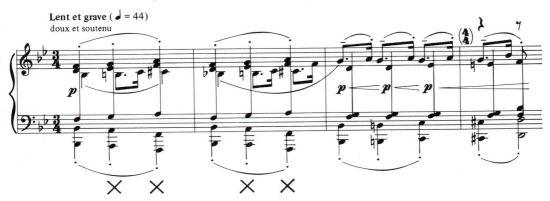

Finally, look once more at the Hindemith excerpt, Example 3–25. We have analyzed the chords in this excerpt as secundal chords, as mixed-interval chords, and as 13th chords; we can see now that they are also whole-tone chords, each one being derived from one of the two whole-tone scales.

POLYCHORDS

A polychord combines two or more chords into a more complex sonority, but it is crucial that the listener be able to perceive that separate harmonic entities are being juxtaposed if the result is to be a true polychord. Any 11th or 13th chord could be explained as a combination of two simpler sonorities, but this would be an incorrect analysis if we do not hear them that way.

EXAMPLE 3–29   Apparent Polychords

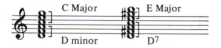

EXAMPLE 3–30   Vincent Persichetti: *Little Piano Book*, Op. 60 (1953), "Prologue," mm. 1–4   (© 1954 Elkan-Vogel, Inc. Used by permission of the publisher.)

In order to be heard as a polychord, the individual sonorities that make up the polychord must be separated by some means such as register or timbre. In Example 3–30 the first and last chords could easily be heard as 11th chords, but in the rest of the phrase the different registers and the pervading contrary motion between the two chordal units result in an unambiguous polychordal texture. Persichetti concludes another of his works, the Symphony for Band, Op. 69 (1956), with a spectacular polychord that combines four registrally distinct sonorities: B♭ major, A major 7th, B major 7th, and F major with an added 9th. The resulting polychord contains all twelve pitch classes.

EXAMPLE 3–31 Stravinsky: Petrushka (1911), Second Tableau *(© Copyright by Edition Russe de Musique; Copyright assigned to Boosey & Hawkes, Inc. Revised edition © Copyright 1947, 1948 by Boosey & Hawkes, Inc. Copyright Renewed. Reprinted by permission.)*

Stravinsky's famous "Petrushka chord" combines two triads a tritone apart: C major and F♯ major. This polychord is seen in Example 3–31, along with another polychord: F♯ major/G major. In the orchestral version, the ascending figures are played on a piano, the descending ones on clarinets.

The constituents of polychords are usually tertian triads or 7th chords, but all of the other kinds of sonorities discussed in this chapter could also conceivably be susceptible to polychordal treatment. For instance, at the end of Example 2–7 (p. 29) there is a 3×4 chord on E in the upper staff of the accompaniment and a D♭ major triad in the lower staff. The only requirement for a polychord is that the listener be able to perceive the chords as separate entities. There will inevitably be ambiguous cases, however, where one listener hears a polychord and another hears a single complex sonority.

SUMMARY

The harmonies of tonal music were limited for the most part to tertian triads and 7th chords. In contrast, composers of the twentieth century have felt free to make use of any conceivable combination of pitches. In the most simple terms, there are four possibilities for chord construction:

Secundal chords (also tone clusters)
Tertian chords (including 9ths, etc.)
Quartal chords (also quintal chords)
Mixed-interval chords

Tertian chords, the most traditional of the four types, have been subjected to some new variations:

> Added notes
> Split chord members
> Open 5ths

One special case, especially important in the early part of the century:

> Whole-tone chords

And finally, the possibility of juxtaposing two or more aurally distinguishable sonorities:

> Polychords

It is frequently the case that a particular sonority is open to more than one interpretation. This is particularly true with mixed-interval chords, many of which can be arranged to resemble secundal, tertian, or quartal chords. The student must be sensitive to the context and the voicing in attempting to choose the best analytical approach. The three chords in Example 3–32, though containing the same pitch classes, obviously must be analyzed differently.

EXAMPLE 3–32   Three Different Chords Containing the Same Pitch Classes

NOTES

1. The omnibus progression is discussed in Kostka and Payne, *Tonal Harmony*, pp. 439–40, and in Piston, *Harmony*, pp. 443–46.
2. Another approach to chords with added notes and split chord members is taken by Bryan Simms in *Music of the Twentieth Century*, pp. 55–58. He identifies nine

pairs of "triadic tetrachords"—that is, four-note chords that contain a major or minor triad. The first chord of each pair is a major triad plus one of the other nine notes of the chromatic scale, while the second chord of each pair is the mirror inversion of the first.

3. Some writers use the term *compound chord*.

4. Some theorists use the term *whole-tone dominant* for whole-tone chords that have a traditional dominant function.

EXERCISES

Part A: Fundamentals

1. Review the nine chord types in the Summary section. Then find one example of each type in the example below.

2. Make up one example of each of the nine chord types and notate them on staff paper. Try not to duplicate any of those found in the text. Label each chord.

3. Find the doubly chromatic mediant relationship in Example 3–9.

4. Name the scales used in the following excerpts.

    a. Example 3–3, treble-clef melody

    b. Example 3–9, last four measures (without the E♭; C is tonic)

    c. Example 3–15

    d. Example 3–21

    e. Example 3–25, cello only (missing an A)

Part B: Analysis

1. Debussy: Preludes, Book I, "The Engulfed Cathedral," m. 1–5.

There are three planes to the texture of this excerpt. One is the static three-note chord in the highest register, another is the quarter-note chords, and the third is the three-note chords in the lowest register. What kind of chord do all three planes make use of? To what scale do the quarter-note chords belong?

2. Stravinsky: *The Rake's Progress* (1951), III.

What kind of sonority predominates in this passage?

3. Debussy: *The Joyous Isle* (1904), mm. 152–55.

And in this one?

4. Ravel: "Minuet on the Name of Haydn" (1909), mm. 50–54.

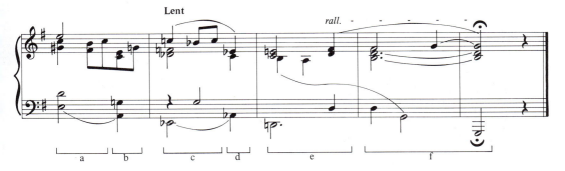

The chords here are tertian. Label the six bracketed chords with Roman numerals.

5. Ravel: *Sonatina* (1905), I, mm. 79–84.

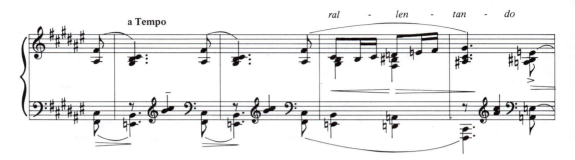

This excerpt contains several sonorities that could be analyzed as added-note chords. Find them, as well as an unconventional German augmented-6th chord.

6. Charles Ives: Violin Sonata No. 4 (1915), II.

Explain or discuss each of the five labeled chords.

Used by permission of G. Schirmer, Inc. and Associated Music Publishers.

7. Alban Berg: "Warm Is the Air," ("Warm die Lüfte"), Op. 2, No. 4 (1910), mm. 20–25.

(Reprinted by permission of the original publisher, Robert Lienau, Berlin.)

This is a complicated and intriguing excerpt from early in Berg's compositional output. Our analysis will be concerned only with the piano part, while recognizing that the relationship between the voice and the accompaniment would have to be considered in a complete analysis.

a. There are at least two ways to approach chords a–f analytically. One is to understand how they are "generated"—that is, how they come about. What sort of pattern does the bass line under chords a–f follow?

b. Meanwhile, the right hand in chords a–f moves a three-note chord down chromatically. How would you classify that chord?

c. The second way of dealing with chords a–f is to analyze each individually. The last of them could be analyzed as a dominant 7th with split 3rd: B7(3!). The others appear to be mixed-interval chords, but closer inspection reveals that they could also be analyzed as tertian chords. Which chords out of a–e could be analyzed as incomplete dominant 7th chords with split 3rds?

d. And which could be analyzed as incomplete 13th chords (or dominant 7th chords with split 7ths)?

e. Of the remaining chords (g–l), list any that are identical to or are transpositions of one of the earlier chords (a–f).

f. What single category would best describe chords g, i, and k?

g. What pattern seems to emerge in chords g and i?

h. Considering your answer to the preceding question, what note seems to be missing from chord k?

Part C: Further Reading

CHRIST, WILLIAM, AND OTHERS. *Materials and Structure of Music*, Vol. 2. See the sections titled "Tertian Chords," "Nontertian Chords," and "Stacked Chords" in Chapter 15.

DALLIN, LEON. *Techniques of Twentieth Century Composition*. See Chapter 6, "Chord Structure."

HARDER, PAUL O. *Bridge to 20th Century Music*. See Chapters 11 and 12, "Expanded Chord Vocabulary I" and "II."

KOSTKA, STEFAN, AND DOROTHY PAYNE. *Tonal Harmony*. See the section titled "Chord Structure" in Chapter 28.

PERSICHETTI, VINCENT. *Twentieth-Century Harmony*. See Chapter 3, "Chords by Thirds"; Chapter 4, "Chords by Fourths"; Chapter 5, "Added-Note Chords"; Chapter 6, "Chords by Seconds"; Chapter 7, "Polychords"; and Chapter 8, "Compound and Mirror Harmony."

PISTON, WALTER. *Harmony*. See pp. 499–507 in Chapter 31, "Scalar and Chordal Types."

REISBERG, HORACE. "The Vertical Dimension in Twentieth-Century Music," in Gary Wittlich, ed., *Aspects of Twentieth-Century Music*. See pp. 322–72.

SIMMS, BRYAN R. *Music of the Twentieth Century*. See the section titled "Triads and Triadic Extensions" in Chapter 3.

ULEHLA, LUDMILA. *Contemporary Harmony*. See Chapter 11, "The Tritone, the Whole-Tone Scale, and Whole-Tone Dominants," the sections titled "Polychords" and "Double Inflections" in Chapter 13, and Chapter 17, "Fourth Chords and Perfect Fifths."

4

The Horizontal Dimension: Melody and Voice Leading

INTRODUCTION

Voice leading—how chords are created by the motion of individual voices—is one of the main concerns of conventional tonal theory.[1] Even today the voice-leading conventions followed by composers of the tonal era occupy an important part of the course of study in colleges and universities around the world. But a glance at the table of contents of this book will reveal that voice-leading conventions are not a central issue in much of the music of the twentieth century. In fact, as we shall see later in this chapter, one of the most hallowed principles of voice leading was an early casualty of the assault on musical conventions made by a number of composers around the turn of the century.

Melody, on the other hand, is usually slighted in courses in music theory, perhaps because we tend to think of such courses as dealing with tonal *harmony* rather than with tonal *music*. Nevertheless, all of us probably have a pretty good notion of what conventional tonal melodies are like, even if we have never actually tried to analyze one. The first part of this chapter will examine some of the new melodic techniques that have been used by composers in the twentieth century. But before looking at some twentieth-century examples, it might be worthwhile to spend a little time with a familiar tonal melody.

TONAL MELODY

The last movement of Mozart's Piano Sonata in D Major, K. 284, is a set of variations on an original theme (that is, on a theme composed by Mozart himself and not borrowed from someone else). Of course, the theme consists of not just the melody, but also the accompaniment, texture, harmony, dynamics, register, articulation, and so forth; in this discussion, however, we will concentrate on the melody, given in Example 4–1. Like many fine melodies, this tune is deceptively simple. Its four phrases begin in mm. 1, 5, 9, and 14, each phrase preceded by an anacrusis. In every case the anacrusis consists of two A's, but in the pickup to m. 9 the A's are ornamented with G♯ neighbors. In every case but m. 9, the pickups are followed by a strong half-note D on the downbeat. Not only do all the phrases begin the same, but they also end the same, with a two-note stepwise descent

EXAMPLE 4–1   Mozart: Piano Sonata, K. 284 (1775), III, mm. 1–17 (melody only)

beginning on the strong beat of the fourth measure of the phrase. Again the third phrase offers some contrast by augmenting the rhythm of the cadential figure (m. 12). Finally, each phrase reaches its highest pitch—the climax or focal point—in the second or third measure of the phrase, giving them a certain similarity of basic contour.

The unity that is provided by the consistent beginnings and endings of the phrases and by their contours is complemented by an interesting motivic organization within and between the phrases. The interior of phrase 1 uses two motives, marked "a" and "b" in the example. Motive "a" is used in contrary motion (or inversion) in m. 2, and motive "b" is used in sequence in m. 3. Phrase 2 begins after the pickup figure with inversions of both "a" (m. 5) and "b" (m. 6) and introduces a new figure, "c," which is used twice in m. 7. The third phrase offers more contrast motivically just as it did in its use of the anacrusis and cadence figures. The figures in m. 9 are heard as variants of "c," but just as apparent to the listener is the chromatic descent in the same measure: A–G♯–G–F♯, possibly a compressed version of "a" in contrary motion. Motive "a" is heard sequentially three times in mm. 10–11, the last time in rhythmic augmentation. Another interesting way to hear m. 11 is as a sequential continuation of the stepwise descent from m. 9, with m. 10 serving as a *forte* interruption. Finally, phrase 4 begins with a literal return of mm. 1–2 (except for the dynamics), followed by a literal transposition of mm. 7–8! That is, phrase 4 joins the first half of phrase 1 to the second half of phrase 2 to effect a shortened return of the opening period.

Slightly over half of the melodic intervals in Mozart's melody are major or minor 2nds, and 2nds and 3rds together account for seven eighths of the intervals. All but two of the thirteen leaps larger than a 3rd are followed by motion contrary to the direction of the leap. One thing accomplished by the 3rds and the larger intervals is clarification of the harmonic structure. In mm. 16–17, for example, the implied harmonies are obviously I–IV (or ii)–I–V7–I. Though the harmonies are not always so unambiguous, the basic harmonic structure implied by the melody is usually clear.

To summarize:

1. The melody exhibits a high degree of motivic unity, brought about through such devices as repetition, return, sequence, and inversion.

2. Each phrase has a single highpoint somewhere near the middle of the phrase.

3. The melody moves primarily in 2nds and 3rds, with larger leaps usually being followed by a change of direction.

4. The basic harmonic structure is implied by the melody.

It would certainly be incorrect to assume that the basic characteristics of Mozart's melody have been discarded by all composers in the twentieth century. With the exception of the fourth item in our list above, it would be safe to say that a great many twentieth-century melodies make use of the same compositional devices employed by Mozart. Nevertheless, we will frequently encounter differences that will help us to understand what it is that gives twentieth-century melody its characteristic sound.

SOME NEW STYLISTIC FEATURES OF TWENTIETH-CENTURY MELODY

To illustrate this part of the discussion we will begin with a famous theme by Richard Strauss, a theme that belongs more to the late Romantic era than to the twentieth century, but one that exemplifies how melody had developed since Mozart's time.

One of the first things that one notices about this melody is its wide range—from E♭2 to D5, just short of three octaves—with most of this span occurring in the first measure. While stepwise motion accounts for about half of the intervals, large leaps (larger than a 3rd) are much more prevalent than in Classical style. The rhythm, too, offers a contrast to Mozart's melody, the rhythmic variety, for example, being much greater in the Strauss excerpt. Other features of this melody, including motivic organization, are similar to Mozart's.

EXAMPLE 4–2   Strauss: *Ein Heldenleben, (A Hero's Life)*, Op. 40 (1898), mm. 1–13 (melody only)

Large leaps occur still more frequently in the Hindemith theme discussed in Chapter Two (Example 2–18, p. 37). Notice that in this theme there are no 3rds at all, whereas about half of the intervals are perfect 4ths or perfect 5ths. Though the range of this melody is not wide in comparison to Mozart's, the effect when it is played on the trombone is of a wider range than is actually the case. The chromatic scale that is the source of the pitch material in this melody is, of course, only one of the new scale resources available to the composer.

It would be misleading to imply that all twentieth-century melodies span a wide range and use a large number of leaps. Though this would be true of many melodies, others do just the opposite. The range of the melody in Example 4–3 is only a perfect 5th, and the largest interval is a minor 3rd. One aspect that gives this melody its twentieth-century sound is its chromaticism. Each phrase (if we take each slurred segment as a phrase) uses some segment of the chromatic scale:

Phrase 1	M3	(A–C♯)
Phrase 2	tt	(A–E♭)
Phrase 3	P4	(B–E)
Phrase 4	P4	(B♭–E♭)

In each case, the second part of the phrase fills in chromatic notes missing from the first part. Another feature of this melody is its unconventional rhythm. While details of twentieth-century rhythm are the topic of a later chapter, we can observe here that, in spite of the carefully notated changes in time signature, the listener perceives only an unpredictable mixture of eighths and quarters, with stressed notes coming at irregular intervals.

EXAMPLE 4–3   Bartók: *Music for String Instruments, Percussion, and Celesta* (1936), I, mm. 1–4   *(© Copyright 1937 by Universal Edition; Copyright Renewed. Copyright and Renewal assigned to Boosey & Hawkes, Inc. for USA only. Reprinted by permission.)*

The examples discussed so far have been instrumental melodies, but the developments in the vocal idiom have been similar. Turn back to the Berg excerpt, Example 3–B–7 (p. 75), and you will notice the same tendency toward more and wider leaps, the comparatively wide range, especially for such a short excerpt, and its use of the chromatic scale. The rhythm, while perhaps not unconventional, is more varied than in the Mozart theme. Observe also that the melody does not imply the harmonic structure, in that you could not predict the chords that Berg would choose to harmonize this melody; in fact, about half of the vocal pitches are not contained in the chords that accompany them. The same proportion of notes might be nonchord tones in a tonal song, but in the Berg many of the "nonchord tones," such as the first and last notes of the excerpt, are left unresolved.

Two points made so far can be reviewed with the help of Example 4–4. Beginning with the flute part (the flute in G sounds a perfect 4th lower than written), notice the extreme range of almost three octaves, with most of that occurring within m. 2 alone, and the overwhelming preponderance of leaps, especially wide ones, over stepwise motion. The vocal range is not so extreme, but the voice part is equally disjunct and difficult to perform. Both parts draw their pitch material from the chromatic scale and employ unconventional rhythmic techniques. Both parts also use more expression marks (dynamics, articulation) than was customary in earlier styles, which, while not strictly a melodic phenomenon, certainly contributes to the effect. The Boulez excerpt is an example of an important trend among some twentieth- century composers to write what many would call less lyrical

EXAMPLE 4–4   Pierre Boulez: *Le marteau sans maître (The Hammer Without a Master)*, (1955), III, mm. 1–15   *(Copyright 1954 by Universal Edition (London) Ltd., London. Final version © copyright 1957 by Universal Edition (London) Ltd., London. Poems de René Char © copyright 1964 by Jose Corte, Editeur, Paris. Copyright renewed. All rights reserved. Used by permission of European American Music Distributors Corporation, sole U.S. agent for Universal Edition.)*

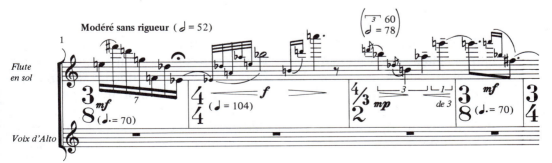

melodies—that is, melodies that seem inherently less vocal, less flowing, more angular, and frequently more fragmented than we might expect from a tonal melody. Other composers—Gershwin, Hanson, Sibelius, and many others—have kept more faithfully to the lyrical tradition of melody writing. A fine twentieth-century example of a long, flowing melody in the lyrical tradition is the opening theme of William Walton's Violin Concerto (see Example 4–5). This melody contains the numerous leaps so characteristic of many twentieth-century melodies, but its implied tertian harmonies, its straightforward tonality (with some modal flavor), and above all its mode of expression are obviously more Romantic than modern in conception. Some composers in more recent years have shown a renewed interest in melodicism in the traditional sense, either through the quotation of melodies from earlier times or through the composition of new, more lyrical melodies. Both of these aspects will be discussed in later chapters.

EXAMPLE 4–5   William Walton: Violin Concerto (1939), I, mm. 1–18 (solo violin
          only)   (© 1939 by Oxford University Press. Reproduced with permission.)

Finally, we might observe that music of the twentieth century seems to be less concerned with melody in general. While much of tonal music is essentially homophonic—melody with accompaniment—the tendency in the twentieth century has been to put more emphasis on other aspects of music, such as rhythm, texture, and timbre.

SOME ASPECTS OF MELODIC ORGANIZATION

The motivic devices such as those seen in Mozart's melody—repetition, return, sequence, inversion—occur also in twentieth-century melodies. Surely the melodies in this chapter by Strauss, Bartók, and Walton could be discussed in those terms. Repetition and sequence were also seen in previous examples by Debussy (Example 3–21, p. 61) and Hindemith (Example 3–25, p. 65). Other motivic devices peculiar to the twentieth century have also come into use. Study Example 4–6, paying special attention to the three phrase marks. The three segments that occur under the phrase marks, though not related in traditional ways, are related nevertheless. The segments are:

1. A–C–C♯
2. D♯–F♯–D
3. C♯–B♭–D–C♯

Each of these segments contains three pitch classes. If we rearrange them, we see that each segment spans a major 3rd and the interval content of each segment is identical:

1. A–C–C♯ = m3 + m2
2. D–D♯–F♯ = m2 + m3 (same intervals in reverse order)
3. B♭–C♯–D = m3 + m2

EXAMPLE 4–6 Anton Webern: Five Canons, Op. 16 (1924), I, mm. 2–5 (voice only)   (© 1928 by Universal Edition. Copyright renewed. All rights reserved. Used by permission of European American Music Distributors Corporation, sole U.S. agent for Universal Edition.)

This kind of motive, really a collection of intervals that can be rearranged and inverted, is often called a *pitch-class cell*. The use of cells, usually of three or four notes each, is an important unifying factor in some twentieth-century music, so important that a special terminology has been developed to deal with it. This terminology will be introduced in Chapter 9.

Another significant factor in the organization of melody has been the development of twelve-tone melody. This term does not refer to just any melody employing the whole chromatic scale, but instead to a melody in which each and every pitch class is used once and only once (tremolo figures and immediate repetitions are allowed). The horn melody in Example 4–7 is such a melody. Once the twelve pitch classes have been presented, another series of twelve pitch classes, related to the first one, can begin. This procedure is discussed in more detail in Chapter 10.

EXAMPLE 4–7 Arnold Schoenberg: Wind Quintet, Op. 26 (1924), III, mm. 1–7 *(Used by permission of Belmont Music Publishers.)*

Two points about the notation of Example 4–7 should be made here. One is that this is a "C score," meaning that all of the instruments sound the pitch classes that are written (although, in the case of some instruments, in a different octave), a development that has no doubt met with the approval of students of music everywhere. The second point concerns the boldface "H" and "N" that appear at the beginning of the excerpt. Schoenberg and others used these letters to designate the *Hauptstimme* (primary voice) and the *Nebenstimme* (secondary voice). The end of the *Nebenstimme* in Example 4–7 is marked in the bassoon at the end of m. 7. In a more complex texture, the *Hauptstimme* and the *Nebenstimme* would be the two most important parts, and it would be up to the conductor and performers to bring them out.

Many melodies are arranged so that there is a single highpoint in each phrase or in the melody as a whole, an approach that has been followed more or less faithfully for centuries. If you look back at the melodies presented in this chapter so far, you will find that this holds true for every one of them.

In more general terms, one could say that melodic organization in the twentieth century tends to be less apparent at the surface level, and the progress of twentieth-century melodies is less predictable than that of tonal melodies. The phrases are less often equal in length, and the clear period forms of the Classical era are the exception. Repetition and sequence, while still found, are often abandoned in favor of other techniques.

VOICE LEADING IN TWENTIETH-CENTURY MUSIC

In the traditional study of tonal harmony, a great deal of attention is paid to the subject of voice leading, or part-writing, and with good reason. Throughout the tonal era and for centuries prior to its beginning, there were voice-leading conventions that were followed by all composers and that did much to contribute to the homogeneity of their styles. This homogeneity was most pronounced among composers who lived during the same period, such as Haydn and Mozart, but some elements are shared by all composers of the tonal era.

Some of the "rules" that we learn in harmony courses are not actually all that general, even when they are tested against tonal music. These include those procedures gleaned from the study of the works of a particular composer (usually Bach) or that are really valid only for a particular medium (usually choral). We learn them in order to begin the study of tonal composition in a controlled and uncomplicated environment. Two conventions that do seem to be applicable throughout the tonal era, however, are the following:

1. Parallel 5ths and octaves, especially the former, should be avoided.[2]
2. Any chord 7th should resolve down by step.

It is, of course, possible to find passages of twentieth-century music that still adhere to these conventions. This seems to be the case in Example 4–8, from a work that may be more familiar to you under the title "Adagio for Strings." The harmonic vocabulary here is tertian, simplifying the task of sorting out the nonchord tones, but there are several places where more than one interpretation is possible. A suggested chordal analysis is included in the example. There are four 7th chords in the excerpt, with the 7th in each case resolving down by step into the next chord; the voice leading in the other instruments follows for the most part the traditional preference for smooth chord connection. Smooth voice leading is also a traditional preference and one that still is often invoked. However, very disjunct voice leading is a characteristic of much twentieth-century music. Examples of disjunct voice leading from earlier in this text include Example 2–7 (p. 29) and Example 2– B–3 (p. 43).

Closer examination of Example 4–8 reveals two sets of parallel 5ths and the same number of parallel octaves. One of the sets of 5ths involves a nonchord tone (mm. 3–4, violin II and cello), so it might conceivably be allowed, and both sets of octaves involve temporary octave doubling between an ornamented melody and its slower-moving accompaniment (mm. 4–5 and 7–8), also possibly acceptable. But the parallel 5ths between violin I and cello in mm. 5–6 cannot be explained at all satisfactorily in traditional terms. This, of course, is not an error on the part of the composer, but instead indicates that one of the most sacred rules of counterpoint no longer has the validity that it once had.

EXAMPLE 4–8   Samuel Barber: String Quartet No. 1, Op. 11 (1936), II, mm. 1–8
Used by permission of G. Schirmer, Inc. and Associated Music Publishers.

Parallel 5ths and octaves may occur incidentally in an otherwise traditional texture, as in Example 4–8, but they frequently play a more significant role. For instance, in Example 3–B–5 (p. 74) Ravel makes consistent use of parallel 5ths in the lowest register. Parallel 5ths also occur in chordal parallelism, a very important development in twentieth-century music. In tonal music the use of first-inversion triads moving in parallel motion was an accepted compositional device, serving in many cases as a connection between two more important chords and in others as a means of thickening a melodic line. The use of a three-part texture resulted in parallel 3rds, 4ths, and 6ths, but no parallel 5ths or octaves occurred. Other uses of harmonic parallelism included parallel °7 chords and, less frequently, parallel °7 chords. Though parallel 5ths might occur on rare occasion, as in one of the Wagner examples (Example 1–7, p. 10), their use was exceptional.

One reason for the traditional avoidance of parallel 5ths and octaves was that these intervals, more than any other consonant interval, when used in parallel motion imply a breakdown of counterpoint—that is, of relatively independent musical lines. We tend to think of counterpoint as something found in fugues, but counterpoint of some kind was the basis of most tonal music, which in fact evolved the way it did largely because of contrapuntal procedures. In the twentieth century, however, composers have been unrestrained in their use of harmonic parallelism and have shown no aversion to the use of parallel intervals of all kinds. This has led to a redefining of some aspects of counterpoint and to new developments in texture. If we can compare a single melodic line to a line drawn on a canvas with a pen, then the analogy used earlier comparing harmonic parallelism to painting with a broad brush may prove helpful. In Example 4–9, for instance, ascending scales in both hands of the piano part are broadened into root-position triads with roots doubled, resulting in parallel 5ths and octaves.

Harmonic parallelism, so typical of much twentieth-century music, is often referred to as "planing."[3] Parallelism may be "diatonic," meaning that it uses only the white keys of the piano or some transposition of them (see Example 4–9), or "real," meaning that the sonority is exactly transposed (see the parallel major triads in the cellos in Example 4–10). Though there are lots of "parts" sounding in Example 4–10, it is really an example of three-part counterpoint, twentieth-century style. The three parts are:

1. Violins and violas. Use of diatonic planing in m. 1 and real planing in mm. 2–4.

2. Cellos and piano. Real planing until m. 4, where two minor triads are employed. The planing in this measure is neither real nor diatonic.

3. Basses.

EXAMPLE 4–9 Bartók Piano Concerto No. 2 (1931), I, mm. 295–304 *(© Copyright 1933 by Hawkes & Son. Copyright Renewed. Reprinted by permission of Boosey & Hawkes, Inc. Reprinted by permission.)*

Notice that the three parts have their own contours and, to some extent, their own rhythms, fulfilling the essential requirements of counterpoint.

Harmonic parallelism that is neither diatonic nor real, as in m. 4 of Example 4–10, is not unusual. Most of the planing in the first two measures of Example 4–11 is diatonic, but Debussy uses an E♮ in one chord, presumably to avoid the sound of a diminished triad at this point; in the last two measures of the excerpt we find real parallelism—the roots outline an A♭ major scale—until the last chord, an unexpected B♭ minor triad.

Triads are not the only sonorities that can be planed. Example 4–12 begins with inverted 9th chords, followed by inverted 7th chords, then root-position 7th chords, and, finally, root-position triads. The progression from complex sounds to simple ones is obvious and effective.

EXAMPLE 4–10   Roger Sessions: Symphony No. 2 (1946), IV, mm. 1–4 (piano and strings only)   *Used by permission of G. Schirmer, Inc. and Associated Music Publishers.*

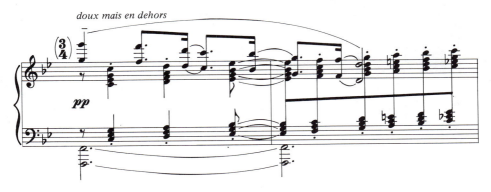

EXAMPLE 4–11   Debussy: Preludes, Book I (1910), "Dancers of Delphi," mm. 11–14

EXAMPLE 4–12   Roy Harris: Symphony No. 7 (1952) (strings only)

Used by permission of G. Schirmer, Inc. and Associated Music Publishers.

EXAMPLE 4–13   Debussy: Preludes, Book II (1913), " 'The Fairies Are Exquisite Dancers' "(" 'Les Fées sont déxguises danseuses' ") mm. 73–78

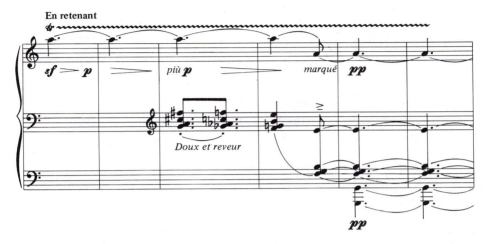

Nontertian sonorities (clusters, quartal chords, and so forth) are frequently planed as well. Real planing of a four-note mixed-interval chord occurs in Example 4–13.

We have seen that the tradition that forbade certain parallels is no longer followed in much music of the twentieth century, but what about the other convention that we discussed, the one about dissonance treatment? In tonal music we sometimes use the term "essential dissonance" to refer to dissonances between members of the same chord (such as between the root and 7th) as opposed to "nonessential dissonances" involving ornamentation (passing tones and so forth). It is usually not difficult when analyzing tonal music to separate the essential dissonances from the ornaments, and the essential dissonances generally resolve the predictable fashion. Neither of these is necessarily true in twentieth-century music. For instance, turn back to Example 4–7 (p. 87) and play it on a piano or listen to a recording. At the beginning, the E♭ in the horn is sustained against G–A–B–C♯ in the bassoon, after which the C♯ is sustained against E♭–C–B♭ in the horn. In neither case is it possible to distinguish essential from nonessential dissonances, since there is no way of identifying the "chords," and the dissonances appear to be approached and left freely.

This free treatment of dissonance, called "emancipation of the dissonance" by Schoenberg,[4] is the norm in a large proportion of twentieth-century works. Many of the examples already used in this text also illustrate free treatment of dissonance, including those listed below. In some of these excerpts the chords are not difficult to identify, but in none of them are dissonances consistently handled in a traditional fashion.

Example 2–7 (Henze, p. 29)	Example 3–23 (Ives, p. 63)
Example 2–11 (Debussy, p. 32)	Example 3–25 (Hindemith, p. 65)
Example 2–16 (Scriabin, p. 35)	Example 3–30 (Persichetti, p. 68)
Example 2–20 (Bartók, p. 39)	Example 3–31 (Stravinsky, p. 69)
Example 3–10 (Stravinsky, p. 54)	Example 4–4 (Boulez, p. 83)
Example 3–15 (Ravel, p. 56)	Example 4–10 (Sessions, p. 92)
Example 3–19 (Copland, p. 60)	Example 4–12 (Harris, p. 94)
Example 3–21 (Debussy, p. 61)	

This "emancipation of the dissonance" has led some to suggest that the whole notion of dissonance should be reevaluated, since a dissonance by some definitions means a sound that requires resolution to a consonance. If sounds need not resolve, are there perhaps no longer any dissonances? This makes very good sense, but we still need a term to label the effect produced by certain combinations of sounds, and "dissonance" remains the most popular choice.

In spite of the repeal of the rules governing parallels and dissonance treatment, there are probably certain basic truths about voice leading that are independent of style. One of them is that counterpoint is threatened whenever voices move in parallel motion, and this is especially true when the intervals between the voices are exactly maintained. For example, parallel major 3rds would tend to destroy a two-voice contrapuntal texture faster than a mixture of major and minor 3rds. Another principle is that the smoothest effect when moving from one chord to another is gained if common tones are maintained where possible and all voices move by the smallest available interval. Finally, the effect of a dissonance can be softened by smooth motion—common tones or steps—into and out of the dissonance.

In the twentieth century these truths are no longer conventions to be followed, but instead merely tools or approaches that are among those available to the composer. So what conventions remain to guide the composer, if the rules concerning parallels and dissonances no longer hold? None, really, which is what Stravinsky meant when he wrote of the "abyss of freedom" and of the "terror" he felt when faced with this multiplicity of choices. He went on to say that he defined a new set of compositional rules

(Stravinsky referred to them as "limitations" and "obstacles") for each work.[5] The task of the composer is to create a work that is consistent, that is stylistically unified within its own self-defined universe. The task of the student is to try to understand what that universe is and how the different aspects of the composition fit into it.

SUMMARY

The traditional approaches to composing melodies are still available to the composer, and certainly there are twentieth-century melodies that exhibit many of them. What interests us here is not so much the traditional aspects of twentieth-century melodies as those aspects that set them apart from the music of the past. Though the fragmentation of styles in the twentieth century makes any generalization difficult, a list of the tendencies seen in twentieth-century melody would include the following:

Wider range

More leaps

More chromaticism

Less lyricism

Unconventional rhythm

More expression marks

Avoidance of traditional harmonic implications

Less regular phrase structure

Motivic use of pitch-class cells

Twelve-tone melody

Less emphasis on melody in general

Voice-leading procedures in the twentieth century are as varied as the multiplicity of musical styles would suggest. The traditional procedures are still available and have not been discarded entirely, but some important conventions of tonal harmony must now be considered as options rather than rules. As a result, parallel motion of all kinds is acceptable, including harmonic planing, while dissonances have been freed from conventional resolutions, and even from any requirement for resolution at all.

NOTES

1. Throughout this chapter and much of the remainder of this book, "tonal" is used to refer to the system of functional harmonic tonality employed in Western art music from around 1600 to around 1900. This use of the term admittedly can be misleading, since it implies that all other music is atonal. The author hopes that this disclaimer will head off any such misconceptions.
2. Parallel octaves were allowed when one part merely doubled another consistently at the interval of an octave. The same cannot be said of 5ths.
3. Some prefer to use the term "organum" for harmonic parallelism in the twentieth century, especially when it involves root-position triads.
4. Arnold Schoenberg, *Style and Idea*, pp. 216–17.
5. Igor Stravinsky, *Poetics of Music*, pp. 63–65.

EXERCISES

Part A: Fundamentals

The Fundamentals exercises in this chapter provide a review of material from earlier chapters.

1. Notate the following scales.

    a. Pentatonic on A♭
    b. Whole-tone on G
    c. Phrygian on F
    d. Dorian on G♯
    e. Octatonic (diminished) beginning D–E

2. Review the summary at the end of Chapter 3. Of the nine chord types listed there, which term best describes:

    a. the chords in mm. 3–4 of Example 4–10?
    b. the chords in Example 4–12?

Part B: Analysis

1. Alban Berg: Violin Concerto (1935), I, mm. 84–93 (solo violin only).

Discuss this melody, including the following points:

  a. What elements are especially typical of twentieth-century melody?

  b. Is any part of this melody a twelve-tone melody?

  c. Does this melody make use of pitch-class cells?

2. Edgard Varèse: *Density 21.5* (1936, 1946), mm. 1–17.

Discuss this melody, including the following points:

a. Which of its elements are especially typical of twentieth-century melody?

b. Is any part of this melody a twelve-tone melody?

c. What is its motivic organization?

3. Karl Korte: *Aspects of Love* (1965), I, mm. 1–3.

Write out the bass line of this excerpt, and under each bass note label the root and quality of the chord (except for the open 5ths, where the quality cannot be determined). Some of the chords are spelled enharmonically. Then answer the following questions.

a. In what ways does the voice leading in this excerpt depart from tonal practice? Be specific.

b. Discuss the reasons for the enharmonic spellings. What other options could have been followed?

4. Review the discussion of Example 4–10. Then briefly discuss the texture of Example 4–11, using a similar approach.

5. Study the voice leading in the following examples.

Example 2–4 (p. 27)   Example 3–10 (p. 54)   Example 3–23 (p. 63)
Example 2–9 (p. 31)   Example 3–20 (p. 61)   Example 3–B–7 (p. 75)
Example 2–11 (p. 32)   Example 3–21 (p. 61)

Then answer the questions below, using each example only once.

a. Which one features two sets of parallel 5ths in imitation?

b. Which one uses diatonic planing of triads?

c. Which one uses real planing of triads?

d. Which two use real planing of nontertian sonorities?

e. Which one features clusters in parallel motion?

f. Which one features unresolved dissonances?

g. Which one adheres most closely to traditional voice leading?

Part C: Composition

1. Compose a melody exhibiting several of the characteristics of twentieth-century melody discussed in the Summary (but not including pitch-class cells or twelve-tone melody), and list those characteristics. Try not to let your melody sound too random, and see that every phrase includes a single highpoint.

2. Compose a melody following the preceding instructions, but using the cell E–G–G♯ and its mirror inversion E–C♯–C as a unifying factor. The

cell and its inversion may be used in any transposition and in any octave, and the notes of the cell may be used in any order. Label each appearance of the cell with brackets.

3. Compose an adagio melody in the same style as the horn melody in Example 4–7 (p. 87), using the pitch classes from that melody, but in reverse order.

4. Compose a short example in which a Phrygian melody is accompanied by planed triads (diatonic planing).

5. Continue the following example, using real planing throughout.

6. Compose an excerpt similar in style to Example 4–B–3, following these guidelines:

   a. Use triads, 7th chords, and open 5ths only.

   b. Approach each 7th by step or common tone.

   c. Leave each 7th by step up or leap down.

   d. Include some parallelism.

   e. Be sure that each part is easy to sing.

Part D: Further Reading

CHRIST, WILLIAM, AND OTHERS. *Materials and Structure of Music.* Vol. 2. See Chapter 14, "Melody in Twentieth-Century Music."

DALLIN, LEON. *Techniques of Twentieth Century Composition.* See Chapter 4, "Twentieth Century Melodic Practices," and the section titled "Parallelism" in Chapter 7.

KLIEWER, VERNON L. "Melody: Linear Aspects of Twentieth-Century Music," in Gary Wittlich, ed., *Aspects of Twentieth Century Music.*

PERSICHETTI, VINCENT. *Twentieth-Century Harmony.* Much of Chapters 3–7 is devoted to details of voice leading.

ULEHLA, LUDMILA. *Contemporary Harmony.* See Chapter 10, "Unrestricted Melodic Movement of All Chord Members."

5 | Harmonic Progression and Tonality

INTRODUCTION

The late nineteenth and early twentieth centuries saw the decline of the tonal system, which had been an important organizing factor in music since the early Baroque. In its place came not a new system but a splintering, a multiplicity of solutions to the problems of harmonic progression and tonality. At the most general level, music is either tonal or not tonal (usually termed atonal), but various approaches may be taken in both of those categories. As we shall see, even the tonal music of the twentieth century was of a new sort, one without a standardized vocabulary of harmonic progressions.

TRADITIONAL APPROACHES TO HARMONIC PROGRESSION

The beginnings of triadic tonality can be found in music composed many years before the beginning of the tonal era. Through evolutionary processes (influenced by voice-leading conventions and the nature of musical acoustics), certain chord successions became standard cadential formulas long before tonal harmony came into being and even longer before the development of the theory of chord roots. Chief among these was the progression that would later be analyzed as a V–I cadence, but other cadences, such as IV–I, vii°6–I, and iv6–V, were also used. As the language of tonality developed, the V–I progression became the prototype of the normative harmonic progression, as seen in the diatonic circle-of-5ths progression:

$$I–IV–vii°–iii–vi–ii–V–I$$

or

$$i–iv–VII–III–VI–ii°–V–i$$

All of the roots in these progressions move by descending diatonic 5th, either perfect or diminished. The same is true in the following progressions, which use some altered chords. Notice that leading-tone chords can substitute for dominant chords of equivalent function.[1]

V7/V–V–I	vii°7/vi–vi–vii°7/V
VI–N6–V	V7/vi–vii°7/ii–V7/V

If the subdominant triad is allowed to substitute for the supertonic triad, putting ii–V and IV–V in the same category, and vii° is allowed to substitute for V, we find that most of the standard chord progressions of tonal music are circle-of-5ths types. Exceptions include those that involve "linear" chords, such as augmented-6th chords, and others used to extend the phrase, such as the "deceptive" progression (V–vi).

This system turned out to be extremely flexible. It allowed a broad range of expression and made possible the composition of long works organized over a background harmonic structure. But late in the nineteenth century and in the early decades of the twentieth, compositional assaults on the system became so insistent that traditional tonality and its associated harmonic progressions all but disappeared from the works of "serious" composers. The procedures that have been discussed in earlier chapters—the introduction of new scales and chord types and the redefinition of the fundamental principles of voice leading—had much to do with the decline of tonal harmony.

Conventional harmonic progressions still occur with some frequency, especially at cadences, in works from the early part of the twentieth century. Two such examples from earlier in this text are Example 3–3 (p. 51), by Debussy, and Example 3–B–4 (p. 73), by Ravel. Examples of conventional progressions from later in the century generally are found in works with a nationalistic or folk-music background, such as Copland's *Billy the Kid*; in the works by staunchly conservative composers such as Rachmaninoff; or in works of a lighter, more entertaining sort, like Menotti's *The Telephone* (see Example 3–11, p. 55). Since the 1970s, conventional tonal music has found new life in an important style called "neo-Romanticism," to be discussed in Chapter 15.

Perhaps the healthiest and most vital continuation of traditional harmony was in the "popular" music of the twentieth century, which includes everything from Broadway musicals to folk music to jazz to rock music. The harmonizations of most of this music can be analyzed using traditional approaches, but the analysis should concentrate on the composer's actual harmonization, not on the chord symbols that often appear in popular-music editions and which are frequently incorrect. More recent rock music, especially since the introduction of electronic synthesizers, has shown an increasing tendency to leave behind its harmonic roots in the blues tradition and to concentrate on unconventional timbres and nonstandard progressions.

NEW APPROACHES TO HARMONIC PROGRESSION

We might expect that, as the older system declined, a new one would have developed to take its place, perhaps one built on root movements of a 3rd or on more-involved cycles of root movements. In fact this did not happen. There is no common harmonic language shared by all composers, although composers are free to devise and follow their own stylistic "rules" (recall the Stravinsky quote on p. 96).

Even twentieth-century modal music tends to avoid root movements by 5ths, as well as the voice-leading constraints of traditional major-minor music. But there are exceptions, as in Example 2–B–4 (p. 44), where a simple modal melody is accompanied by tertian chords. The harmonization of most of this excerpt is quite traditional, although the supertonic $\frac{6}{4}$ chords in mm. 10 and 12 and the altered dominant in m. 18 are not. Nevertheless, this is a fairly close modal equivalent of a conventional tonal progression.

Composers who still make use of tertian sonorities generally do so in the context of unusual or unpredictable harmonic successions. In Example 3–9 (p. 54) Debussy ended a piece with the following progression:

Em–AM–Fm–CMadd9

This succession of chords is surely intended to be unpredictable to the listener, to delight and surprise rather than to perform the task of most tonal progressions, which is to satisfy expectations. It is of no help to the listener that a similar progression appeared earlier (mm. 4–5), because the similarity is one of gesture rather than of detail:

E♭M–A♭M–G♭M–Dm

Much of the element of surprise in these two passages is provided by doubly chromatic mediant relationships: A major–F minor and G♭ major–D minor.

Examples of such successions—one hesitates to call them progressions—abound in twentieth-century tertian music. Example 5–1 is simpler, the chords consisting of an A minor tonic triad and its B♭ minor neighbor.

The subject of harmonic progression becomes even murkier when nontertian chords are considered, because the roots of such chords are not defined by any generally accepted theory or by the common agreement of listeners. The most successful attempt to develop a universal theory of chord roots was carried out by Paul Hindemith in his *Craft of Musical Composition*,[2] first published in 1937. Although his theory does account for

EXAMPLE 5–1 Aram Khachaturian: Piano Concerto (1936), II, mm. 1–8 *(Copyright © 1947 by LEEDS MUSIC CORPORATION. Copyright renewed. Rights administered by MCA MUSIC PUBLISHING, A Division of MCA INC., New York, NY 10019. Used by permission. All rights reserved.)*

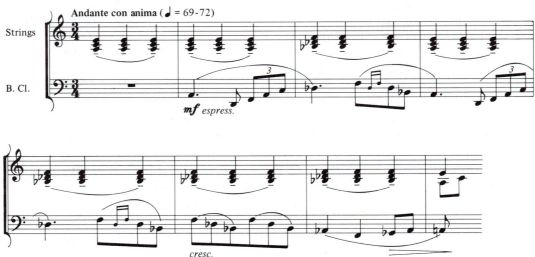

all possible chords (with the exception of microtonal chords) and had a certain amount of influence in the middle of the century, it has since fallen into disfavor, largely because, as Hindemith himself wrote, "A true musician believes only in what he hears,"[3] and his fellow musicians remained unconvinced.

If it is no longer possible to create meaningful harmonic progressions based on chord roots, are there other possibilities? One would be to arrange a succession of chords according to some measurement of the tension, or dissonance, that each contains. Again, Hindemith was one of the few to attempt a systematic approach to harmonic tension that would account for all possible sonorities. He devised six chord groups, with six subgroups bringing the total number of classifications to twelve. To most of these were assigned a relative degree of harmonic tension, which, along with other aspects of his theory, allowed Hindemith to propose "progressions" of chords arranged according to their tension.[4] As with his theory of chord roots, this aspect of Hindemith's theory has not withstood the test of time. Nevertheless, it would be foolish to dismiss out of hand the considered opinions of an accomplished composer, and the interested reader is urged to study his theory in its entirety.[5]

Even without a universally accepted theory, a composer is, of course, free to attempt progressions of tension. Other possibilities might include progressions of register, chord type, density, numbers of pitch classes, and so forth. We are on unfamiliar ground here, as we often are in approaching twentieth-century works, and imagination and flexibility of approach are important analytical tools.

NONHARMONIC MUSIC

In its broadest definition, harmony means the vertical aspect of music, and a harmony, or chord, is any collection of pitch classes sounded simultaneously. Such broad definitions are sometimes useful, but they may also distract us from the fact that a good deal of twentieth-century music is not harmonic in conception. Sometimes the "simultaneities" in a piece are just that—the more or less uncontrolled coming-together of very independent lines. Although Schoenberg was certainly not completely indifferent to the vertical dimension, it would appear that the primary emphases in Example 5–2, for instance, is on lines, rather than the chords that they produce. (Remember that the bass clarinet will sound a major 9th lower than written.) The term "linear counterpoint" is often used for music of this sort, where the compositional method is evidently overwhelmingly linear. This approach is typical of much atonal music, but it occurs in other styles as well.

EXAMPLE 5–2   Schoenberg: *Pierrot Lunaire,* Op. 21 (1912), "Madonna, mm. 1–4   *(Used by permission of Belmont Music Publishers.)*

ESTABLISHING A TONAL CENTER

Before examining how tonality is established in twentieth-century works, let us review how this was accomplished in traditional tonal harmony. One important element was a descending perfect-5th root movement to tonic combined with a half-step leading-tone motion, also a tonic. The tonicizing effect was often made more convincing by a harmonic tritone formed by scale degrees 7 and 4 resolving stepwise to 1 and 3. Other elements were important also, such as melodic emphasis on 1, 3, and 5, melodic skips between 1 and 5, and formal considerations.

All of these elements may be present to some degree in twentieth-century music that has a tonal center, but a traditional V7–I cadence would be exceptional. Instead, other ways have been devised to make the tonal center clear to the listener. Essentially, these methods establish tonic by assertion—that is, through the use of reiteration, return, pedal point, ostinato, accent, formal placement, register, and similar techniques to draw the listener's attention to a particular pitch class. When analyzing the tonality of a passage, it is important to pay attention to melodic aspects as well as harmonic ones, since melodic factors are often crucial in determining the tonality.

For instance, what is it about Example 5–3 that leads us to hear E as the tonal center? Clearly, in the absence of conventional harmonic progressions, it is the E pedal point and the fact that the melody begins and ends on E.

EXAMPLE 5–3   Prokofiev: Piano Sonata No. 6 (1940), II, mm. 1–4   *(Excerpted from the International Music Co. Edition, New York, NY 10018.)*

Example 5–1 convinced us that A is the tonal center of the passage without the use of a pedal point. There is also no hint of dominant harmony or of any conventional scale on A, and the leading tone appears only once (in m. 7, as A♭); in addition, there are just as many measures of B♭ minor chords as there are of A minor chords. Yet we hear A as the tonal center because it was there first, before the melody began, and because A is important both melodically and harmonically at the beginning and end of the phrase. The B♭ minor triads, while interesting, do not distract our attention from the true tonal center.

We will use the term "neotonality" in reference to music that is tonal but in which the tonal center is established through nontraditional means. Though not an ideal term, it will help us to distinguish between the tonal music of the seventeenth through nineteenth centuries and the neotonal music of the twentieth century.

TERTIAN AND NONTERTIAN NEOTONALITY

As we examine additional neotonal examples, we will attempt to categorize them into one of two types: tertian neotonality and nontertian neotonality. As the terms imply, the first type uses primarily chords built from 3rds, whereas the second type usually avoids such sonorities, except perhaps at cadences. Many examples will be of a mixed type, displaying features of both.

Examples 5–1 and 5–3 are both examples of tertian neotonality. Example 5–3 is not quite as clear an instance as Example 5–1, but most of the sonorities appearing above the pedal point in Example 5–3 appear to be tertian in origin. A conservative example of tertian neotonality is seen in Example 2–B–4 (p. 44), whose harmonic progression was discussed earlier in this chapter. In that excerpt, the tonality of D is clearly established, both melodically and harmonically. Melodically, D is established by formal placement (beginnings and ends of phrases), by agogic accent, and by the frequent reiteration of D. The harmonic aspects that establish D as the tonal center include formal placement, pedal point, reiteration, and (in mm. 18–19) a V–I root movement (although not a traditional V7–I progression).

Much of the composition in which Example 5–4 appears is in a tertian neotonal style, but the excerpt shown here is nontertian. Even though there is an open 5th on D at the end of the excerpt, suggesting a tertian harmony, the excerpt is basically nontertian, since there is little else about the harmony or melody that suggests tertian construction. The tonality of D in Example 5–4 is established by both melodic and harmonic factors. Notice that the first phrase in the flute begins on A and ends on D, while the second begins on F (E♯) and ends on A, which is followed by F♯ and D. All of these notes are members of major or minor triads on D. In the piano part the emphasis on the pitch classes D and A is obvious. Even though this music is basically nontertian, the traditional dominant-to-tonic relationship is employed to help establish the tonality.

Example 5–5 seems to have a mixture of tertian and nontertian elements. It begins with an F major triad, the third chord is an F minor triad, and the last sonority is an open 5th on F, but the other four chords in the excerpt sound more like quartal or mixed-interval chords. The tonality in Example 5–5 is established by several factors. The melody obviously centers around F, and the harmony of the phrase begins and ends on F, while in the inner voices there is a double pedal point in F and C. Another interesting feature is the duet between alto and bass, moving in parallel major 10ths until the last two chords, where contrary motion takes over.

POLYTONALITY

Polytonality is conceptually similar to the polychord, which was defined in Chapter 3 as a combination of two or more aurally distinguishable sonorities. Likewise, polytonality is the simultaneous use of two or more aurally distinguishable tonal centers, almost all examples consisting of two tonal

EXAMPLE 5–4   Walter Piston: Flute Sonata (1930), I, last 6 measures

EXAMPLE 5–5   Hindemith: *Ludus Tonalis* (1943), Interlude (No. IX), mm. 8–10   *(© Schott & Co., Ltd., London, 1943. Copyright renewed. All rights reserved. Used by permission of European American Music Distributors Corporation, sole U.S. agent for Schott & Co., Ltd.)*

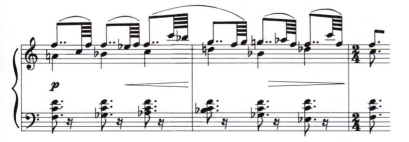

centers rather than three or more. The term "bitonal" is sometimes used for polytonal music with two tonal centers. As a general rule, each tonal layer in a polytonal passage will be basically diatonic to its own scale.

The last section of Debussy's "Fireworks" begins in D♭, over which is superimposed a C major melody and its counterpoint. Only in the last three measures is the polytonal conflict resolved, with the D♭ tonality winning out (see Example 5–6).

In Example 5–7 bitonality occurs in a modal setting. Here the first violin is in E♭ Dorian, while the cello is in D Dorian. Meanwhile, the other instruments are playing only D's and E♭'s. In both Example 5–6 and Example 5–7 the tonalities were a minor 2nd apart, but this is in no sense a "rule" of bitonality. Other relationships can and do occur.

An interesting example of polytonality involving four tonal levels is

EXAMPLE 5–6   Debussy: Preludes, Book II (1913), "Fireworks" ("Feux d'artifice") mm. 91–99

EXAMPLE 5–7   Bartók: String Quartet No. 3 (1927), II   *(© Copyright 1929 by Universal Edition; Copyright Renewed. Copyright and Renewal assigned to Boosey & Hawkes, Inc. for USA only. Reprinted by permission.)*

found in the second movement of Henry Brant's *Angels and Devils* (1932, 1947), where a pair of piccolos and three pairs of flutes are notated in four different keys. It would take a sharp ear indeed to sort all of this out aurally, but most listeners are probably aware that some sort of polytonality is involved.

ATONALITY

Atonality was a development even more radical than the various sorts of neotonality in twentieth-century music. The ways in which atonality has been achieved and the analytical approaches that have been developed for atonal music are extensive and will be discussed in later chapters. For now it will suffice to define atonal music as music in which the listener perceives no tonal center. Since this is a subjective definition, listeners will not always agree as to whether a particular example is tonal or atonal, but the following examples from earlier in the text would probably be heard as atonal by most musicians.

Example 2–7 (Henze, p. 29)
Example 2–16 (Scriabin, p. 35)
Example 2–B–3 (Webern, p. 43)
Example 4–4 (Boulez, p. 83)
Example 4–7 (Schoenberg, p. 87)
Example 5–2 (Schoenberg, p. 108)

PANDIATONICISM

Most atonal music, as well as a large proportion of other works composed in the twentieth or late nineteenth century, is based on the chromatic scale. Presumably as a reaction against such unremitting chromaticism, some composers have employed a style known as *pandiatonicism*. The term *pandiatonic* is used to describe a passage that uses only the tones of some diatonic scale but does not rely on traditional harmonic progressions and dissonance treatment. Such passages are generally neotonal and may be tertian or nontertian. An earlier excerpt by Ives, Example 3–23 (p. 63), illustrates nontertian pandiatonicism. Most of the sonorities in the excerpt are clusters derived from the C major scale. The three altered notes that appear do not seem to destroy the basic pandiatonic sound. The tonality is not obvious, but it is probably G, which at the end is both the highest and the lowest pitch class.

The pandiatonic passage in Example 5–8 makes use of the C major scale. It is best classified as tertian, but the chords are sometimes difficult to identify with certainty. Later in the piece, the music "modulates" through several pandiatonic areas, including C♯, G♭, and F. Other famous pandiatonic passages occur in Stravinsky's *Petrushka* and Copland's *Appalachian Spring*.

SUMMARY

Traditional tonal harmony and the circle-of-5ths progressions associated with it survived in various kinds of popular music as well as in a small proportion of "classical" music in the twentieth century. Otherwise, har-

EXAMPLE 5–8   Stravinsky: *Serenade in A* (1925), I, mm. 52–58   *(© Copyright 1926 by Edition Russe de Musique; Copyright Renewed. Copyright and Renewal assigned to Boosey & Hawkes, Inc. Reprinted by permission.)*

monic progression has to be regarded as a non-issue in an era without a common harmonic vocabulary and no generally accepted theory of chord roots. The declining interest in the vertical dimension is typified by linear counterpoint, in which the "chords" seem truly to be mere simultaneities created by the relatively uncontrolled relationships between independent lines.

For the most part, at least after the first few decades of the century, "serious" music has been either neotonal or atonal. Neotonal music, whether tertian or nontertian, has had to rely on methods other than the V7–I progression for establishing a tonality. These methods include such devices as pedal point and ostinato, accent (metric, agogic, or dynamic), and formal placement. Melodies play a larger role in determining the tonality than was the case in tonal music.

Other developments in twentieth-century tonality include: polytonality, the employment of two or more tonal centers simultaneously; atonality, the avoidance of a tonal center; and pandiatonicism, the use of a diatonic scale in a neotonal style.

NOTES

1. See Kostka and Payne, *Tonal Harmony*, p. 277.
2. Paul Hindemith, *Craft of Musical Composition*, Vol. I.
3. Hindemith, *Craft*, p. 156.
4. See especially pp. 158–60.
5. Other attempts have been made to compute the dissonance level of chords, but none has had the influence of Hindemith's. One example is in Wallace Berry, *Structural Functions in Music*, pp. 107–11.

EXERCISES

Part A: Fundamentals

Define each of the following terms.

1. Chromatic mediant relationship

2. Cluster

3. Mode of limited transposition

4. Neotonality

5. Pandiatonicism

6. Pitch-class cell

7. Planing

8. Polychord

9. Real sequence

Part B: Analysis

Each of the following excerpts for analysis is to be approached in the same way:

    a. Assuming the excerpt is neotonal (and they all are), what is the tonal center, and what melodic and harmonic factors contribute to establishing that tonality?

    b. Is the neotonal style tertian, nontertian, or a mixture of the two?

    c. Is the excerpt polytonal? If so, discuss.

   d. Is the excerpt pandiatonic? If so, discuss.

   e. Do you find any evidence of traditional harmonic progressions? Explain your answer.

1. Example 2–4, p. 27 (Bartók: *Bluebeard's Castle*).

2. Example 2–11, p. 32 (Debussy: "Footprints in the Snow").

3. Example 3–5, p. 52 (Prokofiev: Flute Sonata).

4. Example 3–B–5, p. 74 (Ravel: *Sonatina*).

5. Example 3–B–7, p. 75 (Alban Berg: "Warm Is the Air").

6. Copland: *El Salón México* (1936).

7. Darius Milhaud: *Saudades do Brasil* (1921), "Copacabana," mm. 1–9.

Part C: Composition

As an alternative to any of the following exercises, disregard the music that is provided and compose your own example, illustrating the specified techniques.

1. Continue in B♭, illustrating tertian neotonality.

2. Continue in a mostly nontertian neotonal style. Try to convince the listener of a tonal center on D.

3. Compose an excerpt using polychords with A as a tonal center. End your example with the following cadence.

4. Continue, illustrating C major pandiatonicism and the use of an ostinato.

5. Use bitonality (B and D) at the beginning of this example, resolving into a single tonality at the end.

Part D: Further Reading

CHRIST, WILLIAM, AND OTHERS. *Materials and Structure of Music*, Vol. 2. See the section titled "Harmonic Succession" in Chapter 15; also Chapter 16: "Tonality and Atonality in Twentieth-Century Music."

DALLIN, LEON. *Techniques of Twentieth Century Composition*. See Chapter 7: "Harmonic Succession," Chapter 8: "Tonality," and Chapter 9: "Cadences."

HARDER, PAUL O. *Bridge to 20th Century Music*. See Chapter 1, which deals with melodic tonality.

HINDEMITH, PAUL. *Craft of Musical Composition*, Vol. I. See especially the sections on interval roots (pp. 68–74, 79–89), chord roots (pp. 94–106), and harmonic tension (pp. 106–8, 158–164).

KOSTKA, STEFAN, AND DOROTHY PAYNE. *Tonal Harmony*. See the section titled "Pandiatonicism," pp. 477–78.

PERSICHETTI, VINCENT. *Twentieth-Century Harmony*. See the sections on "Progression" (pp. 182–88) and "Cadential Devices" (pp. 206–9), as well as pp. 248–61 in Chapter 12, "Key Centers."

REISBERG, HORACE. "The Vertical Dimension in Twentieth-Century Music," in Gary Wittlich, ed., *Aspects of 20th Century Music*. See the section titled "Negation of Harmony," pp. 372–85.

ULEHLA, LUDMILA. *Contemporary Harmony*. See the section on "Linear Tonality" in Chapter 18 and Chapter 19, "The Control of Dissonance."

ZIELIŃSKI, TADEUSZ A. "Harmony and Counterpoint," in John Vinton, ed., *Dictionary of Contemporary Music*.

6 | Developments in Rhythm

INTRODUCTION

One of the many features distinguishing the music of the twentieth century from that of the tonal era is its preoccupation with rhythm. Though rhythm is an important element of tonal music, perhaps in ways that are still not completely understood, the surface rhythm of most tonal pieces is relatively straightforward and easy to comprehend, so much so that analyses of such pieces often make little or no mention of the rhythmic dimension. In contrast, in many twentieth-century compositions the focus is on rhythm at least as much as on pitch, and the surface rhythms are frequently varied and complex. This chapter will explore some of the ways that these varieties and complexities are achieved, but first it will be useful to review some terminology.

Rhythm—The organization of the time element in music.
Beat—The basic pulse.
Simple beat—Division of the beat into two equal parts.

Compound beat—Division of the beat into three equal parts.

Meter—The grouping of beats into larger units.

Duple meter—The grouping of beats into twos.

Triple meter—The grouping of beats into threes.

Quadruple meter—The grouping of beats into fours.

Measure—One full unit of the meter.

In simple beat, the beat note has traditionally been as large as a half-note and as small as a sixteenth-note. The customary time (meter) signatures for simple beat, then, have consisted of a 2, 3, or 4 over a 2, 4, 8, or 16. In compound beat, the custom has been for the top number of the meter signature to be the number of *divisions* of the beat that may occur in the measure; thus, the top number will always be 6, 9, or 12, for duple, triple, or quadruple meters, respectively. The bottom number specifies the duration of the division of the beat, traditionally a quarter-note, an eighth-note, or a sixteenth-note. The usual time signatures for compound beat, then, have consisted of a 6, 9, or 12 over a 4, 8, or 16.

	Duple				Triple				Quadruple			
Simple	$\frac{2}{2}$	$\frac{2}{4}$	$\frac{2}{8}$	$\frac{2}{16}$	$\frac{3}{2}$	$\frac{3}{4}$	$\frac{3}{8}$	$\frac{3}{16}$	$\frac{4}{2}$	$\frac{4}{4}$	$\frac{4}{8}$	$\frac{4}{16}$
Compound	$\frac{6}{4}$	$\frac{6}{8}$	$\frac{6}{16}$		$\frac{9}{4}$	$\frac{9}{8}$	$\frac{9}{16}$		$\frac{12}{4}$	$\frac{12}{8}$	$\frac{12}{16}$	

The listener perceives the beat type (simple or compound) by listening to the way the beat divides (into twos or threes); the meter type is conveyed by the characteristic pattern of accents. These accents can be of any type, but dynamic and agogic accents are most commonly used to express the meter. The traditional patterns of metric accents are shown below, with ">" indicating an accent, "(>)" indicating a weaker accent, and "–" indicating no accent.

```
Duple        1   2  |  1   2  |
             >   –     >   –
Triple       1   2   3  |  1   2   3  |
             >   –   –     >   –   –
Quadruple  1   2   3   4  |  1   2   3   4  |
           >   –  (>)  –       >   –  (>)  –
```

SYNCOPATION

Syncopation is a term used either when a rhythmic event such as an accent occurs at an unexpected moment or when a rhythmic event fails to occur when expected. Syncopation is an important element of twentieth-century music, and one that is so familiar that it probably does not need much discussion here. An excerpt containing syncopation was seen in Example 5–8 (p. 115). In that example the syncopation comes about by denying an articulation on the fourth eighth-note of the melody in the first three measures of the excerpt as well as on the downbeat of the last measure.

Syncopation that follows any kind of perceptible pattern may indicate that some other rhythmic device is being employed. In the Stravinsky excerpt (Example 5–8; p. 115), the melody in the first 3½ measures could be heard in a variety of meters, including $\frac{3}{4}$ and $\frac{4}{4}$, as well as the notated $\frac{6}{8}$. Even when syncopation does not follow a pattern, one listener may hear it as a change of meter while another hears it as a syncopation within a single meter. This brings us to one of the main difficulties of rhythmic analysis: the necessity of recognizing that what is perceived is often different from what is written.

WRITTEN RHYTHM AND PERCEIVED RHYTHM

Of course, it is perfectly possible to compose music in such a way that the listener will not be able to perceive the notated beat type or meter type or both. The first of Chopin's Preludes, Op. 28, is heard in compound time, but it is notated in $\frac{2}{8}$, with most of the beats being divided into sixteenth-note triplets. Contradictions between the way rhythm is heard and the way it is written are especially common in twentieth-century music. An example similar to the Chopin prelude, but more complex, is the second movement of Webern's *Variations for Piano*, Op. 27 (1936). Although written in a very fast simple duple, it seems to most listeners to be in a slower compound meter, with occasional odd-length beats thrown in. The beginning of the piece is seen in Example 6–1, with the perceived rhythm notated below. (It could also be heard in $\frac{3}{8}$.) Notice the extra eighth-note rest in the second measure.

Often the conflict between written and perceived rhythms arises out of consideration for the performer. The top staff of Example 6–2 shows us an excerpt as it was conceived by the composer, Olivier Messiaen, while the

EXAMPLE 6–1   Webern: *Variations for Piano,* **Op. 27, II, mm. 1–4**   *(Copyright 1937 by Universal Edition. Copyright renewed 1965. All rights reserved. Used by permission of European American Music Distributors Corporation, sole U.S. agent for Universal Edition Vienna.)*

EXAMPLE 6–2   Messiaen: *The Technique of My Musical Language* **(1944), Examples 68 and 69**   *(© 1966 Editions Alphonse Leduc. Used by permission of the publisher.)*

bottom staff shows us the same music written in what Messiaen calls the "fourth notation," the one that he feels is "easiest for performers, since it disarranges their habits in no way."[1] Presumably a sensitive performance of the "fourth notation" in Example 6–2 would help us to perceive the passage as it is written on the top staff.

In many of the examples discussed in this chapter, it will be necessary to distinguish between rhythm as written and rhythm as perceived. In all cases we will take the perceived rhythm as the true rhythm.

CHANGING TIME SIGNATURES

Though changing from one time signature to another in the course of a movement is not a device exclusive to the twentieth century, it is certainly one that has seen more use in the twentieth-century than in the tonal era. Terms for this technique include *changing meters*, *mixed meter*, *variable meter*, and *multimeter*. Changing meters can be implied by shifted accents or syncopations, or they can be explicitly notated by the composer. Several examples have already illustrated changing time signatures, among them the following:

Example 3–20 (p. 61): $\frac{3}{4}$ $\frac{5}{8}$ $\frac{4}{8}$

Example 4–7 (p. 87): $\frac{6}{4}$ $\frac{7}{4}$

Example 4–8 (p. 89): $\frac{4}{2}$ $\frac{5}{2}$ $\frac{4}{2}$

A more problematical example was Example 4–9 (p. 91), where the meter signatures fluctuated between $\frac{3}{8}$ and $\frac{2}{8}$, even though the perceived rhythm of the solo piano part remained steadfastly in $\frac{2}{8}$. A closer examination of the accompanying orchestral parts, however, reveals that the changing time signatures do reflect the rhythm of the accompaniment. This example will be discussed in more detail later.

NONTRADITIONAL TIME SIGNATURES

The list of time signatures given at the beginning of this chapter has been considerably expanded by twentieth-century composers. Of greatest signif-icance has been the use of values *other* than 2, 3, 4, 6, 9, or 12 for the top number of a time signature. While 5 and 7 have been especially favored (this is why some employ the term *asymmetrical meter* for this device), others such as 1, 8, 10, and 11 have not been completely neglected.

The notated time signature in Example 4–12 (p. 94) is $\frac{4}{4}$, but it is obvious from the phrasing and accents that the *perceived* meter is $\frac{5}{4}$. Most examples of nontraditional meters can easily be heard as changing meters, and this is also true of Example 4–12, which sounds like $\frac{2}{4}$ alternating with $\frac{3}{4}$. However, Example 4–10 (p. 92), also in $\frac{5}{4}$, does not seem to divide clearly into 2 + 3 or 3 + 2. In Example 5–7 (p. 113), the divisions of the $\frac{5}{8}$ measures seem to imply 1 + 2 + 2, 2 + 2 + 1, and 2 + 3, with the first violin and the cello not always in agreement in any particular measure.

Example 5–B–6 (p. 117) illustrates several nontraditional time signa-tures: $\frac{8}{8}$, $\frac{11}{8}$, and $\frac{5}{8}$. Of course, $\frac{8}{8}$ contains the same number of eighth-notes as

$\frac{4}{4}$; Copland presumably used $\frac{8}{8}$ to call our attention to the irregular division of the measures into $3+5$ and $5+3$ eighth-notes (instead of the customary $4+4$). The term *additive rhythm* is sometimes used for passages such as this, where some short note value (here the eighth-note) remains constant but is used in groups of unpredictably varying lengths.

When a traditional time signature is transformed into a nontraditional one by the use of a nonstandard metric accent, one approach is to indicate the new metric accent with dotted lines, as in Example 5–B–6. Another way is to specify the new pattern of metric accents in the time signature itself, as Bartók did in the "Scherzo" of his String Quartet No. 5 (1934). There he transforms $\frac{9}{8}$ (traditionally $3+3+3$) into a nontraditional $4+2+3$ by use of a $\frac{4+2+3}{8}$ time signature, a type sometimes referred to as a *complex meter*. At a vivace tempo, the listener hears three beats of unequal length per measure, a variation on the traditional $\frac{3}{4}$ scherzo. The trio is in an unusual quadruple meter, predominantly $\frac{3+2+2+3}{8}$. Another approach to transforming traditional time signatures is to use the traditional signature, but to use accents and phrase marks to indicate the metric accent. This is the case in Example 6–3, where the two hands play groups of sixteenth-notes of varying length in notated $\frac{4}{4}$ and $\frac{3}{4}$ meters.

	m. 9	m. 10	m. 11	m. 12
R.H.:	rest	$6+6$	$6+6$	$1+5+2+4$
L.H.:	$5+1+4+2$	$4+2+5+1$	$6+6$	rest

EXAMPLE 6–3 Milton Babbitt: *Three Compositions for Piano* (1947), No. 1, mm. 9–12
(© copyright 1957 by Boelke-Bomart, Inc., Hillsdale, NY.)

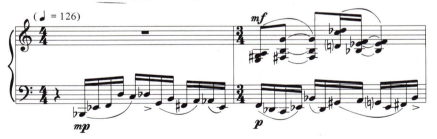

The nontraditional time signature that is the most difficult for performers is probably the fractional time signature. In the third measure of Example 4–4, (p. 83) Boulez writes 4/3 over 2, meaning four beats, each of them the length of one-third of a half-note. Note also the use of $\frac{5}{8}$ and $\frac{7}{8}$ in the example, the latter apparently being divided into two $\frac{7}{16}$ segments. Although each note value maintains a nearly constant metronomic duration in this excerpt (the quarter-note, for example, equals M.M. 104 or 105 throughout), the effect is of a fluid and constantly fluctuating tempo.

POLYMETER

The metrical equivalent of polytonality is *polymeter*, the simultaneous use of two or more aurally distinguishable time signatures. There are three possibilities: same time signature, but displaced (Example 6–4a); different signatures, with barlines coinciding (Example 6–4b); and different signatures, with barlines not coinciding (Example 6–4c). Though all three of these combinations occur, the third is perhaps the most striking aurally and

EXAMPLE 6–4   Polymeter

the most frequently employed. Remember that in each case we are referring to the aural effect, not necessarily to the actual notation.

In Example 6–5 the polymeter (type c) is explicitly notated in the viola
and cello parts. It comes about through the canon at the octave, with the
viola leading the cello by one measure. The fourth and fifth measures of the
viola part are in $\frac{3}{4}$ and $\frac{2}{4}$, while beneath those measures the cello plays the
third and fourth measures of the canon with time signatures of $\frac{2}{4}$ and $\frac{3}{4}$.

Music with barlines that do not coincide, as in Example 6–5, may be
troublesome for an ensemble or a conductor, so polymeter is often implied
instead of explicitly notated. This is the case in Example 6–6, a few pages
later in the same quartet—again a canonic example, this time between the
two violins. Here the viola and cello are clearly in $\frac{3}{8}$, but the violins sound

EXAMPLE 6–5 Bartók: String Quartet No. 3 (1927), II   *(© Copyright 1929 by Universal Edition;*
Copyright Renewed. Copyright and Renewal assigned to Boosey & Hawkes, Inc. for USA only.
Reprinted by permission.)

EXAMPLE 6–6   Bartók: String Quartet No. 3 (1927), II   *(© Copyright 1929 by Universal Edition; Copyright Re-*
newed. Copyright and Renewal assigned to Boosey & Hawkes, Inc. for USA only. Reprinted by permission.)

EXAMPLE 6–7   Explicit Polymetric Notation

as if they are in a polymetric canon (type a) with each other, as well as being polymetric (type c) with the accompaniment. The rhythms might be re-barred as in Example 6–7.

A less complicated example of implied polymeter was seen in Example 4–9 (p. 91), discussed above in connection with changing time signatures. In this instance the piano maintains a steady $\frac{2}{8}$ meter, although it is notated to conform with the changing meters of the brasses.

EXAMPLE 6–8   Stravinsky: *Petrushka* (1911), **first tableau**   *(Excerpted from the Norton Critical Edition. Used by permission of W. W. Norton & Co., Inc., and Edwin F. Kalmus & Co., Inc.)*

Polymeter with coinciding barlines (type b) is probably the least commonly used. Remember that the simultaneous use of $\frac{2}{4}$ and $\frac{6}{8}$, for instance, is not really polymeter but instead poly*division* of a single meter. One example of polymeter type b is seen in Example 6–8, where $\frac{7}{8}$ occurs against $\frac{3}{4}$, and $\frac{5}{8}$ against $\frac{2}{4}$. Here most of the orchestra alternates between $\frac{3}{4}$ and $\frac{2}{4}$, but the trumpets, oboes, and piccolos are in $\frac{7}{8}$ over the $\frac{3}{4}$ measures and $\frac{5}{8}$ over the $\frac{2}{4}$ measures. Because the downbeats of all the measures coincide, there is little of the feeling that we usually associate with polymeter in such a passage. Instead, the eighth-notes in the $\frac{7}{8}$ and $\frac{5}{8}$ measures seem to be new durations in their own right, slightly faster than the eighth-notes in the piano, but slower than the sixteenth-notes in the violins.

Similar in concept to polymeter but much less often encountered is *polytempo*, the simultaneous use of two or more aurally distinguishable tempos. One example of this is the second movement of Ives's Symphony No. 4 (1916). The movement begins with most of the orchestra playing in $\frac{6}{8}$ at ♩. = 50, while a second conductor leads the basses at ♩ = 80 and cues the bassoons, who are to play at ♩ = 70. Neither the basses nor the bassoons have a time signature. Various other combinations occur in the movement. At rehearsal no. 8 Conductor I leads part of the orchestra (chiefly strings and percussion) in an adagio $\frac{3}{2}$ while Conductor II leads the rest in an allegro $\frac{4}{4}$.

AMETRIC MUSIC

We recognize the beat and meter type of a passage by listening to the way that the beat divides and the way that beats group into larger units. Once we have grown used to devices such as changing meters and nontraditional meters, we are able to identify them aurally as well. Yet some music seems to exhibit no perceivable metric organization, a style we will refer to as *ametric*. Gregorian chant is a good example of ametric music, as is much electronic music. An example of music in the plainchant style was seen above in Example 3–16 (p. 57).

Some writers use the term "arhythmic" for music in which rhythmic patterns and metric organization are not perceivable. But if we accept a very general definition of rhythm as covering "all aspects of musical movement as ordered in time,"[2] then music cannot be arhythmic, but only ametric.

Not all music written without a time signature is ametric. For instance, four of the five movements of Hindemith's String Quartet No. 3 (1921) have no meter signature at all, but the music is barred, and the implied time signatures are clear both to the eye and to the ear. At the same time, some music notated *with* a time signature is written in such a way as to sound ametric. A good example of this is the Boulez excerpt discussed earlier in this chapter (Example 4–4, p. 83), which, while precisely notated, sounds free and improvisionary to the listener.

Music without barlines may be metric or not, depending on the composer's intention and the listener's interpretation. Although Ives used no time signature and no barlines in Example 3–B–6 (p. 74), a listener still might hear a steady $\frac{2}{4}$ organization. But Example 3–23 (p. 63), also by Ives, is almost certainly ametric, as is the rest of the movement from which it is excerpted.

Many passages exhibit some ametric features but also have some elements of metric organization. One such excerpt was Example 2–19 (p. 38), which employs no time signature but uses both a traditional barline and a shorter one to indicate two levels of metric organization. From the notation it is clear that the metric scheme is $\frac{3}{4}$–$\frac{7}{4}$–$\frac{3}{4}$–$\frac{6}{4}$, but whether the listener would be able to hear this metric organization might depend on various factors, including the listener's familiarity with the piece.

Luciano Berio's *Sequenza I* (1958) also uses a short barline (see Example 6–9), and the "measure" itself is assigned a specific tempo—M.M. 70 at the beginning. This composition is definitely ametric, however, because the actual durations are specified only by the placement of the notes within the measure. In the first measure, for example, the G5 is to be given the longest duration, because it occupies the greatest portion of the measure. Notation of this sort is sometimes called *proportional notation*. Accidentals in this excerpt affect only the notes they precede.

EXAMPLE 6–9   Berio: *Sequenza I* (1958), first staff

Many techniques developed after 1960 result in ametric effects, often involving some degree of improvisation, as in Example 6–9 and in the next excerpt. In Example 6–10 the temporal organization is determined by timed segments, with unmetered improvisation going on within them. These and other improvisatory techniques will be covered in more detail in Chapter 14.

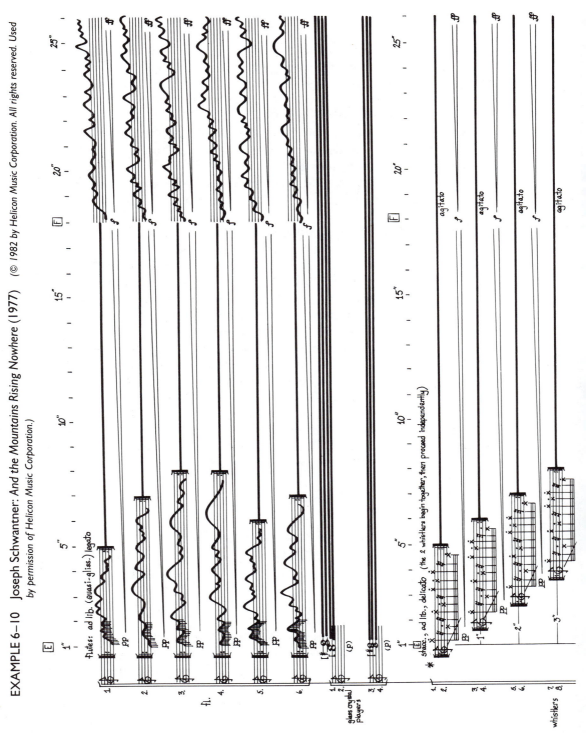

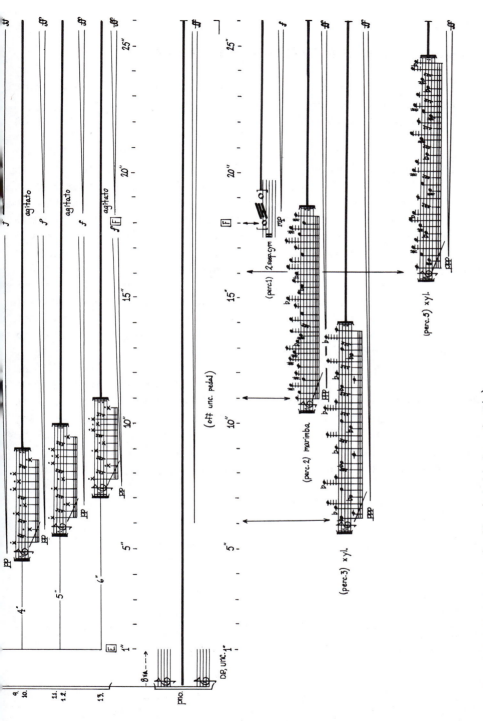

* whistle short "stacc." pitches (specific pitches not indicated, only general register)

133

ADDED VALUES AND NONRETROGRADABLE RHYTHMS

Two techniques from the fertile imagination of Olivier Messiaen will be discussed here. The first one, called *added values*, involves complicating an otherwise simple rhythmic pattern by the addition of a short duration in the form of a dot, a note, or a rest. In Example 6–11 each added value is identified by a " + ". The first three measures would clearly be in $\frac{4}{4}$ without the added values; with them, the effect is still of quadruple meter, but with one or two longer beats in each measure. The rest of the example is more complicated rhythmically and would probably be perceived as ametric.

A *nonretrogradable rhythm* is simply a rhythmic pattern that sounds the same whether played forward or backward (in retrograde). A trivial example would be a group of four eighth-notes, but Messiaen is interested in more complicated patterns. The rhythm of each measure in Example 6–12 is nonretrogradable, and each measure also contains added values. Notice that the rhythmic activity builds gradually to a climax in the seventh measure, followed by a immediate relaxation through longer note values. Both of the Messiaen examples are drawn from the sixth movement of his *Quartet for the End of Time* (1941).

Another way to look at nonretrogradable rhythms is that each one contains some rhythmic pattern followed by its retrograde, resulting inevitably in a rhythmic *palindrome*, a term used for any structure in language or music that reads the same forward as it does backward. Therefore, any piece that makes use of rhythmic retrogrades on a larger scale could also be considered an example of nonretrogradable rhythms. For instance, the second movement of Webern's Symphony, Op. 21 (1928), begins with an eleven-measure theme that is a rhythmic palindrome, a technique that is found through much of the movement.

EXAMPLE 6–11 Messiaen: *The Technique of My Musical Language*, Example 13, mm. 1–6   (© 1944 Editions Alphonse Leduc. Copyright renewed 1966. Used by permission of the publisher.)

EXAMPLE 6–12   Messiaen: *The Technique of My Musical Language*, Example 33   *(© 1944*
Editions Alphonse Leduc. Copyright renewed 1966. Used by permission of the publisher.)

TEMPO MODULATION (METRIC MODULATION)

Elliott Carter is generally credited with being the first to use a particular method of changing tempos precisely by making some note value in the first tempo equal to a different note value (or at least to a different proportion of the beat) in the second tempo. For example, to "modulate" from ♩ = 80 to ♩ = 120, one could begin using eighth-note triplets in the first tempo. These triplet eighths have a duration of 240 per minute (three times the ♩ = 80 rate). This rate of 240 turns out to be the rate of the division of the beat (the eighth-note) at the new tempo of ♩ = 120. (See Example 6–13). This device has been called "metric modulation" because it usually involves changing time signatures; however, a change of tempo is the real objective, so we will use the term *tempo modulation*. This technique does bear a resemblance to the common chord modulation of tonal music, in that one or more measures will contain elements of both tempos.

Carter evidently employed tempo modulation for the first time in his Cello Sonata (1948). A relatively simple example is found in Movement II,

EXAMPLE 6–13   A Simple Tempo Modulation

which begins in cut time at $\half = 84$. Later the meter changes to $\frac{6}{8}$ with the eighth-note remaining constant. The most reliable way to calculate the new tempo is to first compute the tempo of the common note value in the first tempo:

If $\half = 84$, then $\eighth = 4 \times 84 = 336$.

and then to figure out what that means in terms of the beat in the second tempo:

If $\eighth = 336$, and the new beat is the dotted quarter, then the new tempo is $336/3 = 112$.

A more complex example occurs in the third movement, which begins in $\frac{3}{4}$ with $\eighth = 70$. The tempo modulation then follows these steps:

1. Change to $\frac{6}{16}$, keeping the beat constant, so $\eighthdot = 70$.
2. Change to $\frac{21}{32}$, keeping the 32nd-note constant. This unusual time signature is *not* compound septuple, as one might expect. Instead, it is a *triple* meter, with each beat equaling a doubly dotted eighth-note. When $\eighthdot = 70$ (above), $\thirtysecond = 420$ (because there are six 32nds in one dotted eighth). Since the 32nd remains constant, and there are seven 32nds in the new beat value ($\eighthdotdot$), the new tempo is $420/7 = 60$.
3. Change to $\frac{2}{8}$, keeping the beat constant, so $\eighth = 60$.

SERIALIZED RHYTHM AND ISORHYTHM

The term *serialized rhythm* is generally used in connection with pieces in which the rhythmic aspects are governed by some preconceived series of durations. This will be discussed in more detail in Chapter 13.

We will use the term *isorhythm* to refer to the use of a rhythmic pattern that repeats using different pitches. The pitches may or may not themselves form a repeating pattern, but if they do, they are of a different length than the rhythmic pattern. If the rhythm and pitch patterns are the same length, we use the term *ostinato* rather than isorhythm.

Isorhythm is not a widely used device in twentieth-century music, but it can be very effective. Much of Act III, Scene 3 of *Wozzeck* is based on the rhythmic pattern seen in the first 3½ measures of the bottom staff in Example 6–14—in fact, all of the music in the example is derived directly from that pattern. The effect here is polymetric, the 3½-measure pattern in the low register rising inexorably over two whole-tone scales a major 7th apart, while Wozzeck tries desperately to explain to Margaret how blood got onto his hand.

EXAMPLE 6–14   Berg: *Wozzeck* (1921), Act III, Scene 3, mm. 187–98   *(Copyright 1931 by Universal Edition A. G. Wien. Copyright renewed. All rights reserved. Used by permission of European American Music Distributors Corporation, sole U.S. agent for Universal Edition.)*

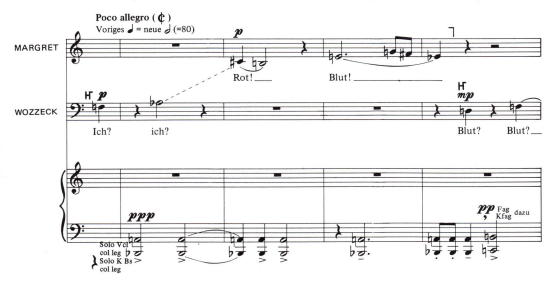

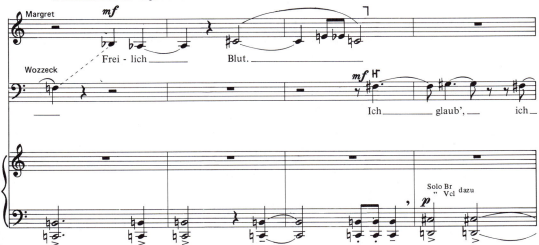

SUMMARY

One aspect of rhythm in twentieth-century music that must catch the attention of any performer is its difficulty. Certainly there was nothing in the rhythm of the tonal era to parallel the complexity of twentieth-century rhythms, and one might have to go back to the late fourteenth century to find a comparable preoccupation with complicated rhythms. While most musicians could perform the rhythms of a tonal work at sight, it is doubtful that they would be as successful with the works from which Example 4–4 (p. 83) and Example 6–12 (p. 135) are drawn.

Some of the specific techniques discussed in this chapter have included the following:

Syncopation
Changing time signatures
Nontraditional time signatures
    Using 5, 7, etc., for the top value
    Fractional top values
    Complex meters such as $\frac{3+2+3}{8}$
Additive rhythm
Polymeter
    Same signature, barlines not coinciding

> Different signatures, barlines coinciding
> Different signatures, barlines not coinciding

Polytempo

Ametric music

Proportional notation

Added values

Nonretrogradable rhythms

Tempo modulation

Serialized rhythm

Isorhythm

Certainly this chapter has not exhausted all of the details of rhythm in the twentieth century, but it has brought up some of the main points. One problem that you will discover if you do more reading in this area is that terminology relating to rhythm is not standardized. You will encounter terms such as "cross-rhythm" and "combined meters" that were not used in this chapter but refer to techniques discussed here using different terminology.

Finally, it is most important to remember that music is an aural experience, and you cannot always make an intelligent observation about the rhythm of a piece by a casual glance at the score. Such devices as polymeter and changing time signatures may be quite perceptible aurally, even though they are not explicitly notated. In all such cases, analyze the music by the way it sounds, not by the way it looks.

NOTES

1. Messiaen, *The Technique of My Musical Language*, Vol. 1, p. 29.
2. Harold S. Powers, "Rhythm," in *The New Harvard Dictionary of Music*.

EXERCISES

Part A: Fundamentals

1. Which example in this chapter was the best illustration of pandiatonicism?

2. On what scale is Example 6–1 based?

3. Which example best illustrates quintal chords?

4. In Example 6–8, will the eighth-notes in the piccolos be exactly the same length in the $\frac{7}{8}$ and $\frac{5}{8}$ measures, assuming that the quarter-note in the rest of the orchestra remains constant? Explain.

5. The following questions dealing with tempo modulation are based on techniques used by George Perle in his String Quartet No. 5 (1960, 1967).

   a. In the first movement, Tempo I is ♩ = 96. In order to get to Tempo II, Perle specifies that the old triplet eighth-note (one-third of a quarter-note) be equal to the new sixteenth-note. What is the tempo of the quarter-note (not the half-note) in Tempo II? Show your work.

   b. In the third movement, Tempo II is ♩ = 96. In order to get back to Tempo I, Perle specifies that the old dotted half-note be equal to the new half-note tied to an eighth. What is the tempo of the quarter-note in Tempo I? Show your work.

   c. Also in the third movement, Tempo III is ♩ = 120. In order to get back to another tempo, Perle specifies that the old eighth-note be equal to one-fifth of the new half-note. Is the new tempo Tempo I or Tempo II? Show your work.

6. Be able to perform the rhythms of the following examples:

   a. Example 2–20 (p. 39)—right hand only, with the eighth-note as the beat note.

   b. Example 3–20 (p. 61)—top staff only.

   c. Example 3–31 (p. 69)—top staff, with the eighth-note as the beat note.

   d. Example 4–2 (p. 81).

   e. Example 4–3 (p. 82).

   f. Example 4–7 (p. 87)—top staff with the right hand, bottom with the left.

   g. Example 4–B–2 (p. 99).

   h. Example 5–7 (p. 113)—top staff with the right hand, bottom with the left.

   i. Example 5–B–6 (p. 117)—bottom staff, vivace.

   j. Example 6–2.

   k. Example 6–5—bottom two staves.

   l. Example 6–6—top two staves.

   m. Example 6–11.

n. Example 6–12.

o. Example 6–13.

p. Example 6–14—Wozzeck's line and the bottom staff.

Part B: Analysis

1. Example 2–20 (p. 39) has nine eighth-notes to the measure, but the time signature is not $\frac{9}{8}$. What do you think would be an appropriate time signature for this example?

2. Discuss the rhythm and meter of Example 4–3 (p. 82), concentrating on those aspects that are characteristic of twentieth-century music.

3. Analyze Example 6–3 (p. 125) in more detail. (Note: Each accidental affects only the note it precedes.) Do any measures share identical patterns of rhythms or accents? Are any the retrograde (reverse) of others? Are there any repeated or retrograded pitch patterns?

4. Analyze Example 6–12 (p. 135) in more detail. Can you find any relationship between the rhythms of successive or nonsuccessive measures? Is there any logic or pattern to the pitch choices?

5. Bartók: *Forty-four Violin Duets* (1931), No. 33, "Song of the Harvest," mm. 6–15.

Discuss rhythmic and tonal aspects of this excerpt. To what scale does the combined pitch material of both staves conform?

6. Francis Poulenc: *Promenades* (1921), V, "En avion," systems 3 and 4.

Discuss rhythmic and pitch aspects of this excerpt, including consideration of chord types and tonality.

Part C: Composition

1. Compose an example for clarinet or trumpet using several different nontraditional time signatures. All of the pitch material should be from a single diminished scale.

2. Compose a short polymetric passage for two violins in the Phrygian mode.

3. Compose a four-part clapping piece employing tempo modulation.

4. Compose and be able to perform a melody illustrating added values and nonretrogradable rhythms.

5. Compose an isorhythmic passage for three instruments in your class. Try to employ some of the techniques seen in Ex. 6–14.

6. Compose and perform an example that uses time signatures and strict tempos, yet sounds ametric to the listener.

Part D: Further Reading

CHRIST, WILLIAM, AND OTHERS. *Materials and Structure of Music*, Vol. 2. See the section titled "Rhythmic Structure" in Chapter 14.

DALLIN, LEON. *Techniques of Twentieth Century Composition*. See Chapter 5, "Rhythm and Meter."

KOSTKA, STEFAN, AND DOROTHY PAYNE. *Tonal Harmony*. See the section titled "Rhythm and Meter" in Chapter 28.

SIMMS, BRYAN R. *Music of the Twentieth Century*. See pp. 92–108 of Chapter 5, "Rhythm and Meter."

SMITHER, HOWARD E. "The Rhythmic Aspect of 20th-Century Music." See pp. 71–84.

SMITHER, HOWARD E., AND FREDERIC RZEWSKI. "Rhythm," in John Vinton, ed., *Dictionary of Contemporary Music*.

WINOLD, ALLEN. "Rhythm in Twentieth-Century Music," in Gary Wittlich, ed., *Aspects of 20th Century Music*.

7

Form in Twentieth-Century Music

INTRODUCTION

All of the formal structures and procedures found in the tonal era survived into the twentieth century. That is, in twentieth-century music we still encounter sonatas and rondos, canons and fugues, sectional and continuous variations, and binary and ternary forms. Not surprisingly, many works employing traditional formal structures date from the first few decades of the century or were composed by relatively conservative composers, but this is not always the case. Schoenberg, for instance, hardly considered by his contemporaries to be a conservative, often composed his serial works in classical forms.

Yet to many musicians some of the older forms seem strangely uncomfortable in twentieth-century garb. The reason for this may well lie in the weakening of tonal centricity in almost all music of the twentieth century, to the point of its total avoidance in atonal styles. The essence of sonata form, in particular, involved a dramatic conflict of tonalities—a large-scale tonal dissonance established in the exposition and resolved in the recapitulation. It can be argued that once that conflict of tonalities loses its impact, to the point that it seems to make little difference to the listener at what pitch level the piece ends, the drama of the sonata is lost.

Tonality is less of an issue in the traditional contrapuntal forms—canon and fugue, especially—which may explain in part their healthy survival in this century. The same could also be said of variations, whether sectional or continuous, and both have aged well. Ternary form, one of the most basic musical structures, has perhaps weathered the storm best of all, since its design—statement, contrast, return—can be applied to a wide variety of styles, from tonal to electronic.

We will survey in this chapter the survival of these and other forms from earlier periods, as well as the appearance of forms unique to the twentieth century. Because it is beyond the scope of this text to present long works or even extended excerpts, there are few musical examples in this chapter. However, all of the works referred to are readily available in both score and recording. In addition, a number of references will be made in the text and exercises to works found in the following three excellent and widely used anthologies. The three-letter abbreviations in parentheses will be used when referring to them.

> Charles Burkhart. *Anthology for Musical Analysis*, 4th ed. New York: Holt, Rinehart and Winston, 1986. (BUR)
>
> Ralph Turek. *Analytical Anthology of Music*. New York: Alfred A. Knopf, 1984. (TUR)
>
> Mary H. Wennerstrom. *Anthology of Twentieth-Century Music*. 2nd ed. Englewood Cliffs, N.J.: Prentice-Hall, 1988. (WEN)

The reader is assumed to have a general understanding of the terminology of musical form as it relates to tonal music. One departure from conventional terminology should be noted: no distinction is made in this chapter between "part forms" or "song forms" and the longer "compound forms." For instance, ABA will be labeled "ternary" and ABACA will be labeled "rondo" without regard to the length or complexity of the component parts.

BINARY FORM

Binary form (AA' or AB) is found as the structure of short pieces or movements or of sections within longer works. Examples are as varied as Hindemith's "A Swan" (1939) (BUR, p. 530), John Cage's *Sonatas and*

Interludes (1948), Nos. 1 and 5 (TUR, p. 829), and "Vocalise 2: Invocation," from George Crumb's *Apparition* (1980) (WEN, p. 91). In its application, the binary principle is little changed in the twentieth century from earlier times, except that the traditional |I–V||V–I| and |i–III||III–i| tonal schemes are seldom used.

TERNARY FORM

The ternary principle is a flexible one that can be applied to small or large segments of music, and the contrast can be achieved in various ways. In a simple tonal piece like Schumann's "Humming Song" (1848) (BUR, p. 339), the contrast provided by the B section might be in little more than pitch level. More often, though, the contrast involves several elements. In Kenneth Gaburo's *Exit Music II: Fat Millie's Lament* (1965), an electronic piece, the A sections use voice and percussion sounds recorded at various tape speeds, while the B section is an excerpt from a jazz piece by Morgan Powell, providing a contrast in almost every aspect of the music.[1]

Many full-length movements are in ternary form, one example being the first movement of Poulenc's Flute Sonata (1957), but it is also not uncommon to cast individual themes or sections in ternary form. An instance of this is the second theme, mm. 41–63, of the first movement of Hindemith's Piano Sonata No. 2 (1936) (BUR, p. 532).

One of the most obvious examples of ternary form in tonal music is the *song form with trio*, which is often found as a minuet or scherzo with trio, followed by a *da capo*, in multimovement sonatas (symphonies, string quartets, piano sonatas, and so forth). While less common in the twentieth century, such forms do occur, as in the fifth movement of Schoenberg's *Suite*, Op. 25 (1923) (WEN, p. 175). A more complicated example is the third movement of Bartók's String Quartet No. 5 (1934). Here the trio is differentiated from the scherzo partly by its time signature ($^{4+2+3}_{\quad 8}$ in the scherzo, $^{3+2+2+3}_{\qquad 8}$ in the trio) and partly by its faster tempo, as well as by more traditional thematic means. The *da capo* is written out and considerably varied, concluding with a coda (m. 58) that starts out with some very fast polymetric imitation.

Ternary form in tonal music generally exhibits something of a balance between the two A sections, whereas works with a shortened return of the A material are categorized by some writers as *rounded binary*. No such balance is expected in twentieth-century ternary forms, and no distinction need be made between ternary and rounded binary. An example of an unbalanced ternary structure from Debussy's Preludes appears in Example 7–1. Here the A section is found in mm. 1–10, the B in mm. 11–24, and the return of A in mm. 25–31. Actually, only two measures of the A material return (mm. 25–26), but this reference to the opening of the piece is enough to give the listener a feeling of return after contrast, the essence of ternary form.

EXAMPLE 7–1   Debussy: Preludes, Book I (1910), "Dancers of Delphi" (complete)

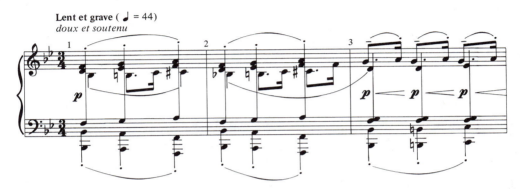

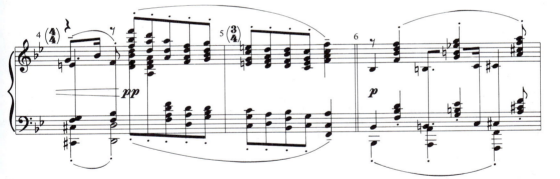

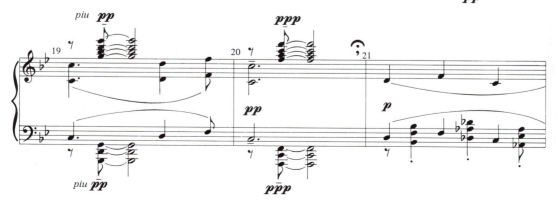

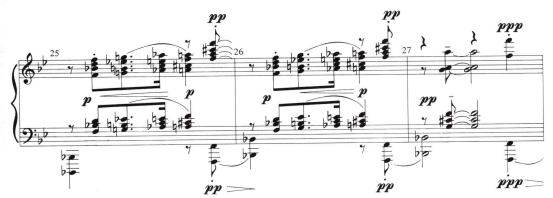

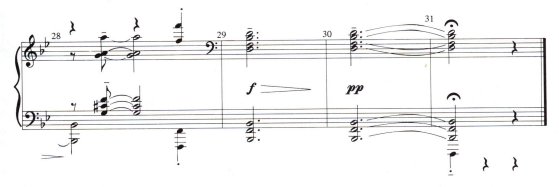

The ternary principle is found in vocal compositions as well. In Ives's song "The Indians" (1921) (BUR, p. 471), it is difficult to say just where a B section might begin, but the return of the opening measures following the climactic passage in mm. 11–13 creates a definite ternary effect. The return of the A section in Copland's "The World Feels Dusty" (1951) (BUR, p. 541) is more subtle. At m. 17 the piano returns to the accompaniment figure of the A section, while the voice continues with music that is not an obvious return of earlier material until m. 22. A similar treatment occurs in "Mary's Birth" (TUR, p. 818) from Hindemith's *The Life of Mary* (*Das Marienleben*) (1923, 1948).

RONDO FORMS

The usual outlines of the rondo form in tonal music were the five-part rondo (ABACA or ABABA) and the seven-part rondo (ABACABA). The term *sonata rondo* is sometimes used for the seven-part structure, especially if the C part includes development of earlier material. The key structure of the rondo required that the A theme always occur in the tonic key and that the B and C themes provide some kind of tonal contrast, except that the return of the B theme in the seven-part rondo was in the tonic key. Unlike sonata form, however, tonal contrast in a rondo could be achieved simply through change of mode. This occurred most often in the C themes of both five- and seven-part rondos.

Both five- and seven-part rondos are found in twentieth-century music, but the traditional tonal plans are not always used. Debussy's "Reflections in the Water" ("Reflets dans l'eau") (1905) follows fairly closely the conventional tonal scheme of a five-part rondo:

A	B	A	B	A
D♭	A♭	D♭	B	D♭

The second movement of Hindemith's String Quartet No. 3 (1921) (WEN, p. 125) is somewhat less conventional in its key relationships:

A	B	A	B	A
C♯	E♭	C♯	A	E♭, C♯

In addition, the B section is bitonal at its beginning, the E♭ harmonies supporting a melody that starts out in E Lydian. Bitonality is carried much further in "Song of the Harvest" from Bartók's *Forty-Four Violin Duets* (1931) (WEN, p. 9). In this miniature five-part rondo the first four sections are bitonal, the two keys in each case being a tritone apart, and the A theme is in a different tonal setting in each appearance (the first B theme appears in Example 6–B–5, p. 141).

The third movement of Prokofiev's Piano Sonata No. 4 (1914) follows the traditional outline for a seven-part rondo:[2]

A	B	A	C	A	B	A
C	G	C	E♭	C	C	C

Since the rondo form is somewhat more dependent than some others (notably sonata form) on contrast of themes as opposed to contrast of key centers, it would seem better suited to the atonal style. The fourth movement of Schoenberg's Wind Quintet, Op. 26 (1924), is a seven-part rondo written using the twelve-tone technique, usually associated with atonality. The B theme is at a different pitch level when it returns, as one would expect, but the A theme also varies in pitch level (and in other ways) at each recurrence, a departure from the classical norm. Interestingly, the movement emphasizes E♭ at its beginning and end, and E♭ remains an important pitch class at the beginning and often at the end of each movement of this otherwise atonal work.

OTHER PART FORMS

Part forms other than binary, ternary, and rondo are frequently encountered, but many of them can be thought of as variants of more traditional structures. One that is very similar to the seven-part rondo is ABACADA. Examples of this form can be found in the last movement of Barber's *Capricorn Concerto* (1944) and in the "Interlude" from Debussy's Sonata for Flute, Viola, and Harp (1916). In the Debussy example the D section also contains elements of C. Another part form that resembles a seven-part rondo is ABACBA, one example of this occurring in the fourth movement of Bartók's *Concert for Orchestra* (1943).

The interest that some composers have in various kinds of symmetry is reflected in their use of *arch form*, a term for any formal structure that reads the same forwards and backwards. Some conventional forms, such as ternary and seven-part rondo, are examples of arch form, but we usually reserve the term for less-conventional formal structures.

Ternary:	A	B	A								
Seven-part rondo:	A	B	A	C	A	B	A				
Arch:	A	B	C	B	A or A	B	C	D	C	B	A etc.

Examples of arch forms in music range from single movements to entire multimovement works. The third movement of Debussy's String Quartet (1893) can be analyzed as a ternary form or as a five-part arch form:

Ternary:	A	Ba	Bb	Ba	A
Arch:	A	B	C	B	A

The third movement of Bartok's *Music for String Instruments, Percussion, and Celesta* (1936) is a modified arch form, two of the parts being recapitulated simultaneously.

A   B   C   D   C+B   A

Bartok's String Quartet No. 5 is an arch form in terms of its overall plan:

I. Allegro

II. Adagio Molto

III. Scherzo and Trio (Vivace)

IV. Andante

V. Finale (Allegro Vivace)

The first movement of this work combines sonata form with the arch idea in various ways, the most obvious being a reverse recapitulation.[3]

Some part forms show the influence of the sonata by including a development. The second movement of Ravel's String Quartet (1903) combines the statement of new material with the development of previous material. The A and B parts each contain two themes:

A   A   B+Dev   A   Coda
a,c♯   a,C   unstable   a,c♯   a

Another movement containing a development is the fourth movement of Debussy's String Quartet, which contains elements of both rondo and sonata forms:[4]

A   B   A   C   Dev

Still other part forms are unique in that they do not seem to be similar to any more conventional form or to conform to the arch principle. One example is the "Interlude" that precedes the "Fugue in A" from Hindemith's *Ludus Tonalis* (1942) (WEN, p. 140), which has the following structure:

|: A :|: B :|: C :| A C C

SONATA FORM

Sonata form was the most important musical form of the Classical and Romantic periods. Its essence involved a conflict between tonalities that would arise early in the exposition and continue until its resolution in the recapitulation. Thematic contrast was a frequent element in movements in sonata form, but it was by no means essential, as the many "monothematic" sonatas of the Classical period prove. Nor was it required that the recapitulation return the material in the original order (the "reverse recapitulation" was a possibility), or that it all return in the tonic key (the "subdominant recapitulation" brought back the first theme in the subdominant), or even that the first theme be recapitulated at all (see the first movements of Chopin's Piano Sonatas, Op. 35 [1839] and Op. 58 [1844]). Instead, the crucial elements seem to have been that the tonal conflict must be resolved by returning to the tonic key well before the end of the movement, and that any important thematic material that had been presented in a contrasting key in the exposition must return in the tonic key.

Movements in sonata form are frequently encountered in twentieth-century music. Some of them even make use of the traditional key relationships in the exposition of tonic-dominant (as in Piston's Quintet for Flute and Strings (1942), I) or tonic-relative major (as in Ravel's Sonatina (1905), I), but more often the tonalities in twentieth-century sonata forms are not the traditional ones. More problematical, however, are those movements in sonata form—and there are many—in which the tonality of one or both of the main themes is unclear. Obviously, a struggle between tonalities cannot occur if the tonalities are not firmly established. Some would say that other elements replace the tonal aspect in such pieces; others might argue that a movement based upon a contrast of themes, for example, might be good music but is not a sonata.

The single movement of Berg's Piano Sonata, Op. 1 (1908), is an interesting mixture of traditional and experimental approaches to sonata form. The first theme, while tonally unstable, does cadence in B minor in the third measure of the exposition (although it does not do so in the recapitulation), and the exposition is even repeated. But Theme 2 (m. 29), which is tonally unstable, begins over an A9 chord in the exposition (implying D major) and a B9 in the recapitulation (implying E major), while the closing theme (m. 49) actually begins at the same.pitch level in the exposition and the recapitulation.

Similar problems are encountered in the first movement of Bartók's String Quartet No. 6 (1939) (WEN, p. 11). In this work the first theme (m. 24) is in D, but the listener might be forgiven for not being certain about this until m. 60, where the first triad on D is heard. The second theme (m.

81) begins over a C pedal, which is apparently the dominant of the tonality of F, reached in m. 94. A third theme, tonally unstable and largely chromatic, begins at m. 99, climaxing at m. 110 on an E♭, but the exposition ends clearly on F at m. 157. In the recapitulation, the first theme returns in D, more or less, but the second theme returns over a C♯ pedal (m. 312), presumably the dominant of F♯, but certainly not in the tonality of D. The third theme climaxes on a B♭ chord at m. 343, but a D major triad is reached at m. 352, and the remainder of the movement is in D.

Tonal uncertainty is obviously a problem, in regard to sonata form, in the Berg and Bartók works discussed above, and the traditional objectives of sonata form are clearly achieved in neither instance. This is not a criticism, of course; both compositions are highly organized in their own ways, and each is a successful and well-known work. What is interesting here from a formal point of view is the effort to make a tonal form function in an increasingly nontonal environment.

The whole notion of a tonal dissonance to be resolved in the recapitulation is essentially moot in any composition that is decidedly atonal, yet a good number of atonal pieces are cast in what appears to be sonata form. A good example is the first movement of Schoenberg's Wind Quintet, Op. 26 (1924), an early twelve-tone atonal composition. In this movement the first theme (m. 1) is recapitulated at the same pitch level (m. 128), whereas the second and closing themes (m. 42 and m. 55) are brought back a perfect 5th lower or a perfect 4th higher, a remarkable duplication of the traditional relationships found in a major-mode sonata form.

SECTIONAL VARIATIONS

The term *sectional variations* is used here to distinguish the theme with variations from the ground bass or continuous variations (passacaglia and chaconne). Many sets of sectional variations have been composed in the twentieth century, works as diverse as Ravel's hyperemotional and tonal *Bolero* (1927) and Babbitt's cerebral and atonal *Semi-Simple Variations* (1957) (TUR, p. 843; BUR, p. 553). While the compositions just cited use original themes, others such as Ralph Vaughan Williams's *Fantasy on a Theme by Thomas Tallis* (1910) and Zoltán Kodály's *Variations on a Hungarian Folksong* (1939) use borrowed material for the theme.

The theme of a traditional set of variations was relatively simple in order to allow for subsequent embellishment, and it was clearly set off from the music that followed so that the listener could easily identify and remember the theme. This is essentially the case with Copland's *Piano Variations* (1930) (TUR, p. 813), using a ten-measure theme that is set off from the first variation by a fermata. Carter's *Variations for Orchestra* (1955), on the other hand, begins with an introduction that is dovetailed into the beginning of the theme through sustained violin tones. The theme begins at the second of two tempo modulations that slow the tempo from allegro to andante, which does somewhat help the listener to identify the beginning of the theme. The theme itself is complex texturally and rhythmically; after 47 measures it runs into Variation I without pause but with another change of tempo. The nine variations are quite free, presenting a real challenge to the listener attempting to hear the relationship between them and the theme.

Some twentieth-century works that are called variations are not variations in the customary sense. This tends to be especially true of serial, or twelve-tone, "variations" such as Webern's Piano Variations, Op. 27 (1936), and Luigi Dallapiccola's Variations for Orchestra (1954). In both of these works the theme of the variations is not a short composition, as in traditional variations, but instead is the twelve-tone series itself; and though the series in both cases surely helps to unify the composition as a whole, the series is not presented initially as a tune or theme for the listener to remember. On the other hand, in some twelve-tone "variations" there is a true theme on which the subsequent variations are clearly based, an example being Shoenberg's *Variations for Orchestra*, Op. 31 (1928) (TUR, p. 768; WEN, p. 179).

CONTINUOUS VARIATIONS

The traditional forms of continuous variations are the *passacaglia*, based on a repeating bass line, or ground, and the *chaconne*, based on a repeating harmonic progression.[5] Though both forms have seen use in this century, the decline of a common harmonic language has been paralleled by the relative decline of the chaconne as a compositional option.

As one would expect, passacaglia themes in the twentieth century tend to be complicated and nondiatonic. The fourth movement of Hindemith's String Quartet No. 4 (1921) consists of a passacaglia and a fugato based on the passacaglia theme, which is shown in Example 7–2. Notice that in the course of its seven measures this theme sounds every pitch class but one (E). Passacaglias using all twelve pitch classes have been used, a famous example being the passacaglia in Act I, Scene 4, of Berg's *Wozzeck*(1921). An intriguing passacaglia with a twelve-tone theme is "Little Blue Devil," from Gunther Schuller's *Seven Studies on Themes of Paul Klee* (1959) (WEN, p. 194). In this work a "jazzy" nine-bar bass line makes its way through three different (but related) twelve-tone "sets." This bass line, first heard in mm. 15–23, serves as the passacaglia theme for the movement.

EXAMPLE 7–2   Hindemith: String Quartet No. 4, Op. 32 (1921), IV, mm. 1–8   *(© by B. Schott's Soehne, Mainz, 1924. Copyright renewed. All rights reserved. Used by permission of European American Music Distributors Corporation, sole U.S. agent for B. Schott's Soehne.)*

Another example is Alexei Haieff's *Saints' Wheel* (1960), a piano composition that uses a complete circle of 5ths (C, G, . . . , F) as its passacaglia theme. The rhythm of the pitch series varies throughout the piece, but the series is maintained until the coda, where it is inverted (C, F, . . . , G).

The use of isorhythms (review Chapter 6, p. 136) can be thought of as an extension of the passacaglia principle. This is especially true when there is a pitch pattern associated with the rhythmic pattern, as in the "Crystal Liturgy" from Messiaen's *Quartet for the End of Time* (1941) (TUR, p. 823). Of course, the pitch pattern (the *color*) must not be the same length as the rhythmic pattern (the *talea*), or an ordinary ostinato would result. In the Messiaen work the rhythmic pattern contains 17 attacks and the pitch pattern contains 29 notes (10 different pitch classes), so the rhythmic pattern would have to be repeated 29 times before the beginnings of the two patterns would again coincide (because 493 is the lowest common multiple of 17 and 29). Messiaen stops the process long before that point.

CANON AND FUGUE

Canon and fugue are not "forms" in the sense that rondos and sonatas are. Instead, they are contrapuntal procedures that can be cast in any of a number of formal designs. Nevertheless, musicians customarily have referred to both "homophonic forms" and "contrapuntal forms," and it will be convenient in this chapter to follow that tradition.

The canon, a form that saw relatively little use in the century and a half after Bach, has enjoyed a new popularity among twentieth-century composers. Whole sets of canons have been written, such as Webern's Five Canons, Op. 16 (1924) (WEN, p. 271), and canons frequently appear as a major portion of a longer work, examples being the trio of the minuet from Schoenberg's Suite, Op. 25 (1923) (WEN, p. 177), and the second movement of Webern's Variations for Piano, Op. 27 (1936) (BUR, p. 524). In both of these works, the canonic imitation happens to be by contrary motion. Canons also frequently appear as passages in otherwise noncanonic movements. For instance, although Schoenberg's "Summer Morning by a Lake," Op. 16, No. 3 (1909) (BUR, p. 459), is not a canon, it contains canonic passages, two of the clearest being mm. 3–9 and mm. 32–38.

Much of the challenge in writing a canon in the tonal idiom is to control the dissonance while at the same time creating harmonic interest. To a certain extent these difficulties are alleviated in twentieth-century music because of the "emancipation of the dissonance" and the lack of traditional harmonic progressions. Both can be seen and heard in the works cited in the preceding paragraph. In another example, the "Song of Harvest" from Bartók's *Forty-Four Violin Duets* (1931) (WEN, p. 9), the first canonic phrase (see Example 6–B–5 on p. 141) finds the violins a tritone apart, with no attempt at conventional preparation and resolution of the dissonances that result.

Terry Riley's *In C* (1964) (TUR, p. 872) is an interesting canon in which the performers begin together but progress through the music at different rates. Each performer plays the same 53 musical segments for an indeterminate amount of time, usually for at least a minute, with each performer proceeding to the next segment on his or her own initiative, but not without regard for what the other players are doing. The resulting canon is a good example of phase music, or minimalism, to be discussed in more detail in Chapter 15.

The renewed interest in counterpoint in this century can also be seen in the collections of fugues composed after the model of *The Well-Tempered Clavier*. Hindemith's *Ludus Tonalis* (1942) is a famous collection of twelve fugues separated by eleven interludes, the entire work beginning with a prelude and ending with a postlude. Instead of arranging his fugues in chromatic order, as Bach did in *The Well-Tempered Clavier*, Hindemith follows Series 1 from his *Craft of Musical Composition*, an ordering that he first derives when discussing tuning. Hindemith felt that this ordering represented a "diminishing degree of relationship" with the beginning tonality of C:[6]

C G F A E E♭ A♭ D B♭ D♭ B F♯

Another collection of twentieth-century fugues is Shostakovich's *Twenty-Four Preludes and Fugues*, Op. 87 (1951). Here the order of keys is more traditional: C–a–G–e–D–b–A–f♯, etc. As in Bach's collection, each fugue is preceded by a prelude in the same key.

Fugues are also commonly encountered as individual movements within a longer work, as in the first movement of Bartók's *Music for String Instruments, Percussion, and Celesta* (1936) (BUR, p. 487) and the "Fantasy" from Elliott Carter's *Eight Etudes and a Fantasy for Woodwind Quartet* (1950) (WEN, p. 57), or as a portion of a movement, as in Berg's *Wozzeck* (1921), Act III, Scene 1, consisting of a theme with seven variations followed by a fugue based on the theme.

The tonal conventions of the Baroque fugue need not restrict the twentieth-century composer, and frequently they do not, but it is remarkable how often the traditional tonal relationships are found in the expositions of twentieth-century fugues. Three examples:

Bartók: Sonata for Solo Violin (1944), II

Shostakovich: String Quartet No. 8 (1962), V

Rochberg: String Quartet No. 4 (1977), II

Each of the movements cited above begins with a fugue exposition in which the first and third statements of the subject are in the tonic and all the others are in the dominant. Coincidentally, each also happens to be in the key of C.

PROPORTION: THE GOLDEN MEAN

Some twentieth-century composers and writers have been interested in the "golden mean" or "golden section," a proportion used for centuries in art and architecture to obtain aesthetically pleasing designs. To understand this ratio, consider a line $\underline{ac}$ with line segments $\underline{ab}$ and $\underline{bc}$:

```
|_____|_____|
a                b                           c
```

If the proportion of $\underline{ab}$ to $\underline{bc}$ is the same as the proportion of $\underline{bc}$ to the whole line, then $\underline{ac}$ is segmented according to the golden mean. This relationship can be expressed as:

$$\frac{ab}{bc} = \frac{bc}{ac}$$

The resulting fraction is about .618.

Integers (whole numbers) that approximate the golden mean can be generated by means of a *Fibonacci sequence*, an endless series of numbers in which each number is the sum of the previous two. The farther you go in the sequence, the closer you get to the true value of the golden mean:

Integers:	1	2	3	5	8	13	21	34 etc.
Ratios:	.5	.67	.6	.625	.615	.619	.618	

The most obvious way that this ratio can be used musically is in the proportions of a musical form. For example, the beginning of "Minor Seconds, Major Sevenths," from Bartók's *Mikrokosmos* (BUR, p. 483), could be subdivided in this way:

m. 8 = Strong cadence; first whole-note cord.

m. 21 = Strong cadence; first appearance of "glissando."

m. 34 = End of long accelerando and of first main section.

There is some evidence that Bartók used the golden mean not only in formal proportions but in other aspects of his music as well,[7] and this is also true, if to a lesser extent, of some other twentieth-century composers.[8]

NONTHEMATIC DELINEATORS OF MUSICAL FORM

The primary determinants of musical form in tonal music were tonality and theme, with contrast of tonalities being a generally stronger force than contrast of themes. The decline in tonality as an organizing force has often led to a greater reliance on thematic contrast; but in many pieces, themes, in the sense of melodies, play a small or nonexistent part. The most obvious example is electronic music, where texture, register, dynamics, and especially timbre are usually more important as shaping elements than themes are. Rhythmic activity is another organizing factor, as in Bartók's "Increasing—Diminishing" from the *Mikrokosmos* (1937), where rhythmic activity creates an arch form. Other works in which nonthematic elements are important in delineating the form include "They Do Not Think of the Rain, and They Have Fallen Asleep," from George Crumb's *Madrigal's*, Book I (1965) (BUR, p. 586), and the third movement of Paul Cooper's String Quartet No. 5 (1973) (TUR, p. 875).

NONORGANIC APPROACHES TO MUSICAL FORM

A traditional painting depicts something, and if the painting is a good one, every part of the canvas contributes to the effectiveness of the visual message that the artist is trying to convey. In traditional literature every passage has its purpose—fleshing out a character, setting the mood, developing the plot, and so on. The same is generally true of music in the European tradition: the composition is considered to be greater than the sum of its parts, a work of art in which each passage has a function that is vital to the overall plan of a work. Think of any tonal work that you know well, and imagine what it would be like if its parts—themes, transitions and so forth—were randomly rearranged. It might be interesting to see how it would turn out, but the piece would almost certainly not be as effective as a whole.

There has been a reaction by some composers against this traditional "organic" (or "teleological") approach to musical composition. One such reaction led to what Karlheinz Stockhausen has called "moment form," an approach that treats every portion of a piece as an end in itself, without any intentional relationship to what precedes or follows it. The listener is not supposed to try to identify traditional shaping forces such as motivic development, dynamics, and rhythmic activity in an attempt to understand where the music is going, because it is not going *anywhere*, in the traditional sense. Even the beginning and ending of the work lose their traditional functions, because "a proper moment form will give the impression of starting in the midst of previously unheard music, and it will break off without reaching any structural cadence, as if the music goes on, inaudibly, in some other space or time after the close of the performance".[9]

Stockhausen first used the term "moment form" in discussing *Contact* (1960), a work for prerecorded tape, piano, and percussion, but other works by various composers, both before and since, show the same avoidance of linear growth. Some of these are works employing a high degree of chance, an early example being Cage's *Williams Mix* (1952), a tape piece composed by juxtaposing at random hundreds of prerecorded sounds. Tape music and the use of chance in music are both discussed in more detail in later chapters.

SUMMARY

All of the forms of the tonal era survived into the twentieth century, in spite of problems relating to the function of tonality in those forms. Not only was there a decline in the influence of tonality upon form, but in many twentieth-century compositions the "theme" also ceased to be an important element of form. Formal proportions are often less balanced than in the Classical period, but interest in the golden mean by some composers, notably Bartók, shows a desire for a systematic aesthetic. Coexisting with the traditional forms are a large number of works that do not conform to earlier models. Some of these can be thought of as variants of traditional part forms or as related to the sonata; others are arch forms; and still others would seem to be unique in the sense that they do not have traditional analogues. Even more radical is the nonorganic approach to musical form seen in the "moment form" works of Stockhausen and others and in some works composed using chance procedures.

NOTES

1. Barry Schrader, *Introduction to Electro-Acoustic Music*, p. 33.
2. For a detailed analysis of the form of this work, see Wallace Berry, *Form in Music*, pp. 216–24.
3. For a detailed analysis of this movement, see Mary Wennerstrom, "Form in Twentieth-Century Music," in Wittlich, ed., *Aspects of Twentieth-Century Music*, pp. 19–33.
4. For an analysis of this movement, see Gail deStwolinski, *Form and Content in Instrumental Music*, pp. 546–48.
5. These definitions are used for convenience, but the difference between the two was not so clearly defined in the Baroque period, during which both the passacaglia and the chaconne first flourished.
6. Paul Hindemith, *The Craft of Musical Composition*, Vol. I, p. 56. The derivation of this series of tones is found on pp. 32–43.
7. Ernö Lendvai, *Béla Bartók: An Analysis of His Music*.
8. Jonathan D. Kramer, "The Fibonacci Series in Twentieth Century Music."
9. Jonathan D. Kramer, "Moment Form in Twentieth Century Music," p. 180.

EXERCISES

Part A: Score Analysis

Each of the pieces below can be found in one of the three anthologies listed at the beginning of this chapter. Analyze the form of whatever piece you are assigned, including a diagram down to the phrase level, if possible. Be sure to include measure numbers.

1. Bartók: *Mikrokosmos* (1931), No. 91, "Chromatic Invention" (TUR, p. 807).

2. Berg: *Wozzeck* (1921), "Marie's Lullaby" (WEN, p. 28).

3. Cooper: String Quartet No. 5 (1973), III (TUR, p. 875).

4. Debussy: "Hommage à Rameau," from *Images*, Book I (1905) (TUR, p. 665). Analyze the form of this work as well as the form of mm. 1–30.

5. Debussy: Preludes, Book I (1910), "The Engulfed Cathedral" ("La Cathédrale engloutie") (BUR, p. 450).

6. Hindemith: Piano Sonata No. 2 (1936), I (BUR, p. 532). Analyze the form of the movement as a whole, as well as the form of the theme in mm. 1–26.

7. Hindemith: *Ludus Tonalis* (1942), Fugue in C (BUR, p. 537) and Fugue in A (WEN, p. 140). Before beginning work on these fugues, review the terms "double fugue" and "triple fugue."

8. Ives: Sonata No. 2 for Violin and Piano (1910), II (WEN, p. 147). Though this movement is not a canon, it contains some canonic passages. Locate and comment upon each one.

9. Ravel: *Noble and Sentimental Waltzes* (*Valses nobles et sentimentales*) (1911), No. 1 (BUR, p. 474).

10. Schoenberg: *Six Short Pieces for Piano*, Op. 19 (1911), No. 6 (WEN, p. 173).

11. Schoenberg: *Pierrot Lunaire*, Op. 21 (1912), No. 8 (TUR, p. 756).

12. Schoenberg: Variations for Orchestra, Op. 31 (1928), Var. 2 (TUR, p. 768). Concentrate on the issue of imitation in this variation.

13. Stravinsky: Sonata for Two Pianos (1944), II (BUR, p. 505). This set of variations is interesting to study both for variation technique and for the form and compositional techniques used in each section.

14. Webern: *Five Movements for String Quartet*, Op. 5 (1909), IV (BUR, p. 520).

15. Webern: Quartet for Violin, Clarinet, Saxophone, and Piano, Op. 22 (1930), I (BUR, p. 525).

Part B: Aural Analysis

Listen several times to any of the works listed below. Name the form, and provide a diagram of the main parts. Try to sketch the salient features (rhythms, contours, etc.) of each section.

1. Barber: Piano Concerto, Op. 38 (1962), III.
2. Bartók: String Quartet No. 6 (1939), II.
3. Dallapiccola: *Quaderno Musicale* (1952), No. 3.
4. Hindemith: String Quartet No. 3 (1921), V.
5. Prokofiev: Symphony No. 5 (1944), IV.
6. Piston: Symphony No. 5 (1956), I.
7. Walter Ross: Trombone Concerto (1971), II, "Canzona."
8. Shostakovich: String Quartet No. 1 (1935), II.
9. Stravinsky: Septet (1953), I.
10. Stravinsky: *Symphony of Psalms* (1930), II.
11. Stravinsky: Septet (1953), II.
12. Arnold Walter, Myron Schaeffer, and Harvey Olnick: Summer Idyll (1959).

Part C: Further Reading

BERRY, WALLACE. *Form in Music*. This text—like deStwolinski's, cited below—does not deal exclusively with twentieth-century music.

CHRIST, WILLIAM, AND OTHERS. *Materials and Structure of Music*, Vol. 2. See Chapter 17, "Formal Processes in Twentieth-Century Music."

DESTWOLINSKI, GAIL. *Form and Content in Instrumental Music*.

HOWAT, ROY. "Bartók, Lendvai, and the Principle of Proportional Analysis."

KRAMER, JONATHAN D. "The Fibonacci Series in Twentieth Century Music."

_____ "Moment Form in Twentieth Century Music."

LENDVAI, ERNÖ. *Béla Bartók: An Analysis of His Music*. See the sections titled "Golden Section," pp. 17–26, and "Chromatic System," p. 35–66.

WENNERSTROM, MARY. "Form in Twentieth-Century Music," in Gary Wittlich, ed., *Aspects of Twentieth-Century Music*, pp. 1–65.

8

Influences from the Past, the Present, the Exotic

INTRODUCTION

This chapter is concerned with some of the external influences that have had an effect on the music of the twentieth century. These influences have come chiefly from three sources:

The Past
    Neoclassicism
    Quotation

The Present
    Folk music
    Jazz

The Exotic
    Music from other cultures

There is little new technical information in this chapter, and few exercises follow it. In many ways it deals more with music history than with music theory. But the currents outlined here are more important ones, and they had a significant role in shaping the sound of twentieth-century music.

RELICS AND REVIVALS FROM THE PAST

Composers in this century have shown a greater awareness of and concern for the music of past centuries than did any of their predecessors. In earlier chapters we have seen the revival of modal scales and isorhythm, and renewed interest in older forms like the passacaglia. This historical consciousness has also led to the developments discussed in the next two sections: neoclassicism and quotation. *Neoclassicism* was a reactionary movement in the sense that it rejected the chromatic saturation and other characteristics of both the late Romantic style and of atonality. While it was not truly an attempt to revive the Classical style, as the term might suggest, it did reflect a desire for clarity, balance, and greater detachment, and the music of the Baroque and Classical periods provided a starting place for the style.

Quotation of already existing music was not unknown before the twentieth century. The use of plainsong melodies in Renaissance polyphonic compositions and the borrowed themes for sets of variations are but two examples. But quotation in the twentieth century is of a different sort, at times a dramatic juxtaposition of contrasting styles, at others an almost poetic allusion to another author. Thus "quotation music" has become another catchword of twentieth-century music.

NEOCLASSICISM

"Let's say that I was a kind of bird, and that the eighteenth century was a kind of bird's nest in which I felt cozy laying my eggs."[1] In this picturesque way Stravinsky characterized his own involvement in neoclassicism, an approach to composition that was especially widespread from around 1920 to around 1950. Many composers wrote works in the neoclassical style—Hindemith and Poulenc, for example—but the central figure in the movement was Stravinsky. Important neoclassical works by Stravinsky include the Octet for Wind Instruments (1923) the *Symphony of Psalms* (1930), the Symphony in C (1940), and the *Symphony in Three Movements* (1945).

Donald Jay Grout defines neoclassicism as "adherence to the Classical principles of balance, coolness, objectivity, and absolute (as against Romantic program) music, with the corollary characteristics of economy, predominantly contrapuntal texture, and diatonic as well as chromatic harmonies.''[2] William Austin, referring to Stravinsky's neoclassical works in particular, writes:

> They presumed sophistication. They alluded not simply to Bach and Beethoven, but to separate traits of the classical styles. They treated those traits with such dry irony, such jerky stiffness, and such evident distortion that even a sympathetic listener needed several hearings to penetrate beneath the wit and skill to the glowing warmth of the melodies and the subtle continuity of the forms.[3]

From these definitions it is clear that neoclassicism was not an attempt to compose new works in the style of Haydn and Mozart. For one thing, it

EXAMPLE 8–1 Stravinsky: Octet for Wind Instruments (1923), "Sinfonia," last 9 mm.

made use of Baroque techniques as well as Classical ones. But more important, neoclassicism was a reaction against the style of late Romanticism in favor of a sparser texture and less chromaticism, using clear rhythms and definite cadences, all combined with twentieth-century developments in melody, meter, and the treatment of dissonance.

The techniques of neoclassicism are not new, and all of them have been discussed in earlier chapters of this text. The best way to get acquainted with the style is through listening and score study, but Example 8–1 is included here as a representative of several aspects of neoclassicism. Notice first of all the metric subtleties between the bass-clef instruments and the treble-clef instruments. The changing time signatures accurately reflect the rhythm of Trumpet I and Clarinet; however, for Flute and Trumpet II, the $\frac{3}{8}$ measure is related in $\frac{2}{4}$ (four bars from the end). Meanwhile, the bass-clef instruments move along with a steady pattern of eighth-notes followed by eighth rests, sometimes agreeing with the time signature and sometimes not, but contributing a stabilizing third element to this polymetric texture.

Another aspect to be noted in Example 8–1 is the prevailing pandiatonicism (see p. 114). Since Trumpet II sounds in unison with the Flute (but two octaves lower), the only pitches in the excerpt that are not diatonic to Eb major are the Db's in Bassoon I and Trombone II. But there is no harmonic progression in the traditional sense, even though the bass-clef accompaniment is triadic, and no attempt is made to control the dissonances that occur among the treble-clef instruments or between them and the bass-clef accompaniment.

The ballet *Pulcinella* (1920) is one of Stravinsky's earliest neoclassical works. An excerpt from the *Suite Italienne* (1932), derived from the ballet, appeared earlier as Example 3–10 (p. 54), and it will serve as our second example of neoclassicism. Here the rhythm is quite straightforward, as is the harmonic progression, but the nontraditional treatment of dissonance in this excerpt is a fine example of the dry irony to which Austin referred in the passage quoted earlier.

Though the neoclassical style has nearly died out, music of the past still attracts the interest of many composers. A more recent movement, dubbed "neoromanticism," will be discussed in the final chapter of this book.

QUOTATION, ARRANGEMENT, AND PARAPHRASE

Neoclassicism rarely involved the actual quotation of already existing music, exceptions including Stravinsky's *Pulcinella* (1920) and *The Fairy's Kiss* (*Le baiser de la fée*) (1928), which used the music of Pergolesi and Tchaikovsky, respectively. But many other twentieth-century composers not connected with the neoclassical style have quoted, arranged, and paraphrased earlier music extensively. Though this practice has become especially common since the mid-1960s, earlier examples include Debussy, who quoted Wagner in "Golliwog's Cakewalk" from *The Children's Corner* (1908) and Bach in *In Black and White* (*En blanc et noir*) (1915), and Berg, who quoted Wagner in the last movement of the *Lyric Suite* (1926) and Bach in the concluding "Adagio" movement of the Violin Concerto (1935). The style of another composer from the early part of the century, Charles Ives, depended to a great extent on the quotation of music—hymn tunes, popular songs, and the like—familiar to most Americans in the early part of the century. Patriotic songs were grist for his mill as well, as seen in Example 8–2, where "America," "Columbia, the Gem of the Ocean," and the "Marseillaise" can all be heard.

Another work in a similar vein is Stockhausen's *Hymns* (*Hymnen*) (1966), an electronic work that quotes a number of national anthems. Here the "program" is not nationalistic, as Ives's presumably was, but instead is concerned with world unity.

A composer does not always quote existing music for programmatic reasons. The second act of George Rochberg's *Music for the Magic Theater* (1965) begins with a "transcription" (actually a rather free arrangement) of the fourth movement from Mozart's Divertimento in B flat, K. 287 (1777).

EXAMPLE 8–2   Ives: "In Flanders Fields" (1917), mm. 30–35   (© copyright 1955 by Peer International Corporation. Used by permission.)

In the preface to the score Rochberg discusses the reaction of the audience:

> It seems to test the perceptual courage of listeners (musicians and laymen alike) by putting in question the whole concept of what is "contemporary," how far that concept may be stretched today and what it can include. The presence of the transcription abrogates the nineteenth to early twentieth century notion of "originality." . . .[4]

Rochberg goes on to provide more insight into the compositional aesthetic that justifies quotation in his music:

> The world of this music is surreal more than it is abstract. In its combinations of the past and the present, seemingly accidental, unrelated aural images whose placement in time obeys no conventional logic, it attempts to create a musical soundscape which is strangely and oddly familiar.[5]

This idea of juxtaposing seemingly unrelated ideas was encountered in Chapter 7 in the discussion of "nonorganic approaches to musical form." Crumb takes up the same topic in discussing his *Ancient Voices of Children* (1970): "I was conscious of an urge to fuse various unrelated stylistic elements. I was intrigued by the idea of juxtaposing the seemingly incongruous . . ."[6]

The material borrowed by a composer is often transformed, or paraphrased. This was true to some extent of the Ives example above. Electronic compositions might use recorded excerpts, with or without alteration, as in Kenneth Gaburo's *Exit Music II* (see p. 146) and Stockhausen's *Opus 1970* (1969). The pair of excerpts in Example 8–3, drawn from Examples 108 and 109 of Messiaen's *Technique of My Musical Language*,

EXAMPLE 8–3   Messiaen: *Technique of My Musical Language*, Examples 108 and 109 (excerpts) *(© 1944 Editions Alphonse Leduc. Copyright renewed 1966. Used by permission of the publisher.)*

illustrate how Messiaen paraphrased part of a plainchant in the melody of a work for organ.

Quotation in Bernd Alois Zimmermann's music is an important stylistic element rather than the exceptional event, a good example being *Photoptosis* (1968), an orchestral work with quotations from various sources. In *Petroushkates* (1980), Joan Tower has composed a sort of paraphrase variation on Stravinsky's original. Direct quotations in *Petroushkates* are most apparent at the beginning, but chords, rhythms, and melodic figures drawn from Stravinsky can be heard throughout the work, most of which maintains the exhilarating spirit of the opening of *Petrushka*.

Bach's Partita in E Major for solo violin serves as the basis for the third movement of Lukas Foss's *Baroque Variations* (1967). Far removed from the traditional theme and variations, this dramatic and effective work often views the Bach through a wildly distorted lens. Chapter 14 includes additional discussion of this movement.

Perhaps the most famous example of quotation is the third movement of Berio's *Sinfonia* (1968), a work for eight voices and orchestra. The entire movement is based on the third movement of Mahler's Symphony No. 2 (1894), sometimes obviously but often more subtly, with additional quotations from Bach, Berg, Brahms, Debussy, Ravel, Schoenberg, Strauss, Stravinsky, and others, these quotations being alluded to on occasion by the chorus.[7] Most of the text, however, is drawn from Samuel Beckett's novel *The Unnamable*. The connections between Mahler, Joyce, Beckett, and Berio have been convincingly shown, including the suggestion that Joyce's stream-of-consciousness style of writing has its parallel in Mahler's music, and presumably in Berio's as well.[8] The result is a musical collage but also a complex and fascinating work, much more than a haphazard pastiche.

INFLUENCES FROM FOLK MUSIC AND JAZZ

Composers of the nineteenth century were certainly not unaware of folk music, as witnessed by the influence of Polish folk music on Chopin and the arrangements of German folk songs by Brahms. The rise of nationalism in the late nineteenth century spawned an increased interest on the part of composers of all countries in the music that was indigenous to their own cultures, and this interest continued into the twentieth century, especially in the first several decades.

Probably the composer whose name first comes to mind in connection with folk music in the twentieth century is Béla Bartók. Shortly after the beginning of the century, he and his compatriot Zoltán Kodály began a serious study of folk music, at first only Hungarian, but soon including that of neighboring countries as well. Bartók's interest in this area is seen explicitly in the titles of many of his works; for example, the following titles appear in Volumes 4–6 of the *Mikrokosmos:*

100. In the Style of a Folk Song
112. Variations on a Folk Tune
113, and 115. Bulgarian Rhythm
127. New Hungarian Folk Song
128. Peasant Dance
138. Bagpipe
148–153. Six Dances in Bulgarian Rhythm

An excerpt from No. 148 appeared as Example 2–20, (p. 39), and the beginning of No. 112 is given in Example 8–4. The folk-song melody appears in octaves in mm. 1–8. The first variation follows without pause, parallel 6ths in the right hand being imitated canonically in the left hand at the 12th below.

EXAMPLE 8–4   Bartók: *Mikrokosmos* (1926–37), No. 112, mm. 1–17   *(© Copyright 1940 by Hawkes & Son, Ltd. Copyright Renewed. Reprinted by permission of Boosey & Hawkes, Inc.)*

The music of composers like Bartók, Kodály, and the Czech composer Leoš Janáček often shows the influence of folk music even when folk materials are not being explicitly quoted—hence the frequent references to their "folklike" melodies and rhythms. But it would be a serious mistake to think of the music of these composers only in terms of folk songs. Though folk music is an important element in their work, it merges with the currents of change in twentieth-century music, to which these composers made significant contributions.

Interest in folk music was of some importance in all European countries, but less in countries like Germany that had a great musical tradition of their own. Spain had a particularly strong nationalist movement in the music of Isaac Albéniz, Enrique Granados, and Manuel de Falla. Representative figures in the New World included Heitor Villa-Lobos in Brazil and Carlos Chávez and Silvestre Revueltas in Mexico.

In the United States the influence of folk song is seen in the music of Ives, Copland, and Roy Harris, among others. One of the first to make use of the folk songs of black Americans was the English composer Samuel Coleridge-Taylor, whose father was African. His *Twenty-Four Negro Melodies* (1905) may have inspired the black American composers William Grant Still and William Dawson. Another English work that uses black folk music is Michael Tippett's *A Child of Our Time* (1941), an oratorio dealing with racial persecution.

Jazz music first caught the attention of "serious" composers around the end of World War I (1918). A large number of works were composed over the next few decades that borrowed certain obvious features from jazz. Some of the better-known of these compositions include:

Igor Stravinsky: *Ragtime* (1918)

Paul Hindemith: *Chamber Music No. 1* (*Kammermusik No. 1*) (1922)

Darius Milhaud: *The Creation of the World* (*La création du monde*) (1923)

George Gershwin: *Rhapsody in Blue* (1924)

Aaron Copland: *Music for the Theater* (1925)

Aaron Copland: Piano Concerto (1927)

Ernst Křenek: *Johnny Plays On* (*Jonny spielt auf*) (1927)

Kurt Weill: *The Three Penny Opera* (*Die Dreigroschenoper*) (1928)

Maurice Ravel: *Concerto for the Left Hand* (1930)

George Gershwin: *Porgy and Bess* (1935)

Igor Stravinsky: *Ebony Concerto* (1945)

EXAMPLE 8–5 Stravinsky: *The Soldier's Tale (1918),* "Ragtime," mm. 1–8 *(© 1924 J. & W. Chester/Edition Wilhelm Hansen London Limited. Reproduced by kind permission.)*

One of the first such pieces was the "Ragtime" from Stravinsky's *The Soldier's Tale* (*L'histoire du soldat*) (1918), the beginning of which is seen in Example 8–5. The syncopations and dotted rhythms are evident here, as is an imitation of the functions of bass and percussion in an early jazz band, while later in the piece "jazzy" trombone glissandos are used. Of course, this music does not really sound like jazz, any more than neoclassical music sounds Classical; in fact, Austin's comment concerning Stravinsky's neo-classical style (see p. 166) is equally appropriate here.

With some important exceptions, jazz does not seem to have exerted much influence on concert music after World War II (i.e., since 1945). The main exception to this has been the so-called Third Stream movement, chiefly associated with Gunther Schuller, which attempted to blend jazz and concert music without condescending to either. In Example 8–6 Schuller evokes the sound of a blues through the "walking" bass line in the bassoon, the prevailing compound meter (Schuller instructs the performers to accent the eighth-note in any ♩♪ figure), the bends and glissandos in the horn, and other means as well.

Third Stream music never seemed to "catch on" to the extent that might have been expected, but jazz-influenced music is still being created by composers such as David Amram and Anthony Davis, whose opera *X (The Life and Times of Malcolm X)* (1986) resembles Gershwin's *Porgy and Bess* in its combination of jazz idioms with serious subject matter. Nevertheless, Reginald Smith Brindle is no doubt correct when he points out that most jazz has three characteristics that innovative composers since 1945 generally

EXAMPLE 8–6   Schuller: *Suite for Woodwind Quintet* (1957), II, mm. 16–23   *(Copyright © 1957 by Josef Marx. Used by permission of McGinnis & Marx Music Publishers.)*

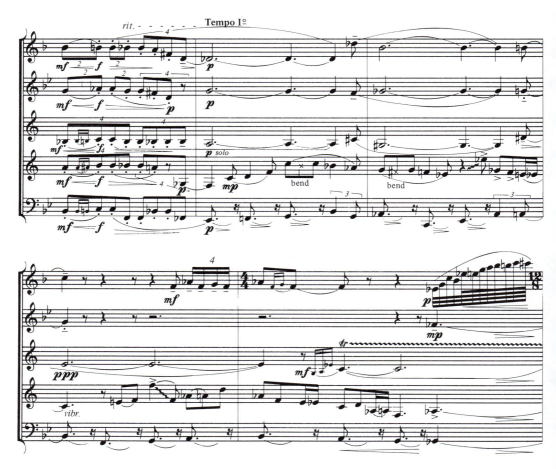

have wanted to avoid: clear melodic lines, conventional harmonic progressions, and a strong beat.[9] Ironically, "progressive jazz" itself seems to have done away with those characteristics one at a time—first by means of the disjunct, complex melodies of bebop in the 1940s, then through the harmonic stasis of the "time—no changes" style associated with Miles Davis in the 1960s,[10] and finally, in the performances of musicians like Keith Jarrett, by the development of an ametric approach to rhythm. In fact, some of the experimental jazz ensembles that exist today play compositions that resemble in significant ways some postwar avant-garde music.

All jazz by definition contains some improvisation, usually a significant amount, and this is the primary difference between jazz and most of its concert-hall derivatives. But improvisation has been an important aspect of certain "serious" music in recent decades (see Chapter 14), and the improvisatory styles of Charlie Parker and his heirs may well have had an influence on the performers of this kind of music. In addition, some of the instrumental timbres introduced into concert music in the twentieth century—notably the vibraphone and the cup mute for brass instruments—probably got there by way of the jazz band.

EXOTICISM

Composers have shown occasional interest since the late eighteenth century in the music of "exotic" lands, which in this context means anything from the islands of the Western Pacific to the Middle East to Africa. A broader definition could easily include Hungary and Spain, since each had absorbed a certain amount of Eastern culture through long periods of occupation. Under such a definition, Debussy's "La Puerta del Vino" (1910) and Ravel's *Bolero* (1927) would be examples of musical exoticism.

Until the twentieth century, most examples of musical exoticism, such as the "Alla Turca" movement from Mozart's Sonata in A Major K. 331 (1783) and Rimsky-Korsakov's *Scheherazade* (1888), made use of only the most superficial elements of the musical style being imitated. Two obvious ways of evoking the sound of the Orient are through timbre—the use of gongs, wood blocks, and pitched percussion instruments in imitation of the gamelan orchestra—and through certain compositional techniques such as parallelism and pentatonic scales.

Debussy makes use of some of these in Example 8–7. The upper two voices move in parallel motion up and down a four-note scale: (C♯–D♯–F♯–G♯), while the entrance of the bass in m. 29 provides a B, which when added to these four produces a pentatonic scale. The middle

EXAMPLE 8–7 Debussy: *Estampes (Stamps)* (1903), "Pagodas," mm. 27–30

voice in the texture moves more quickly than the bass but more slowly than the upper pair, and it seems to emphasize the important notes of the topmost voice. The total effect—pentatonicism, slow-moving bass, heterophony between topmost and middle voices—resembles some of the characteristics of the Javanese gamelan orchestra, indicating that Debussy had perhaps absorbed more of the authentic technique of exoticism than had his predecessors.

Composers became still more sophisticated about the music of other cultures as the century progressed: Messiaen, who studied the music of India and adapted its rhythms and scales to his own purposes, and Lou Harrison, who studied in Japan, Taiwan, and Korea, are but two examples. Some representatives works:

Gustav Holst: *Choral Hymns from the Rig-Veda* (1910)

Albert Roussel: *Padmâvatî* (1914)

Henry Cowell: *Persian Set* (1957)

Lou Harrison: *Concerto in Slendro* (1961)

Alan Hovhaness: *Fantasy on Japanese Woodprints* (1965)

Karlheinz Stockhausen: *Telemusik* (1966)

This blending of Western and Eastern musical styles has been furthered by various non-Western composers, including the Japanese composers Toru Takemitsu and Toshiro Mayuzumi, the Chinese Chou Wen-chung, and Jacob Avshalomov, a Chinese-born American.

Oriental philosophy (or at least the Western understanding of it) has also been important for some twentieth-century composers, especially for John Cage. Questioning the whole notion that art can "communicate" anything, Cage turned to Indian aesthetic theory, where he found the idea that "the purpose of music is to sober and quiet the mind, thus making it susceptible to divine influences."[11] His study of Zen, which "leads to a mistrust of the rational mind and a searching out of ways to nullify its powers of decision,"[12] led Cage to compose music by chance, the compositional decisions being made by the use of chance procedures from the *I-Ching*, a Chinese treatise on probabilities (discussed in more detail in Chapter 14). For Cage the influence of Zen was central to his development as a composer; he has said that "without my engagement with Zen I doubt whether I would have done what I have done."[13]

SUMMARY

In many ways the music of the twentieth century has broken with the past as completely as has any period in history. Neoclassicism and quotation, while providing important connections to the music of earlier times, are in no sense equivalent to the veneration of the past represented by the *stile antico* of the Baroque. As if to fill the void, some composers have reached out in other directions—to folk music, to jazz, to the music of other cultures—and have adapted these new materials and techniques to their own needs. These trends are an important part of the amazing diversity of styles found in twentieth-century music.

NOTES

1. Robert Craft, *Stravinsky: The Chronicle of a Friendship, 1948–71*, p. 103.
2. Donald Jay Grout, *A History of Western Music*, pp. 714–15.
3. William Austin, *Music in the 20th Century*, p. 330.
4. George Rochberg, *Music for the Magic Theater* (Bryn Mawr: Theodore Presser, 1972), p. 6. "Notion" appears as "notation" in the original.
5. Rochberg, *Music for the Magic Theater*, p. 6.
6. George Crumb, *Ancient Voices of Children* (New York: C. F. Peters, 1970).
7. A thorough list is given in Chapter 4 of David Osmond-Smith's *Playing on Words*.
8. Michael Hicks, "Text, Music, and Meaning in the Third Movement of Luciano Berio's *Sinfonia*" in *Perspectives of New Music*.
9. Reginald Smith Brindle, *The New Music*, pp. 137–38.
10. Ian Carr, *Miles Davis*, p. 145.
11. Ev Grimes, "Ev Grimes Interviews John Cage," in *Music Educators Journal*, p. 48.
12. Brindle, *The New Music*, p. 123.
13. Michael Nyman, *Experimental Music*, p. 43.

EXERCISES

Part A: Analysis

1. Bartók: *Fourteen Bagatelles*, Op. 6 (1908), No. 4, mm. 1–8. This excerpt contains the beginning of a folk-song harmonization by Bartók (the remainder of the piece simply repeats mm. 5–8). Bartók uses different compositional techniques in the harmonization of each phrase. Analyze both the song and the accompaniment in detail, summarizing your findings in prose with musical examples. Do not neglect such issues as voice leading and scale formations.

2. List the chords used in the accompaniment (bassoons and trombones) in Example 8–1. How much of this conforms to traditional harmonic progressions in E♭? Point out some dissonances between the accompaniment and the upper parts that would be difficult to explain in traditional terms. Comment on imitation in this excerpt.

3. A very basic harmonic pattern for a twelve-bar blues in B♭ is:

| B♭ |✠| B♭7 |✠| E♭7 |✠| B♭ |✠| F7 | E♭7 | B♭ |✠||

Discuss how Example 8–6 compares to the first eight measures of that pattern. Remember to transpose the clarinet and horn parts.

4. The B♭ "blues scale" can be derived by combining the three chords listed in the previous exercise, producing a nine-tone scale: B♭–C–D♭–D–E♭–F–G–A♭–A. Part of the flavor that we associate with the blues results from the use, either melodically or harmonically, of the altered and unaltered "blues notes" (D♭/D and A♭/A) in close proximity. Point out any examples that you can find of this technique in Example 8–6.

Part B: Listening

Listen to as many examples as you can. For each one, explain how the example is relevant to the present chapter, and try to describe how the music *sounds*—how the use of folk materials or quotation, for example, helps to give the music its own particular sound.

1. David Amram: Triple Concerto for Woodwind, Brass, and Jazz Quintets, and Orchestra (1970), I

2. Béla Bartók: *Fifteen Hungarian Peasant Songs* (1917)

3. Luciano Berio: *Sinfonia* (1968), III

4. Aaron Copland: *Appalachian Spring* (1944)

5. Manuel de Falla: *Nights in the Gardens of Spain* (1916)

6. Lou Harrison: Double Concerto for Violin and Cello with Javanese Gamelan (1982)

7. William Grant Still: *Afro-American Symphony* (1933)

8. Igor Stravinsky: Octet for Wind Instruments (1923)

Part C: Further Reading

BRINDLE, REGINALD SMITH. *The New Music*. See Chapter 13, "The Search Outwards—The Orient, Jazz, Archaisms."

CHOU, WEN-CHUNG.   "Asian Concepts and Twentieth-Century Western Composers."

GRIFFITHS, PAUL.   *Modern Music*. See Chapter 11, "Quotation—Integration."

GROUT, DONALD JAY.   *A History of Western Music*. See the sections titled "Musical Styles Related to Folk Idioms," pp. 685–700, and "Neo-Classicism and Related Movements," pp. 700–22.

RINGO, JAMES.   "The Lure of the Orient."

SIMMS, BRYAN R.   *Music of the Twentieth Century*. See Chapter 10, "Neoclassicism in France, Germany, and England," and Chapter 15, "Eclecticism."

9 | Nonserial Atonality

INTRODUCTION

In the first decade of the twentieth century, a few composers developed an approach to composition that, in retrospect, was perhaps inevitable. The chromaticism of the nineteenth century had chipped away at the tonal system so successfully that it was only a natural outcome for the system eventually to be abandoned altogether. This new music without a tonal center eventually became known as "atonal" music, although not without objection by some of the composers who originated the style.

Atonality is one of the more important aspects of twentieth-century music, and it is a major factor that distinguishes much of the music of this century from any other music in the Western tradition. Nonserial, or "free," atonality led in the 1920s to a more organized atonal method called *serialism* or *twelve-tone music*, but nonserial atonal music continued to be composed and is still being composed today. We will discuss serialism in later chapters. For now we are concerned only with nonserial atonal music, which, for the present, we will refer to simply as atonal music.

It is not surprising that the analysis of atonal music has required the development of new theoretical terms and approaches. Though analytical methods are still being developed and experimented with, most of the current literature derives from the work of Allen Forte, whose book *The Structure of Atonal Music* is a standard reference on the subject.[1] Most of the information in this chapter derives from Forte's work or from that of his followers, and it may be totally unfamiliar to you. The concepts are not very difficult, however, and you will find them applicable to a wide range of twentieth-century styles.

CHARACTERISTICS OF ATONAL MUSIC

There are several characteristics of atonal music that set it apart from other styles. The first is that it lacks a tonal center. This aspect is a subjective one, for any two listeners might differ concerning the degree to which a tonality is audible in a particular work; nevertheless, a great many pieces are widely accepted as being atonal. This atonality is achieved by avoiding the conventional melodic, harmonic, and rhythmic patterns that help to establish a tonality in traditional music. In their place we find unresolved dissonances, a preponderance of mixed-interval chords, and pitch material derived from the chromatic scale. Textures are often contrapuntal, with themes or melodies in the traditional sense occurring less often, and the metric organization is frequently difficult for the listener to follow.

Example 9–1 is from the beginning of one of the earliest atonal works. While not the most representative example that could have been chosen, it does have the advantage of being easy to play, and you will get more out of the following discussion if you play the example several times while reading it. The piece opens with a slow tremolo between D and F over a sustained F, perhaps suggesting D minor. Octave doublings such as the octave here on F were soon discarded in atonal music on the theory that they put too much emphasis on a single pitch class. The melody that enters in m. 2 does nothing to confirm D as a tonality. Two short melodic phrases, one beginning in m. 2 and the other in m. 3, use the pitch classes C, D♭, D, E♭, A♭, and A, with many of these pitches being freely dissonant against the accompaniment. If these phrases suggest any tonal center at all, it is D♭. Following the rest under the fermata, a third phrase interrupts the tremolo figure in the low register and closes the excerpt. Melodically this third phrase begins with an expressive motion up to D (notice the accompanying chords here do not suggest a D tonal center), followed by the same pitch classes that ended the second phrase: C–E♭–D♭. The tremolo figure re-

EXAMPLE 9–1 Schoenberg: *Three Piano Pieces* (1909), Op. 11, No. 2, mm. 1–5 *(Used by permission of Belmont Music Publishers.)*

turns as the melody settles in on its last two notes. While in this excerpt the D/F dyad (pair of notes) in the accompaniment is clearly in opposition to the D♭ in the melody, neither D nor D♭ is strongly established as a tonal center, and this, along with the prevailing chromaticism, leads us to classify this music as atonal rather than polytonal (review Chapter 5).

It is doubtful that the listener would be able to identify the time signature used in these opening measures. The opening undulating figure is notated in groups of three notes but contains only two pitches, so the listener is not sure whether the first six eighth-notes constitute two or three beats (assuming the eighth-note is heard as a division of the beat). The melody in its first phrase works out nicely in $\frac{12}{8}$, but, to express the meter as notated, the melody should start at the beginning of the measure instead of on the third eighth-note. The melody of the second phrase could easily be heard as two measures of $\frac{3}{4}$ with an anacrusis. Later portions of the piece (not shown) suggest $\frac{3}{4}$, $\frac{2}{4}$, and $\frac{6}{4}$, among others, although there are passages that are clearly in $\frac{12}{8}$.

PITCH-CLASS SETS

It soon became clear to musicians that the pitch aspect of atonal music required a new vocabulary if the analysis of this music was ever to be more than descriptive. It was recognized that atonal music often achieved a certain degree of unity through recurrent use of a new kind of motive. This new kind of motive was given various names, including *cell*, *basic cell*, *set*, *pitch set*, *pitch-class set*, and *referential sonority*. It could appear melodically, harmonically, or as a combination of the two. The set could also be transposed and/or inverted (that is, in mirror inversion; for example, G–B–C inverts to G–E♭–D), and its pitches could appear in any order. Most pieces were found to employ a large number of different kinds of pitch sets, only a few of which might be important in unifying the piece. The analysis of atonal music has largely become a process of identifying and labeling these important pitch sets, a process referred to as *segmentation*.

This process of segmentation is in some ways much more difficult than the analysis of chords in traditional tonal music. The first problem is that, when beginning the analysis, one usually does not know which sets will turn out to be significant in the piece and which ones will not, meaning that various musically convincing segmentations may have to be tried and discarded before the significant ones appear. We will demonstrate the process of segmentation throughout this chapter.

A second problem is labeling the sets for ease of comparison, and it is in this area that Allen Forte's work has proved so helpful. Since an atonal chord or melodic fragment can consist of any combination of pitches, thousands of different sets are possible. As we shall see, Forte's system of pitch-class sets reduces this number considerably.

OCTAVE EQUIVALENCE, TRANSPOSITIONAL EQUIVALENCE, AND NORMAL ORDER

In the analysis of tonal music, we routinely reduce sonorities to basic forms. For instance, through the theories of octave equivalence and chord roots we analyze all of the chords in Example 9–2a as C major triads and all of those in Example 9–2b as F major triads. In addition, we consider C major triads and F major triads to be transpositionally equivalent, to be members of a class of sonorities referred to collectively as major triads. These concepts are so obvious to us that it seems trivial to mention them, but in fact the theory that classifies the sonorities in Example 9–2 into one chord type is only a few centuries old.

EXAMPLE 9–2 Major Triads

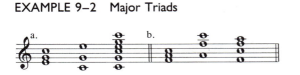

In order to analyze and compare the pitch-class sets in atonal music, we need a process that will reduce any set to some basic form in the same way that we reduce the chords in Example 9–2 to the three notes of the major triad in root position. This basic form in pitch-set analysis is called the *normal order*. The procedure to follow in determining the normal order will be illustrated by means of the segmentations shown in Example 9–3.

EXAMPLE 9–3 Schoenberg: *Three Piano Pieces*, (1909) Op. 11, No. 2, mm. 1–5 *(Used by permission of Belmont Music Publishers.)*

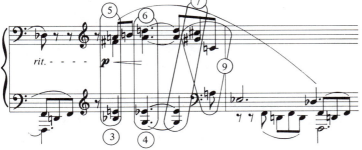

To find the normal order of a set, notate the pitches as an ascending "scale," as in Example 9–4a. You can begin the scale on any one of the notes, and the notes can be spelled enharmonically if you wish. Leave out any duplicated pitch classes. Continue the scale up to the octave (the second

EXAMPLE 9–4   Normal Order of Set 1

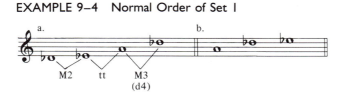

Db in Example 9–4a) and find the largest interval between any two adjacent notes (the tritone in Example 9–4a). The *top* note of this largest interval (the A in Example 9–4a) is the *bottom* note of the normal order. The normal order of set 1 is shown in Example 9–4b. Notice that in Example 9–4 we have labeled the interval A–Db as a major 3rd even though it is notated as a diminished 4th. While enharmonic substitution is discouraged in tonal analysis, it is essential in analyzing atonal music. It may already be obvious to you that Set 2 is transpositionally equivalent to Set 1. Notice that

EXAMPLE 9–5   Normal Order of Set 2

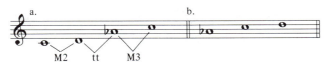

Example 9–5b is equivalent to Example 9–4b, but a minor 2nd lower. Sets 3 and 4 are the three-note chords that accompany the melody in m. 4. The normal orders of these two sets are shown in Example 9–6. Notice that Set 4 is transpositionally equivalent to Sets 1 and 2, but Set 3 is not. Sets 5, 6,

EXAMPLE 9–6   Normal Orders of Sets 3 and 4

and 7 result from a different segmentation of m. 4. Each one contains four pitch classes. The first column of Example 9–7 shows these sets in scalar form, with the largest intervals labeled. Notice that in Set 7 the G♯ and C♯ have been spelled enharmonically for convenience. The normal orders of these sets are shown in the second column of Example 9–7. None of these sets is transpositionally equivalent to any of the others.

Occasionally you will encounter a set in which there is not a single largest interval, but instead two or more intervals that are tied for largest. Set 8 is an example of such a set. Notice in Example 9–8a that there are two

EXAMPLE 9–7   Normal Orders of Sets 5, 6, and 7

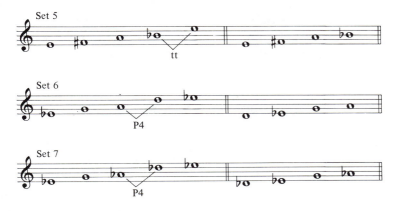

major 3rds and that all of the other intervals are smaller. This means that we have two candidates for the normal order, Example 9–8b and Example 9–8c. The tie is broken by comparing the intervals between the bottom two notes in both versions (A–C♯ in Example 9–8b versus C♯–D in Example 9–8c). The normal order is the version with the *smaller* interval—Example 9–8c.

If the intervals between the bottom two notes in Example 9–8b and Example 9–8c had been the same, we would have proceeded to the intervals between notes 2 and 3, and so on, until the tie was broken. In some sets, however, the tie cannot be broken. Consider the set in Example 9–9a (not taken from the Schoenberg excerpt). It contains two instances of its largest interval, the minor 3rd, so there are two candidates for the normal order. These are shown in Example 9–9b and Example 9–9c. The interval successions in the two versions are identical (because they are transpositionally

EXAMPLE 9–8   Normal Order of Set 8

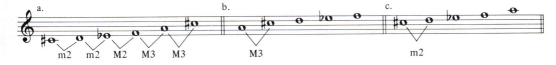

EXAMPLE 9–9   A Transpositionally Symmetrical Set

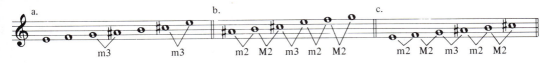

equivalent), so it is impossible to break the tie. In this case, either of the tied forms may be selected as the normal order. A set such as this is called a *transpositionally symmetrical set*, because it reproduces its own pitch-class content under one or more intervals of transposition. In the case of the set in Example 9–9, transposition at the tritone reproduces the set.

INVERSIONAL EQUIVALENCE AND BEST NORMAL ORDER

We have seen that tonal and atonal analyses share the concepts of octave equivalence and transpositional equivalence. Atonal analysis goes a step further, however, and considers pitch-class sets that are related by inversion to be equivalent. This would not be a useful approach in tonal music, because the major and minor triads, for example, are related by inversion, as are the dominant 7th chord and the half-diminished-7th chord, and we need to be able to distinguish between them in tonal analysis. But in atonal music a set and its inversion are considered to be different representations of the same set type.

If we are going to have a single classification for any set and its inversion, then we will have to carry the concept of the normal order a step further, to something called the *best normal order*. This concept is important because the best normal order is the generic representation of all the possible transpositions and inversions of a set. In order to find the best normal order of any set, first find its normal order, then invert the set and find the normal order of the inversion. Finally, compare the two normal orders: the "better" of the two is considered to be the best normal order.

Let us see how this works with Set 1 from Example 9–3. Its normal order was given in Example 9–4. To invert the set, it is best to begin with the normal order. In Example 9–10a the intervals of the normal order are analyzed. These intervals are then inverted in Example 9–10b to form the inversion. We used A as the first note of the inversion, but any other note would have served equally well. Next, in Example 9–10c, we work out the normal order of the inversion and notate it in Example 9–10d. Finally, we choose between the two orders by comparing the intervals between the

EXAMPLE 9–10   Set I and Its Inversion

bottom two notes in both versions, just as we did with Example 9–8; if they are the same, we proceed to the next interval, and so on. We select as the best normal order the version with the smaller interval—in this case, Example 9–11b.

EXAMPLE 9–11   Best Normal Order of Set 1

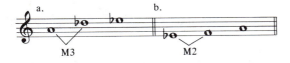

Looking back over Examples 9–4, 9–5, and 9–6, you can see that Sets 1, 2, and 4 were transpositionally equivalent to each other, and that all three were inversionally equivalent to Set 3. In other words, all four sets have the same best normal and therefore are all representatives of the same set type.

Set 5 is analyzed in Example 9–12. The normal order of the original set is in Example 9–12a, and its inversion is in Example 9–12b (starting on B♭, but remember that we could begin with any note). In Example 9–12c the inversion is analyzed, and its normal order is given in Example 9–12d. Comparing the two normal orders, Example 9–12a and 9–12d, the better one is Example 9–12d, because its lowest interval is a minor 2nd, and so it is selected as the best normal order.

In Example 9–13 Set 6 is analyzed. The normal order of the original set, Example 9–13a, turns out to be the best normal order.

EXAMPLE 9–12   Best Normal Order of Set 5

EXAMPLE 9–13   Best Normal Order of Set 6

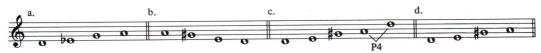

Set 7 is analyzed in Example 9–14. The best normal order is Example 9–14d. Since the best normal orders of Sets 6 and 7 (Example 9–13a and Example 9–14d) are transpositionally equivalent, Sets 6 and 7 are representatives of the same set type.

EXAMPLE 9–14   Best Normal Order of Set 7

It is not uncommon to find a set in which the normal order of the set and the normal order of its inversion are identical or transpositionally equivalent. An example is Set 9, shown in normal order in Example 9–15a. In Example 9–15b the normal order is inverted, starting on A (for no particular reason). The normal order of the inversion, Example 9–15c, is the same as Example 9–15a, but a major 3rd lower. In a case such as this, either version can be selected as the best normal order. A set such as the one in Example 9–15 is called an *inversionally symmetrical set*, because it reproduces its pitch-class content at one or more levels of inversion. In this case, the pitch-class content would have been duplicated if we had begun the inversion in Example 9–15b on C♯ instead of A.

EXAMPLE 9–15   Best Normal Order of Set 9

SET TYPES AND PRIME FORMS

By adopting the concepts of transpositional and inversional symmetry, the thousands of possible pitch combinations have been reduced to a manageable number of best normal orders or pitch-class set types. The table below shows how many set types there are for combinations of from two to ten pitch classes.

6	Dyads (2 pitch classes)
12	Trichords (3 pitch classes)
29	Tetrachords (4 pitch classes)
38	Pentachords (5 pitch classes)
50	Hexachords (6 pitch classes)
38	Septachords (7 pitch classes)
29	Octachords (8 pitch classes)
12	Nonachords (9 pitch classes)
6	Decachords (10 pitch classes)
220	**TOTAL**

The total of 220 set types is far more than the eight or nine chord types that constituted the harmonic vocabulary of tonal music. It would be unreasonable to expect musicians to memorize 220 new names for these set types, and fortunately that is not necessary. Instead, a set type is named by applying numbers to the best normal order, the resulting series of numbers being called the *prime form*. The first number is always 0, and it stands for the lowest note of the best normal order. The other numbers give the distance in half-steps each successive note is above that lowest note. For instance, in Example 9–10d we notated the best normal order of Set 1 as E♭–F–A. Since F is two half-steps above E♭ and A is six half-steps above E♭, the name of this set type is [0,2,6]. Sets 1, 2, 3, and 4 are all [0,2,6] trichords. Notice that the set type is enclosed in brackets and the numbers are separated by commas.

A few more illustrations: The best normal order of Set 5 (Example 9–12d) is E–F–A♭–B♭, yielding [0,1,4,6] as a prime form. The prime form of Set 6 (Example 9–13a) is D–E♭–G–A, or [0,1,5,7], and Set 7 (Example 9–14d) is also a [0,1,5,7] tetrachord. Set 9 (Example 9–15a) is a [0,1,4,5] tetrachord.

SOME HINTS FOR FINDING PRIME FORMS

With a little practice, the task of analyzing a set becomes much less time-consuming, and there are a few shortcuts that may make it easier for you to get to that point. For one thing, it is usually not really necessary to notate the inversion and go through the process of finding its best normal order. For instance, consider Example 9–16, which is a set in normal order, but not necessarily in its best normal order. The normal order of the inversion will simply reverse the order of the intervals: M2–M2–m3 becomes m3–M2–M2. Without bothering to notate the inversion, we can see that Example 9–16 is already in prime form, because its first interval (the major 2nd) is smaller than the first interval of its inversion (the minor 3rd). The prime form, then, is [0,2,4,7].

EXAMPLE 9–16   A Normal Order

The set in Example 9–17a, also in normal order, has the interval succession m3–m2–M2, while the normal order of its inversion will have M2–m2–m3. Since a major 2nd is smaller than a minor 3rd, the inversion will be the best normal order. However, it is still not necessary to write out the inversion; instead, designate the *top* note as 0, and number the others in terms of half-steps below the top note, as in Example 9–17b. Reverse the order of the numbers, and the prime form turns out to be [0,2,3,6].

EXAMPLE 9–17   A Normal Order

Unfortunately, this shortcut will not always work, because the normal order of the inversion is not always the reverse of the normal order of the original, but it usually is. This will work with all twelve trichords. It will also work with all but one of the 29 tetrachords; if you analyze a set as [0,3,4,8], you're wrong—it's [0,1,4,8] instead. This system fails with three of the pentachords and four of the hexachords—too many to memorize. However, it will work with *any* set that contains only a single "largest interval."

Probably the best way to analyze atonal music, as well as tonal music, is at the piano keyboard. Finding the best normal order and prime form becomes considerably faster at the piano. More important, as you work at the analysis you hear the sound of the set and gradually learn to associate the sounds with the set types.

THE INTERVAL VECTOR

Most of pitch-set analysis is concerned with identifying sets that recur in a piece in compositionally significant ways. This includes, of course, transpositions and inversions of the original set, since we recognize transpositional and inversional equivalence. But analytical theory is much less advanced when it comes to comparing nonequivalent sets. Consider, for example, Sets 5 and 6 from the Schoenberg excerpt, reproduced here in best normal order beginning on G.

EXAMPLE 9–18   Sets 5 and 6

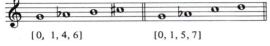

[0, 1, 4, 6]   [0, 1, 5, 7]

It is obvious to us that [0,1,4,6] and [0,1,5,7] are very similar, the only apparent difference being the interval between the second and third notes; thus, [0,1,5,7] is a kind of expansion of [0,1,4,6]. But there are other differences, one of them being that [0,1,5,7] contains two perfect intervals (G–C and G–D), while [0,1,4,6] contains only one (A♭–C♯). This probably means that [0,1,5,7] is potentially a more consonant sound than [0,1,4,6]. One way of comparing sets that contain the same number of notes, as these do, is to tabulate their interval contents. Because inversional equivalence is still in effect, we will consider the minor 2nd and the major 7th to be the same interval, also the major 2nd and the minor 7th, and so forth. We then have six *interval classes* ("interval class" is sometimes abbreviated as "IC"):

Interval Class	Traditional Interval
1	m2, M7
2	M2, m7
3	m3, M6
4	M3, m6
5	P4, P5
6	A4, d5

To analyze a set according to its interval vector, tabulate all the ICs between each note in the set and all the notes *above* it. This way, the interval between each pair of notes in the set will be counted only once. The diagram below demonstrates this procedure for Sets 5 and 6 (refer again to Example 9–18).

	Set 5	
From	**Up to**	**IC**
G	A♭	1
G	B	4
G	C♯	6
A♭	B	3
A♭	C♯	5
B	C♯	2

	Set 6	
From	**Up to**	**IC**
G	A♭	1
G	C	5
G	D	5
A♭	C	4
A♭	D	6
C	D	2

You can see from this that Set 5 contains exactly one occurrence of each IC. Set 6, on the other hand, contains two occurrences of IC5 but none of IC3. This information is usually presented in the form of an *interval vector*, which lists the number of occurrences of each IC, beginning with IC1 and continuing through IC6, with the list enclosed in angles. Set 5, since it contains one of each IC, has an interval vector of <1,1,1,1,1,1>, while the interval vector for Set 6 is <1,1,0,1,2,1>. The interval vectors of Sets 5 and 6 illustrate their similarity and give us a general picture of their potential consonance or dissonance.

The interval vector provides one tool for comparing pitch-class sets of the same size, but it is not without its problems. At the beginning of Example 3–B–7 (p. 75) Berg employs two set types in alternation (the chords marked a, b, c, d, and e). The first two chords are shown in Example 9–19, both in their original versions (but compressed spacing) and in their best normal orders, transposed to begin on G. The first chord is set type [0,1,3,7], and the second is [0,1,4,6], the same as Set 5 from the Schoenberg excerpt. The surprising thing here is that both sets have an interval vector of <1,1,1,1,1,1>. Since they are different set types, we know they are not related by transposition or inversion, yet their interval vectors are identical. Pairs of sets that share the same vector (they come only in pairs) are known as *Z-related sets*. This is the only pair of Z-related tetrachords, but there are three pairs of Z-related pentachords and fifteen pairs of Z-related hexachords. It is obvious from this that the interval vector alone cannot be used to compare set types, although it does provide some useful information.

EXAMPLE 9–19   Two Chords From Berg's "Warm Is the Air"

AGGREGATES

Nonserial atonality does not offer a systematic method of achieving atonality, as serialism does, but atonal composers have at times shown a concern that all twelve pitch classes be heard within a fairly short period, which is one of the fundamental notions of twelve-tone serialism. The term *aggregate* is used to refer to any such statement of all twelve pitch classes, without regard to order or duplication. In atonal analysis, it is sometimes helpful to look for aggregates, especially at the beginning of a piece or major section, or even within certain parts of the texture.

Concerning his *Bagatelles* Op. 9, a nonserial atonal work, Anton Webern wrote, "While working on them I had the feeling that once the twelve tones had run out, the piece was finished."[2] This does not mean that each Bagatelle is only twelve notes long, although they are quite short, but it might mean that Webern has used aggregates in significant ways in these pieces. The first half of the fifth Bagatelle (Example 9–20) contains an extreme example of what Webern was talking about.

In the first measure of this piece, Webern introduces a nearly chromatic set, C–C♯–D♯–E, which is filled in by the D in m. 2, giving us:

```
C    C♯    D    D♯    E
|———————mm. 1–2———————|
```

Measure 3 begins with a chord that extends the chromatic set by two more pitches:

```
B    C    C♯    D    D♯    E    F
3    |———————mm. 1–2———————|    3
```

The chord in m. 4 expands the chromatic set to nine pitches:

```
B♭    B    C    C♯    D    D♯    E    F    G♭
4     3    |———————mm. 1–2———————|    3    4
```

Measure 6 continues the set upwards by two notes:

```
B♭    B    C    C♯    D    D♯    E    F    G♭    G    A♭
4     3    |———————mm. 1–2———————|    3    4    6    6
```

And the chromatic set is completed by the A in m. 7:

```
A    B♭    B    C    C♯    D    D♯    E    F    G♭    G    A♭
7    4     3    |———————mm. 1–2———————|    3    4    6    6
```

What we have in mm. 1–7 is an aggregate, but it is a highly unusual one in that the pitch classes are introduced according to a preconceived pattern and within a single octave (A3 to A♭4). Even the pitch classes that are repeated, like the E and E♭ in m. 3, recur in the same octave, with the single exception of the C5 in m. 5.

Aggregate completion is also important in the first movement of Ligeti's *Ten Pieces for Wind Quintet* (1968). In this 25-measure work the composer employs eleven pitch classes, omitting only C♯, until the middle of m. 16, where C♯s are introduced to produce the climax of the movement.

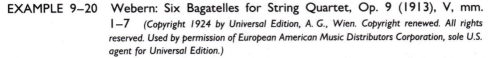

EXAMPLE 9–20   Webern: Six Bagatelles for String Quartet, Op. 9 (1913), V, mm. 1–7 *(Copyright 1924 by Universal Edition, A. G., Wien. Copyright renewed. All rights reserved. Used by permission of European American Music Distributors Corporation, sole U.S. agent for Universal Edition.)*

MORE ABOUT SEGMENTATION

Earlier in this chapter we said that atonal analysis is largely a matter of segmentation, or identifying and labeling significant pitch-class sets. The Schoenberg excerpt provided some experience with this process. Segmentation is largely a hit-or-miss analytical procedure, because a set that occurs only once and is not significantly related to any more important set is not really of much interest. In the Webern excerpt (Example 9–20), for instance, you might isolate these three sets in m. 1:

C–C♯–E   [0,1,4]
C–D♯–E   [0,1,4]
C–C♯–D♯–E   [0,1,3,4]

The fact that the first two sets are representatives of the same pitch-class set is encouraging to the analyst, but they may or may not recur later in the piece. Another segmentation that could be tried would be to join the "melodies" in the violins:

C♯–D♯–D–F–E♭   [0,1,2,4]

Other musically defensible segmentations could be made on the basis of timbre (for instance, *am steg* versus *pizzicato*) or register. The most important thing is that the segmentations should reflect the way the music sounds and should not divide musical units such as chords or melodic figures in unmusical ways. In spite of the mathematical nature of pitch-class sets, atonal analysis requires a high degree of musical sensitivity and a very keen ear.

SUMMARY

The most essential characteristic of nonserial atonal music is its atonality, which is achieved by avoiding the melodic, harmonic, and rhythmic patterns used to establish a tonality in tonal music. Some of the other characteristics of nonserial atonal music include unresolved dissonances, a preponderance of mixed-interval chords, contrapuntal textures, ambiguous metric organization, and use of the chromatic scale.

An important aspect of atonal analysis is the identification of the important pitch sets or cells used in the piece. This part of the analysis, called segmentation, involves arranging each set in normal order and then best normal order for the identification of its pitch-class set type, represented by its prime form. This classification process depends upon both transpositional and inversional equivalence in order to reduce to 220 the number of possible sets of between two and ten pitch classes.

Nonequivalent sets that contain the same number of pitch classes may be compared by means of their interval vectors, as well as by other means not introduced here.

Aggregate completion is another element to look for in the analysis of atonal music, especially at the beginning of a piece.

NOTES

1. Allen Forte, *The Structure of Atonal Music*.
2. Webern, *The Path to the New Music*, p. 51.

EXERCISES

Part A: Fundamentals

1. Analyze the pitches in each exercise below as a single pitch-class set.

Notate the set in its normal order and in its best normal order (which may or may not be different), and put underneath the best normal order the prime form (e.g., [0,1,5,7]).

2. Provide the interval vector for each set in Exercise A.1.

3. Classify each set from Exercise A.1 as (1) transpositionally symmetrical, (2) inversionally symmetrical, (3) both transpositionally and inversionally symmetrical, or (4) neither transpositionally nor inversionally symmetrical.

4. There are twelve possible trichord set types (prime forms). See if you can list them. Be sure none are related by inversion or transposition.

Part B: Analysis

1. See Example 3–21 (p. 61). What trichord type (prime form) is featured in this passage from one of Debussy's tonal compositions?

2. See Example 3–B–7 (p. 75). We saw in connection with Example 9–21 that Berg alternates between [0,1,3,7] and [0,1,4,6] in the first two measures. What trichord type is found in the right hand in those measures? What set type ends the piece?

3. See Example 4–4 (p. 83). What tetrachord begins the flute part? the voice part? Where is the first aggregate completed? Is this a structurally significant location, such as a climactic pitch or the end of a phrase?

4. See Example 4–6 (p. 86). What trichord type appears under each of the three phrase marks?

5. See Example 4–7 (p. 87). Using reasonable segmentations of the bassoon part, find two recurrent tetrachords.

6. See Example 4–13 (p. 95). What tetrachord is Debussy using here? What is its interval vector?

7. See Example 4–B–1 (p. 99). One way to segment this would be into three tetrachords and a final trichord. Analyze each one.

8. See Example 4–B–2 (p. 99). Analyze this melody in terms of set types and large-scale (mostly chromatic) motion.

9. See Example 5–4 (p. 111). What trichord type is most prominent in this excerpt?

10. See Example 9–1. Where in this excerpt is the first aggregate completed? Is this a structurally significant location?

11. Crumb: *Madrigals*, Book I (1965), No. 1, "To see you naked is to remember the earth," mm. 1–6 (see p. 203). This excerpt is based primarily upon one pitch-class set type. Decide what that set type is, and mark its occurrences in the music. Try to make your segmentations musically justifiable.

Part C: Composition

1. Compose an instrumental melody based on the [0,1,5,7] tetrachord in various transpositions and in inversion. Every fourth note should be the end of one statement of the tetrachord and the beginning of another:

Because the [0,1,5,7] tetrachord has an interval vector of <1,1,0,1,2,1>, your melody can have a good deal of intervallic variety. Include an analysis of your melody.

(Crumb: *Madrigal*, Book I (1965), No. 1, "To see you naked is to remember the earth," mm. 1–6)

203

2. Continue the example below or compose one of your own, basing the passage on a single trichord type, used both melodically and harmonically. Circle all occurrences of the set. The trichord used in the example is [0,1,6].

3. Compose a fanfare for three trumpets, based upon one melodic trichord type and a different harmonic trichord type. Label all of the trichords.

4. Compose a harmonic "progression" in four parts using a single tetrachord type. The pitch content of each chord should be a transposition of the preceding one, and you are to use all six ICs as intervals of transposition. Label the transpositions. Keep any invariant pitch classes in the same voices, and move the remaining voices as smoothly as possible. What is the interval vector of your tetrachord? How does that interval vector relate to the invariants?

Part D: Further Reading

BENWARD, BRUCE. *Music in Theory and Practice*, Vol. 2. See pp. 329–39.

FORTE, ALLEN. *The Structure of Atonal Music*. See Part 1, "Pitch-Class Sets and Relations."

LANSKY, PAUL AND GEORGE PERLE. "Atonality," in Stanley Sadie, ed., *The New Grove Dictionary of Music and Musicians*.

PERLE, GEORGE. *Serial Composition and Atonality*. See Chapter 2, " 'Free' Atonality."

RAHN, JOHN. *Basic Atonal Theory*.

SCHMALFELDT, JANET. *Berg's Wozzeck*. See pp. 14–24.

SIMMS, BRYAN. *Music of the Twentieth Century*. See Chapter 2, "Harmonic and Motivic Associations and the 'Emancipation of Dissonance.' "

WINOLD, ALLEN. *Harmony: Patterns and Principles*. See Chapter 28, "Integer Notation and Analysis."

WITTLICH, GARY. "Sets and Ordering Procedures in Twentieth-Century Music," in Gary Wittlich, ed., *Aspects of Twentieth-Century Music*. See pp. 455–70.

10

Classical Serialism

INTRODUCTION

When Schoenberg composed the first twelve-tone piece in the summer of 1921,[1] the "Prelude" to what would eventually become his Suite, Op. 25 (1923), he carried to a conclusion the developments in chromaticism that had begun many decades earlier. The assault of chromaticism on the tonal system had led to the nonsystem of free atonality, and now Schoenberg had developed a "method [he insisted it was not a "system"] of composing with twelve tones that are related only with one another."

Free atonality achieved some of its effect through the use of aggregates, as we have seen, and many atonal composers seemed to have been convinced that atonality could best be achieved through some sort of regular recycling of the twelve pitch classes. But it was Schoenberg who came up with the idea of arranging the twelve pitch classes into a particular series, or row, that would remain essentially constant throughout a composition.

Various twelve-tone melodies that predate 1921 are often cited as precursors of Schoenberg's tone row, a famous example being the fugue

theme from Strauss's *Thus Spake Zarathustra* (1895). A less famous example, but one closer than Strauss's theme to Schoenberg's method, is seen in
Example 10–1. Notice that Ives holds off the last pitch class, C, for 3½
measures until its dramatic entrance in m. 68.

EXAMPLE 10–1 Ives: *Three-Page Sonata* (1905), mm. 62–68 *(© 1949 Mercury Music Corporation. Used by permission of the publisher.)*

In the music of Strauss and Ives the twelve-note theme is a curiosity,
but in the music of Schoenberg and his followers the twelve-note row is a
basic shape that can be transformed in only a few well-defined ways,
thereby assuring a certain unity in the pitch domain of a composition.

This chapter presents the basics of "classical" serialism, the serial
technique developed by Schoenberg and adopted by Webern and Berg
(somewhat more freely by the latter), as well as many other composers.
Chapter 13 will deal with more advanced serial topics, concentrating on
integral serialism.

BASIC TERMINOLOGY

The core of the twelve-tone system is the *tone row* (*basic set*, *series*), an
ordered arrangement of the twelve pitch classes, with each one occurring
once and only once. The row itself has four basic forms:

1. *Prime*: the original set (not to be confused with the prime form of
   an unordered set, discussed in Chapter 9)

2. *Retrograde*: the original set in reverse order
3. *Inversion*: the mirror inversion of the original set
4. *Retrograde Inversion*: the inversion in reverse order

The row that Schoenberg used for his first serial work is shown in its four basic forms in Example 10–2. The notes could have been written in any octave and with enharmonic spellings if desired. We follow the convention here and in similar examples of omitting natural signs; any note without an accidental is natural. The numbers under the notes are called *order numbers* and simply indicate each note's position in the row form.

EXAMPLE 10–2   Schoenberg: Suite, Op. 25 (1923), row forms   *(Used by permission of Belmont Music Publishers.)*

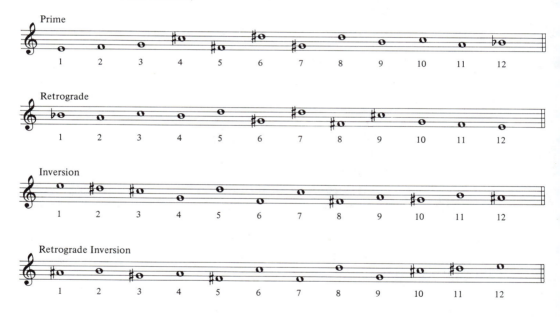

In addition, each of the four basic forms has twelve transpositions—that is, each one may be transposed to begin with any of the twelve pitch classes—so a single row has 4 × 12 or 48 versions that are available to the composer. In simple terms, a twelve-tone work consists of the presentation of various row forms at various transpositions, though the details of how this is done vary from composer to composer and from piece to piece.

When analyzing a serial composition we label the row forms using abbreviations:

P = Prime

R = Retrograde

I = Inversion

RI = Retrograde Inversion

After the abbreviation comes a number, from 0 to 11, which specifies the transposition of the row form in half-steps. The very first row form in a composition is numbered P-0, and the other row forms and transpositions are numbered accordingly.[2] Because all of the row forms shown in Example 10–2 are at their original pitch levels, they would be labeled P-0, R-0, I-0, and RI-0. Notice that I-0 begins on the same note as P-0 does, but that R-0 and RI-0 do not, because they are the retrogrades of P-0 and I-0. A prime version of the row in Example 10–2 beginning on F would be labeled P-1, because it is one half-step above P-0. P-2 would begin on F♯, and P-11 would begin on D♯. Transpositions are always figured *above* the original, regardless of the octave in which they actually occur. Similarly, R-1 would begin on B (one half-step higher than the A♯ that begins R-0), while R-2 would begin with C and R-11 would begin with A.

THE TWELVE-TONE MATRIX

It is sometimes helpful when composing or analyzing serial music to be able to see all 48 versions of the row. The *matrix* or "magic square" allows you to see all 48 versions after writing out only 12 of them. Example 10–3 is the matrix for the row for Schoenberg's Suite. The prime forms can be read from left to right along the rows of the matrix, while the retrogrades are read from right to left. The inversions are read along the columns from top to bottom, and the retrograde inversions from bottom to top. The transposition number is next to the first note of each row form. Looking down the left-hand side of the matrix, you can see that P-0 begins on E, P-11 on D♯, P-9 on C♯, and so on. To fill in the matrix, follow these steps:

1. Fill in P-0 along the top row.
2. Fill in the transposition numbers above P-0 by numbering the pitches chromatically, beginning with a 0 for the first note and moving up by half-step. Write these same numbers beneath the matrix.

EXAMPLE 10–3   Matrix for Schoenberg's Suite, Op. 25

	0	1	3	9	2	11	4	10	7	8	5	6	
0	E	F	G	C♯	F♯	D♯	G♯	D	B	C	A	B♭	0
11	D♯	E	F♯	C	F	D	G	C♯	A♯	B	G♯	A	11
9	C♯	D	E	A♯	D♯	C	F	B	G♯	A	F♯	G	9
3	G	G♯	A♯	E	A	F♯	B	F	D	D♯	C	C♯	3
10	D	D♯	F	B	E	C♯	F♯	C	A	A♯	G	G♯	10
1	F	F♯	G♯	D	G	E	A	D♯	C	C♯	A♯	B	1
8	C	C♯	D♯	A	D	B	E	A♯	G	G♯	F	F♯	8
2	F♯	G	A	D♯	G♯	F	A♯	E	C♯	D	B	C	2
5	A	A♯	C	F♯	B	G♯	C♯	G	E	F	D	D♯	5
4	G♯	A	B	F	A♯	G	C	F♯	D♯	E	C♯	D	4
7	B	C	D	G♯	C♯	A♯	D♯	A	F♯	G	E	F	7
6	A♯	B	C♯	G	C	A	D	G♯	F	F♯	D♯	E	6
	0	1	3	9	2	11	4	10	7	8	5	6	

3. Fill in the transposition numbers along the left border by subtracting each of the numbers on the top border from 12, with the exception of the first number, which is always 0. Write these same numbers to the right of the matrix.

4. Find the horizontal row with a 1 in front of it, and transpose all of P-0 up one half-step into that row.

5. Find the horizontal row with a 2 in front of it, and transpose all of P-1 up one half-step into that row.

6. Continue this process until P-10 is transposed up one half-step into P-11, and the matrix is complete.

A FIRST EXAMPLE

Before going on to some more technical information, it would probably be of interest at this point to see how Schoenberg used the row we have been discussing. The beginning of the work is given in Example 10–4. Since this is the first serial piece that Schoenberg composed, you might expect it to be fairly simple in terms of row usage, but this is really not the case. While reading the discussion that follows the example, be sure to find in the matrix (Example 10–3) every row that is mentioned.

EXAMPLE 10–4   Schoenberg: Suite, Op. 25 (1923), Prelude, mm. 1–5   *(Used by permission of Belmont Music Publishers.)*

The prelude is the first movement of the Suite, and the first row form to be used is designated P-0. Here the first row form occurs in the treble clef, beginning on E and ending on B♭; it is, of course, P-0 in the matrix. P-0 is accompanied at the beginning by P-6, and the careful listener will hear the imitation between the two voices at this point:

P–0: E F G   D♭
     P–6: B♭ C♭ D♭ G

P-6 continues toward the end of m. 2 in the tenor voice: C–A–D–G♯, in imitation of G♭–E♭–A♭–D in the soprano, while beneath the tenor the bass sounds the last four notes: F–F♯–E♭–E. Notice that notes 9–12 here do not follow notes 5–8, but occur simultaneously with them.

The B♭ that ends P-0 becomes the bass for a time, and it also serves as the first note of I-6, the next row form. Trace the first four notes of this row form, B♭–A–G–D♭, as they move from the bottom staff to the top staff and finally, in m. 5, to the melody. Some listeners would be able to recognize that the sixteenth-note line, B♭–A–G, is the inversion of the opening motive, E–F–G. The highest voice from the end of m. 3 through m. 4 is made up from notes 5–8, A♭–C♭–G♭–C, while the alto sounds notes 9–12, E♭–D–F–E.

To recapitulate: We have seen that P-0 and P-6 were used in counterpoint at the beginning, whereas in the next measures a single row form, I-6, accompanied itself. We have also seen that the row does not always have to proceed strictly from the first note to the last, but instead that segments of the row may appear simultaneously.

ANALYZING A ROW

Since the tone row serves as the source of the pitch material of a composition, we really should analyze the row itself before beginning the analysis of the piece. The first step should be to play (or sing) it several times. Listen for sequences or familiar patterns. In general, composers avoid using in a row any combination of pitches that would recall tonal music, such as triads, scale segments, and traditional bass or melodic formulas. If the composer chooses to include such patterns, as occasionally happens, you should make note of this and its effect on the music. For example, play through the series Berg used for his *Lyric Suite* (1926):

F	E	C	A	G	D	G♯	C♯	D♯	F♯	A♯	B
1	2	3	4	5	6	7	8	9	10	11	12

This row contains triads on A minor and D♯ minor, and the row ends with a figure that suggests a B tonality, F♯–A♯–B. (The end of the retrograde, C–E–F, would suggest an F tonality.) The first hexachord (the first six notes) is diatonic to C major or F major, and the second hexachord is diatonic to F♯ major or B major. Schoenberg's row (Example 10–2) contains fewer tonal references, but it ends with the retrograde of the famous B–A–C–H motive (in German B♭ is written as B, and B♮ as H), and we might expect Schoenberg to do something with this in the piece.

The next step in the analysis might be to label the ICs (interval classes; review Chapter 9) found between adjacent notes of the row. For instance, for Schoenberg's Op. 25 we find:

IC:	1	2	6	5	3	5	6	3	1	3	1
Note:	E	F	G	C♯	F♯	D♯	G♯	D	B	C	A	B♭

Totals:	IC1	IC2	IC3	IC4	IC5	IC6
	3	1	3	0	2	2

We see from the totals (do not confuse this interval tabulation with the interval vector, discussed in Chapter 9) that there are no appearances of IC4 (major 3rd or minor 6th) and that IC1 (minor 2nd, major 7th) and IC3 (minor 3rd, major 6th) predominate. Some rows are composed so as to emphasize particular intervals, as is the case here, while others are not. The *all-interval row*, when spelled in an ascending fashion, contains exactly one appearance of each interval, from the minor 2nd through the major 7th. For example, the row from Berg's *Lyric Suite*:

M7	m6	M6	m7	P5	TT	P4	M2	m3	M3	m2
F	E	C	A	G	D	G♯	C♯	D♯	F♯	A♯	B

If the row that you are analyzing has two of each IC except for IC6, which appears once, check to see if it is an all-interval row.

Some rows use the first three, four, or six notes as a pattern from which the rest of the row is derived: such a row is called a *derived set*. In such a set the pattern is transposed, inverted, retrograded, or inverted and retrograded to "generate" the remainder of the set. For example, the first hexachord of Berg's row from the *Lyric Suite* in retrograde and transposed by a tritone would produce the second hexachord, so the row is a derived set. The row of Webern's Concerto, Op. 24 (1934), is generated by applying the RI, R, and I operations to the first trichord:

B	B♭	D		E♭	G	F♯		G♯	E	F		C	C♯	A
1	2	3		4	5	6		7	8	9		10	11	12

pattern   RI of 1–3   R of 1–3   I of 1–3

Even if the row is not a derived set, it may well contain pitch patterns that are transposed, inverted, or retrograded. Patterns of ICs that are repeated or reversed may help us to find these pitch patterns. In Schoenberg's Suite the repeated 3–1 at the end of the row is caused by two overlapping statements of a trichordal pattern:

```
IC:    1    2    6    5    3    5    6    3    1    3    1
Note: E    F    G    C♯   F♯   D♯   G♯   D    B    C    A   B♭
                                         [D    B    C]
                                              [C    A   B♭]
```

The pattern 6–5 within the row is reversed later as 5–6, and it is also part of a larger pattern that reverses itself: 6–5–3–5–6. Such patterns may indicate that a segment of the row is its own retrograde or retrograde inversion. Here the patterns 6–5–3–5–6, 3–1–3 and 1–3–1 are all reversible. With these particular row segments, the retrograde inversion of the segment reproduces the segment (but transposed), as the following diagram shows:

```
ICs       6    5    3    5    6        3    1    3        1    3    1
Prime G   C♯   F♯   D♯   G♯   D | D    B    C    A | B    C    A   B♭
RI    D   G♯   C♯   A♯   D♯   A | A    F♯   G    E | B♭   B    G♯   A
```

These patterns that we have found may have implications in the piece motivically, and in this case they certainly have implications in the area of *invariance*. An invariant pitch class is one that is shared by any two collections of pitches (two chords, for example). Similarly, an *invariant subset* is one that appears intact in two forms of the row. The order of the notes was not important when dealing with unordered sets, but it is important when talking about rows. Looking back at the matrix, Example 10–3, you can see that the notes involved in the 6–5–3–5–6 pattern, G–C♯–F♯–D♯–G♯–D, appear in the same order in both P-0 and RI-1 as do the notes from the 1–3–1 pattern, B–C–A–B♭. In fact, RI-1 is a reorganized form of P-0, beginning with notes 9–12 from P-0, then notes 3–8, and ending with notes 1–2. Each prime row transposition in the matrix has a similar RI "cousin," and there are also twelve similar I/R pairs. The matrix of a derived set may exhibit even more invariance. Berg's *Lyric Suite* set, for instance, has only 24 different row forms instead of the usual 48, because each R form is the same as some P form, and each RI form is the same as some I form.

The next step in a thorough analysis is to analyze the subsets in terms of the pitch-class set types we learned in Chapter 9. This is not the same thing as the row segment analysis we were doing above, because there we were looking for exact transpositions (or inversions, etc.) of row segments. Here we are looking for set types, and we know that the notes of a pitch-class set may appear in any order and may be inverted to find the best normal order and the prime form. For example, there are ten trichords in any row, the first one made up of notes 1–3, the second of notes 2–4, and so on, with the last one made up of notes 10–12. There are also nine tetrachords, eight pentachords, and seven hexachords. The set types contained in Schoenberg's row are the following:

First Note	Trichords	Tetrachords	Pentachords	Hexachords
E	[0,1,3]	[0,2,3,6]	[0,1,2,3,6]	[0,1,2,3,4,6]
F	[0,2,6]	[0,1,2,6]	[0,1,2,4,6]	[0,1,2,3,5,7]
G	[0,1,6]	[0,1,4,6]	[0,1,2,5,7]	[0,1,2,5,6,7]
C♯	[0,2,5]	[0,2,5,7]	[0,1,2,5,7]	[0,1,2,4,7,9]
F♯	[0,2,5]	[0,1,4,6]	[0,1,4,6,9]	[0,1,3,4,7,9]
D♯	[0,1,6]	[0,1,4,7]	[0,1,3,4,7]	[0,1,3,4,6,7]
G♯	[0,3,6]	[0,2,3,6]	[0,1,3,4,6]	[0,1,2,3,4,6]
D	[0,1,3]	[0,2,3,5]	[0,1,2,3,5]	
B	[0,1,3]	[0,1,2,3]		
C	[0,1,3]			
A				
B♭				

In practice, it is usually enough to analyze only the trichords and tetrachords; the first and last hexachords will always be either of the same type or Z-related,[3] and most of the pentachords and hexachords overlap too much to be of interest. The trichord analysis shows us that [0,1,3] and [0,1,6] are unifying elements in the set; the composer might possibly make use of them as melodic motives or as chords to help unify the piece. The set [0,2,5], although it occurs twice, is less useful because its two appearances overlap. The tetrachords [0,2,3,6] and [0,1,4,6] also might fulfill a unifying function, although the two appearances of [0,1,4,6] overlap by two notes.

COMPOSITIONAL USES OF THE ROW

There are a number of ways in which rows are actually used in compositions. Generally, a twelve-tone work consists of the presentation of various
row forms at a number of transpositions, the forms being used sometimes in
succession and sometimes simultaneously. The notes may appear in any
octave, and the order of the notes of each row form is usually preserved, but
there are exceptions. Notes can be sounded simultaneously, as in a chord,
and there is no "rule" as to how the notes in this case must be arranged.
Repeated notes are not considered to alter the order of the row, and neither
are tremolo figures—using two of the notes repeatedly in alternation. Less
common are overlapped segments of a row (as in Example 10–4) and arbitrary reordering of the row for compositional purposes.

Since most music involves more than a single line, the composer must
either present two or more row forms simultaneously or distribute a single
row form among the various voices. Both of these approaches are widely
used, which complicates the task of determining P-0 at the beginning of an
analysis. Turn back to Example 10–4 for a minute, and imagine that you
had no prior knowledge of P-0. You might notice that the melody in the
right hand comes to a stop after eight notes (on the D) and that the left hand
in the same passage contains four notes, making twelve in all, so you would
check out the possibility that P-0 has been distributed between the two
lines. This could have been done in various ways, such as:

```
1   2   3       6   8   9       11   12
        4   5       7       10
```

or

```
1   2   3       4   5   6       7   8
        9   10      11      12
```

The first of these diagrams is the more commonly used method of distrib-
uting a row, but we could not rule out the second possibility. Even if we
want to go ahead on the assumption that the first diagram is basically
correct, we still would not be sure of the entire order, because some of the
notes are played simultaneously (3–4 and 7–8), and notes in a simultaneity
do not have to be arranged in any particular vertical order with respect to
the row. In any case, we would have to analyze more of the piece to find out
the answers to these questions.

As it turns out, we can see that Schoenberg has not distributed P-0 between the two hands, because the eight notes in the treble and the four in the bass include only ten of the pitch classes: C and A are missing, and Db and G occur twice. Instead, P-0 continues through the Bb in m. 3, while P-6 is used in the bottom staff. In mm. 3–6 Schoenberg uses the other basic approach, which is to distribute a single row form among the voices. In this and in some of his other works. Schoenberg breaks his row into three tetrachords which he then uses somewhat independently. That is, he might begin with the third tetrachord in some voice and introduce the first and second tetrachords later. Sometimes the order of pitches within each tetrachord is maintained, and at other times it is not. A more frequently used method is the one shown in the first diagram above, where the notes of the row are presented in order.

Turn back to Example 4–7 (p. 87) for an especially interesting example of row technique. (Remember that in this example the horn is written at concert pitch.) The excerpt, from Schoenberg's Wind Quintet, Op. 26, consists of three statements of P-0 (plus a final Eb) of the following row:

Eb	G	A	B	Db	C	Bb	D	E	F#	G#	F
1	2	3	4	5	6	7	8	9	10	11	12

Schoenberg distributes the notes so that the horn melody (the H symbol designates the primary line) uses each member of the row only once (disregarding immediate repetitions):

```
Horn:      1          6 7              12    2     5     8      11
Bassoon:     2 3 4 5       8 9 10 11      1    3 4   6 7   9 10    12

(Horn, cont.)          3 4           9 10
(Bassoon, cont.) 1 2      5 6 7 8         11 12 1
```

The resulting succession of twelve pitch classes in the horn forms a new twelve-tone row, drawn from but independent of the original row.

SET SUCCESSION

Although a composer has 48 row forms available, few twelve-tone compositions make use of all of them—in fact, some works use P-0 and nothing else. One of these is another of Schoenberg's early serial works, the fourth movement from his *Serenade*, Op. 24 (1923), for voice and seven instruments. The text features eleven-syllable lines, which Schoenberg sets to permutations of his row:

Line 1: notes 1–11
Line 2: notes 12–10
Line 3: notes 11–9
etc.

Not many twelve-tone works are so restricted, however. Most employ all four basic forms and several transpositions. One of the more difficult tasks of the analyst is attempting to determine why a particular row form and transposition have been chosen. It is not enough to put the label "R-3" on the score without considering why a retrograde form was chosen and why R-3 instead of some other transposition, even though we may not be able to find an explanation in every case.

Invariance is frequently a factor in the choice of transpositions. In the Schoenberg excerpt, Example 10–4, B♭ is the invariant pitch class in m. 3 between P-0, where it is the last note, and I-6, where it is the first. It is not uncommon for one or more pitch classes to serve as common tones between two row forms in this manner. Schoenberg's reasons for choosing P-6 as the first row in the left hand are not hard to guess. Presumably he chose imitation at the tritone as an effect analogous to the imitation at the dominant so much a part of Baroque style, and it offered the advantage of keeping intact the pitch classes that form the two tritones in the top voice:

G/D♭ answered by D♭/G
A♭/D answered by D/G♯

Also, Schoenberg's choice of I-6 and P-6 conforms to his overall plan for the work, which is to use only P-0, P-6, I-0, I-6, and their retrogrades. Each of these row forms begins on E and ends on B♭ (or the reverse), and each contains the tritone G/D♭ (or D♭/G).

Luigi Dallapiccola's overall plan for "Fregi," the sixth movement of his *Musical Notebook for Annalibera* (*Quaderno Musicale di Annalibera*) (1952), goes as follows:

1. Using P-0, compose a melody for mm. 1–6 to be played by the right hand.
2. In mm. 7–12, invert that melody and give it to the left hand.
3. In order to carry the idea of inversion a step further, accompany mm. 1–6 with an I form, and mm. 7–12 with a P form.

The prime form of the row is:

A#	B	D#	F#	G#	D	D♭	F	G	C	A	E
1	2	3	4	5	6	7	8	9	10	11	12

Notice that this row has tonal implications (for example, the triads on B and A) that we might expect Dallapiccola to make use of. The melody in mm. 1–6 actually consists of two row forms, P-0 and R-7. Here the link between the rows is the E, which is the *second* note of R-7:

B	E	G	D	C	G#	A	E♭	D♭	B♭	G♭	F
1	2	3	4	5	6	7	8	9	10	11	12

This allows a diatonic "progression" from the A minor triad at the end of P-0 to the E minor triad at the beginning of R-7. It also allows for a quintal chord (A–E–B) that is beautiful in context. All of this happens in the fourth measure of Example 10–5. The accompaniment in mm. 3–6 is provided by I-10:

A♭	G	E♭	C	B♭	E	F	D♭	B	F#	A	D
1	2	3	4	5	6	7	8	9	10	11	12

EXAMPLE 10–5 Dallapiccola: *Musical Notebook for Annalibera (1952)*, "Fregi," mm. 1–8

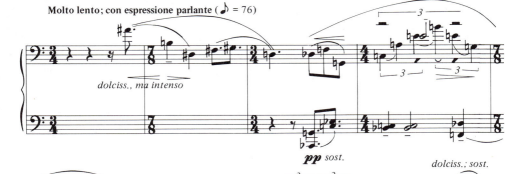

Just as P-0 is ending and R-7 is beginning in m. 4, I-10 in the accompaniment needs an E, the shared pitch class between P-0 and R-7. Dallapiccola puts the E for I-10 in the top staff, stem up, and all three rows come together at this point. The use of I-10 also allows the first half of the piece to end in m. 6 on an inversionally symmetrical sonority, A–D–Gb–F, or [0,3,4,7], which means that when the first half of the piece is inverted, the final sonority will be a (transposed) duplication of this one.

The only remaining row choice to be discussed is the transposition level for the inversion of the melody, which begins with the Cb in the bottom staff at the end of m. 6. The obvious answer is that I-1 is the only inversion that begins with the two notes that began P-0 at the opening of the piece (A♯–B answered by Cb–Bb). Another consideration might have been the nice major 7th sonority in m. 7 formed by the beginning of I-1 and the end of R-7.

COMBINATORIALITY

Sometimes the choice of row forms or transpositions is governed by a desire to form aggregates between portions of row forms. For example, in the following diagram, the row that Schoenberg used for his *Piano Piece*, Op. 33a (1929), is followed by its RI-5 form. Notice that the last hexachord of P-0, when combined with RI-5, forms, an aggregate. In effect, we have created a new row, called a *secondary set*, by combining two hexachords from two different row forms.

```
┌──────────P–0──────────┐      ┌──────────RI–5──────────┐
Bb F  C  B  A  F♯ C♯ D♯ G  Ab D  E    A  B  F  Gb Bb C  G  E  D  C♯ G♯ D♯
1  2  3  4  5  6  7  8  9  10 11 12   1  2  3  4  5  6  7  8  9  10 11 12
          └──────────────aggregate──────────────┘
```

This combining of row forms to form aggregates is called *combinatoriality*, and it is an important aspect of some serial compositions. Most often the combining is done vertically:

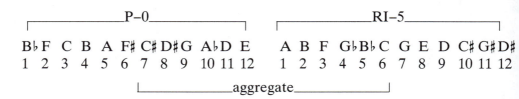

P–0:	Bb	F	C	B	A	F♯	C♯	D♯	G	Ab	D	E
I–5:	D♯	G♯	C♯	D	E	G	C	Bb	Gb	F	B	A
	1	2	3	4	5	6	7	8	9	10	11	12

```
└──────aggregate──────┘  └──────aggregate──────┘
```

This diagram is seen in notation in Example 10–6. The first aggregate occupies m. 14 through the first two notes of m. 16, and the second aggregate occupies the rest of the excerpt. Notice that Schoenberg freely retrogrades or repeats row segments, as in C–B–A–B–C in mm. 14–15. Schoenberg's row is so constructed that any pair of row forms that can be combined hexachordally to form twelve-tone aggregates can also be combined tetrachordally to form three sets of eight pitch classes each:

RI–5:   A   B   F   F♯   A♯   C   G   E   D   C♯   G♯   D♯
R–0:   E   D   A♭   G   D♯   C♯   F♯   A   B   C   F   B♭
        1   2   3   4   5   6   7   8   9   10   11   12

└─octachord─┘   └─octachord─┘   └─octachord─┘

EXAMPLE 10–6   Schoenberg: *Piano Piece, Op. 33a* (1929), mm. 14–18   *(Used by permission of Belmont Music Publishers.)*

Though this does not produce twelve-tone aggregates in the way that the combined hexachords do, the technique is similar. In Example 10–7 each pair of tetrachords occupies approximately one measure.

Other rows are constructed to produce tetrachord aggregates by combining three rows vertically, or trichord aggregates by combining four rows vertically; however, hexachordal combinatoriality is the most commonly used.

Combinatoriality guarantees a more controlled recycling of the twelve pitch classes, and to some it seems a necessary extension of the twelve-tone

EXAMPLE 10–7 Schoenberg: *Piano Piece,* Op. 33a (1929), mm. 3–5   *(Used by permission of Belmont Music Publishers.)*

aesthetic. Schoenberg invented this technique, although he obviously was not using it in his Suite (see the juxtaposed G/D♭ and D♭/G in Example 10–4). Nor was Dallapiccola interested in combinatoriality in his *Notebook* (notice the duplicated G's in m. 3 of Example 10–5). In fact, most rows cannot by their nature be used combinatorially and must instead be specially constructed for that use. But combinatoriality has been of considerable interest to some composers, and a large number of pieces are combinatorial throughout.

THE ANALYSIS OF SERIAL MUSIC

In analyzing the use of rows in a serial piece, it is often enough to label the row forms (P-0, etc.) without writing the order numbers on the music. If the texture is complex or if some unusual row technique is being employed, it may be necessary to write the order numbers near the noteheads and even to join them with lines. Always work from a matrix. If you get lost, try to find several notes that you suspect occur in the same order in some row form, and scan the matrix for those notes, remembering to read it in all four directions.

The labeling of row forms and the consideration of the details of their use is only a part of the analysis of a serial composition, somewhat analogous to identifying the various tonalities of a tonal work. Questions regarding form, thematic relationships, texture, rhythm, and other matters are just as relevant here as in the analysis of more traditional music. The music of classical serialism is not especially "mathematical," and it is not composed mechanically and without regard to the resulting sound or the effect on the listener. Probably the best way to appreciate the processes and choices involved in serial composition is to try to compose a good serial piece. The exercises at the end of this chapter will provide some practice at attempting this.

SUMMARY

The pitch materials of a serial work are derived from the twelve-note row, so an analysis should begin with the row itself. Two special types of row are derived sets and all-interval sets. A composition may make use of the prime row, its retrograde, its inversion, and its retrograde inversion, each of which can appear at any of twelve transpositions. This pitch material may be conveniently displayed in the form of a matrix.

Row forms may be used compositionally in a number of ways. For example, a single row may be distributed among the voices, or more than one row may be used at the same time. The choice of row forms is often related to invariance or combinatoriality, two important but complementary concepts.

Analysis of serial music includes identification of the row forms and consideration of the reasons for choosing a particular row form and transposition, but a thorough analysis cannot be confined only to serial matters.

NOTES

1. Jan Maegaard, "A Study in the Chronology of Op. 23–26 by Arnold Schoenberg." See the chart on p. 108.
2. Other systems in use number the first row P-0 only if it begins on C, use 0–11 for order numbers instead of 1–12, and use O or S instead of P.
3. The so-called "hexachord theorem." See John Rahn, *Basic Atonal Theory*, p. 105.

EXERCISES

Part A: Fundamentals

1. Suppose P-0 begins on G and ends on B♭:

Form	Begins on	Ends on			
a. P–6	_____	_____	e. I–1	_____	_____
b. P–11	_____	_____	f. I–9	_____	_____
c. R–0	_____	_____	g. RI–2	_____	_____
d. R–5	_____	_____	h. RI–7	_____	_____

2. Analyze the row from Dallapiccola's *Musical Notebook for Annalibera* (p. 219).

3. Analyze the row from Schoenberg's Wind Quintet, Op. 26 (p. 217), and construct a matrix.

4. The following set is P-0 from the first of Milton Babbitt's *Three Compositions for Piano* (1947). Analyze it and construct a matrix.

   B♭   E♭   F   D   C   D♭   G   B   F♯   A   G♯   E

5. Do the same for the following set, from Webern's Symphony, Op. 21.

   A   F♯   G   G♯   E   F   B   B♭   D   D♭   C   E♭

Part B: Analysis

1. Turn back to Example 6–3 (p. 125). Analyze the row forms in that excerpt using the matrix you constructed for Exercise A4. (Note: Each accidental affects only the note it precedes.) Is the row usage in mm. 10–11 combinatorial? Explain. Is there a secondary set formed by the last hexachord of m. 9 and the first hexachord in the left hand of m. 10? What about in the right hand from the end of m. 11 through the beginning of m. 12? If so, write them out.

2. Turn back to Example 2–B–3 (p. 43). Analyze the row forms using the matrix you constructed for Exercise A5. (Hint: Four row forms are used simultaneously.) Is this excerpt combinatorial? How can you tell?

3. Schoenberg: Wind Quintet, Op. 26 (1924), III, mm. 8–15.

   This excerpt is a continuation of Example 4–7 (p. 87). We discussed the use of the row in Example 4–7 in the section titled "Compositional Uses of the Row," and you constructed a matrix for this row in Exercise A3. This excerpt features a duet between the clarinet and horn, with a secondary duet in the flute and oboe.

   a. Analyze the row forms in the clarinet and horn. The E♭ in the bassoon is part of the first row, but the F♯ in the horn is not and may be ignored.

   b. Compare the row usage here with that in Example 4–7. Be sure to review the discussion concerning that example.

(Schoenberg: Wind Quintet, Op. 26 (1924), III, mm. 8–15).

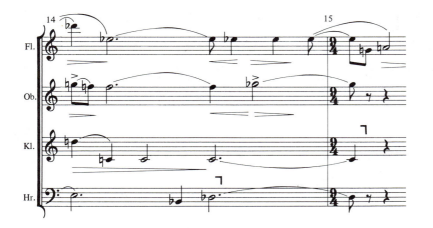

c. Do you find any other similarities between Example 4–7 and this duet between the clarinet and horn?

d. Analyze the row forms in the flute and oboe.

e. In what ways is this duet similar to the one in the clarinet and horn? In what ways is it different?

4. In discussing Example 10–4 we identified P-0, P-6, and I-6. What row form ends the excerpt? Remember (a) that this is one of Schoenberg's tetrachord pieces, in which the three tetrachords of a row form may be introduced in any order, and (b) the possibility of common tones linking the row forms. Use the matrix in Example 10–3 for help.

5. Webern: "Das dunkle Herz" (1934), Op. 23, No. 1, mm. 1–11.

a. In this song P-0 begins with the D that is the first note in the piano. Because of the chords that occur in that piano in the first two measures, you will need to do a certain amount of detective work to determine the correct order for P-0. Once you have discovered P-0, construct a matrix.

b. Label all the row forms used in the excerpt. Remember that notes may occasionally serve functions in two row forms, either in the same part (voice or piano) or between parts.

c. This piece is more concerned with the unifying effect of invariants than it is with combinatorial aggregates. For example, the vocalist enters on an F that has just been heard in the piano and then sings three of the notes contained in the chord at the end of m. 2 (G–E–E♭). Find similar pitch-class connections that help bring the voice and piano parts together. (Obviously, this technique has much to do with explaining why the various row forms were chosen.)

    d. Use the pitch-class set terminology you learned in Chapter 9 to study Webern's use of motives. For example, the four-note chord is an important accompanimental motive. In terms of pitch-class set types, how do these chords compare? Consider the other motives in a similar fashion. Do not neglect the voice. Are there any motivic connections between the two?

6. Play through and sing the row from Dallapiccola's *Musical Notebook for Annalibera* (p. 229) until you are able to sing it without accompaniment. then listen carefully to several or all of the movements from that work. In which ones is the unifying effect of the row apparent? How is this accomplished? Is there any particular part of the row that is more memorable, or perhaps more emphasized by the composer, than others?

Part C: Composition

1. Compose a twelve-tone row that avoids tonal references and is not predictable in its use of patterns. Be sure to do this at a piano or other instrument, and play (or sing) the row as you compose it.

2. Analyze your row, and construct a matrix. Then compose an unaccompanied melody for some instrument in your class, using three different row forms from your matrix. Label the row forms and transpositions. Try to emphasize in some way any recurrent subsets or other significant features that the row contains, and explain what you are attempting. Include tempo, dynamics, and phrasing.

3. Compose an instrumental duet using a single form of your row distributed between the two instruments in a manner similar to that used by Schoenberg in Example 4–7 (p. 87), discussed under "Compositional Uses of the Row." Try to give the duet a musical shape, with some amount of motivic unity and a climax in the second half of the duet. Analyze your work.

4. Use your row for a simple piano piece in a homophonic (melody-and-accompaniment) texture. Use different row forms in the melody and accompaniment. Label all row forms.

5. Compose a twelve-tone row in which the first hexachord contains the notes: C♯, D, E♭, F, A, and B♭. Put the notes in any order you choose, except that D should be the first note. The second hexachord should contain the remaining notes, in any order. Then compose a duet beginning with P-0 in one part and I-5 in the other. These two forms are

combinatorial, so be sure to line up the hexachords to form aggregates. Then continue the duet with two different combinatorial pairs (such as P-2 and I-7). Label the row forms.

Part D: Further Reading

BRINDLE, REGINALD SMITH.   *Musical Composition*. See Chapter 12, "Serialism."

————.   *Serial Composition*. See Chapters 1–7.

CHRIST, WILLIAM, AND OTHERS.   *Materials and Structure of Music*. See pp. 376–81 and 404–410.

DALLIN, LEON.   *Techniques of Twentieth Century Composition*. See Chapter 14, "The Twelve-Tone Method."

FENNELLY, BRIAN.   "Twelve-Tone Techniques," in John Vinton, ed., *Dictionary of Contemporary Music*.

GRIFFITHS, PAUL.   "Serialism," in Stanley Sadie, ed., *The New Grove Dictionary of Music and Musicians*.

KOSTKA, STEFAN AND DOROTHY PAYNE.   *Tonal Harmony*. See pp. 483–91.

KRENEK, ERNST.   *Studies in Counterpoint*.

PERLE, GEORGE, AND PAUL LANSKY.   "Twelve-Note Composition," in Stanley Sadie, ed., *The New Grove Dictionary of Music and Musicians*.

SIMMS, BRYAN R.   *Music of the Twentieth Century*. See Chapter 4, "Serialism," pp. 68–74 and 78–83.

ULEHLA, LUDMILA.   *Contemporary Harmony*. See Chapter 20, "Its Strict Application."

WITTLICH, GARY.   "Sets and Ordering Procedures in Twentieth-Century Music," in Wittlich, ed., *Aspects of Twentieth-Century Music*. See pp. 388–430.

WUORINEN, CHARLES.   *Simple Composition*. See Chapter 7, "The 12-Tone Pitch System: Elements and Operations."

11 | Timbre and Texture: Acoustic

INTRODUCTION

It may be that the way twentieth-century music *sounds* sets it apart from earlier styles as much as anything. This seems obvious, since music is about sound, after all, but what "sound" means in this context is a little narrower. Here we are referring especially to timbre and texture, two aspects of music that have received much attention from twentieth-century composers. *Timbre* means tone color, and it can refer to the tone color of an individual instrument or of an ensemble. As we will see, the timbral ranges of both have expanded greatly in the twentieth century. *Texture* is a little harder to define, although most of us have a pretty good idea of its meaning. We could say that texture refers to the relationships between the parts (or voices) at any moment in a composition; it especially concerns the relationships between rhythms and contours, but it is also concerned with aspects such as spacing and dynamics. Not infrequently the line between timbre and texture is unclear, especially when a large ensemble is involved.

Some of the exploration of new timbres and textures, especially the former, was partly the result of outside influences—jazz and folk music, oriental and Latin American music. In fact, few really new instruments have been invented and successfully introduced in this century, most of the exceptions being percussion instruments (the vibraphone, for instance). A very important exception is electronic music, an area significant enough to require its own chapter (see Chapter 12).

NEW TIMBRAL EFFECTS FROM TRADITIONAL INSTRUMENTS

Composers in the twentieth century have required performers to learn many new techniques of producing sound with traditional instruments, so many that we can only hope to provide a good sampling in this discussion.[1]

Some techniques have been required of all performers, regardless of instrument, including tapping on the instrument or on some other surface, whistling, and a wide variety of vocal sounds. Certain instruments, such as the piano and the harp, have seen an exceptional amount of development as percussion instruments because of the sonorous nature of their bodies. In these cases the performer is not performing as a clarinetist, for example, but as a percussionist, whistler, or vocalist. In Example 6–10 (p. 132) thirteen wind players whistle approximately the same pattern (the exact pitches are unspecified), but beginning at different times and proceeding independently. Notice also in the same example the use of glass crystals, or tuned water glasses. Electronic amplification and distortion are other timbral devices that can be used with any performing medium.

WIND INSTRUMENTS

Some techniques for winds used in contemporary scores are not entirely new but represent an intensification or development of earlier usages. This would include, for example, the use of mutes and glissandi. The brasses use a wider variety of mutes than previously, many of them of jazz origin, and even the woodwinds have been muted in a number of ways. The "bend," which might be considered a special type of glissando, also derives from jazz. Both the bend and the glissando were seen in Example 8–6 (p. 175), where the horn imitates a jazz trombone solo. Other techniques sometimes associated with jazz include the fluttertongue (see mm. 9–12 of Example 4–4, p. 83) and the enharmonic trill, in which the performer rapidly alternates between two fingerings for the same pitch.

Removal of the mouthpiece permits performing on the mouthpiece alone, without the rest of the instrument, or performing only on the rest of the instrument without the mouthpiece. Wind players are also required to produce breath sounds through their instruments instead of pitches, and in some cases to sing and play simultaneously. Harmonics, though not practicable on brasses, have been used on woodwinds, especially the flute and the clarinet. Several of these techniques are illustrated in a lighthearted way in Example 11–1.

An important development, again available only on woodwinds, is the use of *multiphonics*, the production on a single instrument of two or more pitches (as many as six are possible) simultaneously. Multiphonics rarely sound like the instrument played in a conventional manner. In Example 11–2 three flutes using multiphonics combine to produce chords of up to six notes. Notice that multiphonics are not simply two harmonics played at once. None of the multiphonics in Example 11–2 are produced as harmonics, and most of them create dissonant intervals, not the consonances associated with the harmonic series. Multiphonics are often difficult to produce, and in a footnote in the score Heiss suggests that the performers "secure the upper note" of each pair and "let the lower one sound more quietly if necessary." Notice also the fingering instructions in the score. Performance instructions such as these are a feature of many works composed since World War II.

EXAMPLE 11–1 David Amram: Quintet for Winds (1968), III, mm. 106–11 *(© 1971 by C. F. Peters Corporation. Used by permission.)*

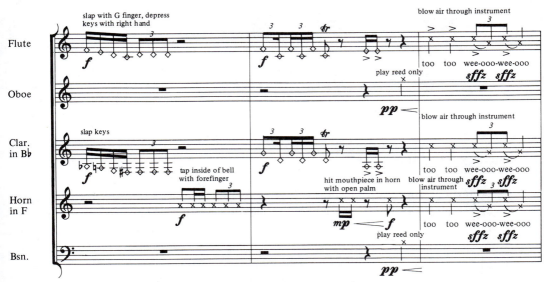

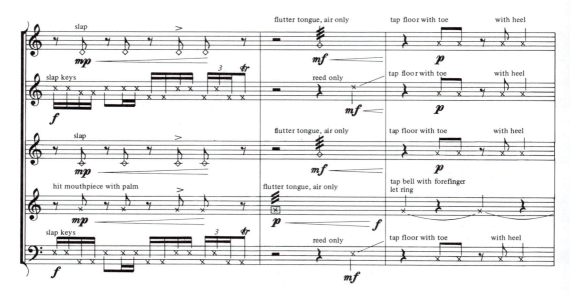

EXAMPLE 11–2 John Heiss: *Four Movements for Three Flutes* (1969), III, mm. 40–45 *(© Copyright 1977 by Boosey & Hawkes, Inc. Reprinted by permission.)*

STRINGED INSTRUMENTS

A large number of special effects are found in the contemporary string repertoire. As with the winds, these devices are in many cases not the invention of twentieth-century composers but are employed much more frequently in contemporary scores. These would include the use of mutes, open strings, harmonics (both natural and artificial), nonstandard tunings (scordatura), multiple stops, and glissandi. In Example 9–B–11 (p. 203) the lowest string of the contrabass, the E string, is tuned to E♭ instead. The same excerpt also illustrates glissandi and natural harmonics. Remember that the contrabass sounds an octave lower than written.

The traditional pizzicato is still used, but other methods have been developed, including left-hand pizzicato, snap pizzicato, nail pizzicato, buzz pizzicato (the string vibrates against the fingernail), plectrum pizzicato (use of a guitar pick), and strumming. A device that might be considered a kind of pizzicato is silent fingering, in which the player only fingers the notes with the left hand, producing a subtle, semipitched sound. An early use of snap pizzicato is seen in Example 11–3, where the device is indicated by the small circle with a line at the top. All of the instruments are being played pizzicato here, the viola and cello triple-stops being strummed. The arrows in the cello part indicate that the strumming is to be in descending fashion; the "O" specifies that the A3 is to be played on an open string.

Bowing techniques in common use in twentieth-century music include tremolo, bowing with the wood, various kinds of rebounding bow strokes, and nonpitched bowing, in which the idea is to obtain a scratchy sound rather than a pitch. In addition to bowing on the usual part of the string, the player may bow at the bridge, as in Example 9–20 (p. 199), or over the fingerboard, or the two may be combined in circular bowing. Other works call for the performer to bow between the bridge and the tailpiece, or under the strings, or on the body of the instrument. Penderecki's *Threnody: To the Victims of Hiroshima* (1961) is famous for its string techniques, among other things. In Example 11–4 each player performs a series of seven special effects as fast as possible. The wavy lines in some of the parts call for a slow quarter-tone vibrato, performed here on the highest possible note for each instrument.

EXAMPLE 11–3 Bartók String Quartet No. 4 (1928), IV, mm. 45–51 *(© Copyright 1929 by Universal Edition; Copyright Renewed. Copyright and Renewal assigned to Boosey & Hawkes, Inc. for USA only. Reprinted by permission.)*

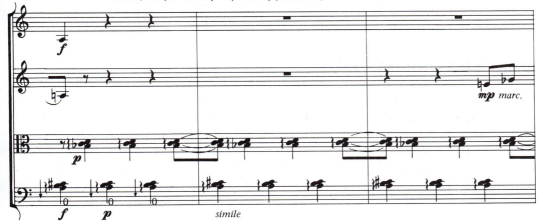

Seven special effects are specified in Example 11–4, and they appear in a different order in each of eight lines in the example. These effects, as seen in the top line of the ten cellos are (1) strike the upper sounding board, (2) play the highest note on the instrument pizzicato, (3) play a fast tremolo between the bridge and the tailpiece, (4) play an arpeggio on the four strings behind the bridge *legno battuto* (beating with the wood of the bow), (5) strike the upper sounding board twice, (6) play the highest note on the instrument arco and tremolo, and (7) play between the bridge and the tailpiece.

New techniques have also been developed for those stringed instruments traditionally played by plucking: the banjo, the guitar, the mandolin, and above all the harp. In fact, according to Gardner Read, "No modern instrument...has undergone such a metamorphosis in the twentieth century as the harp,"[2] with many of the new effects being devised by one composer, Carlos Salzedo. These include a wide variety of glissandi and of ways of activating the strings, as well as a number of percussive effects.

PERCUSSION INSTRUMENTS

One of the most important developments in twentieth-century music is the greatly expanded role of percussion. The percussion section of the orchestra, to be discussed in more detail below, has been expanded from the classical norm of one timpanist to a varying number of performers playing an ever-expanding array of instruments. Some of these instruments are newly invented, but most are instruments that already existed in Western

EXAMPLE 11–4 Penderecki: *Threnody: To the Victims of Hiroshima (1961),* mm. 6–7

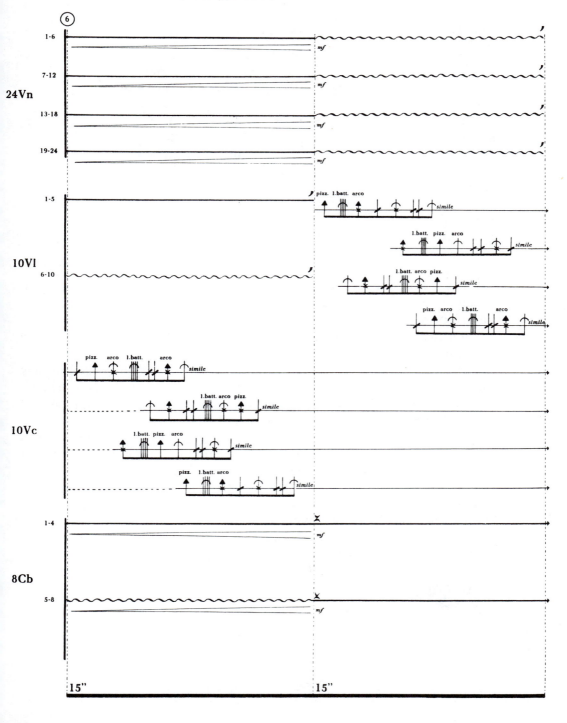

music (in bands or folk music, for example) or in the music of other cultures. An incomplete but representative list of instruments that are now commonly employed would include the following:[3]

Pitched Instruments	*Unpitched Instruments*	
Timpani	Snare drum	Triangle
Tablas	Tenor drum	Cymbals
Roto-tom	Bass drum	Tam-tam
Vibraphone	Tom-toms	Cowbells
Xylophone	Bongos	Anvil
Marimba	Timbales	Steel plates
Glockenspiel	Cocktail drum	Claves
Chimes	Tambourine	Wood block
Gongs	African drum	Temple blocks
Crotales	Chinese drum	Slapstick
Flexatone	Sleighbells	Castanets
Steel drums	Güiro	Maracas
Celesta	Ratchet	Sand blocks

As if this were not enough, composers freely introduce sounds produced by everyday materials. Examples include a resonant piece of furniture to be struck with a club, silk and sheets of paper to be torn apart, a metal tray filled with dishes to smash, a wooden bowl filled with marbles to rattle, and a tree stump to be hit with an ax.[4]

The more traditional percussion instruments are now played in new ways. Most of these basically consist of unconventional methods of striking the instrument (rim shots, dead-stick strokes), unconventional beaters (wire brushes, knuckles), and striking the instrument in unconventional places (the casing, tuning screws). Dead-stick strokes were illustrated in Example 9–B–11 (p. 203). Another interesting technique is the use of a string-bass bow to produce sounds from cymbals and gongs.

The percussion ensemble is one of the more important new ensemble types created in the twentieth century. Example 11–5 is an excerpt from a famous early work for percussion ensemble, in this case an ensemble of thirteen players, each player being responsible for at least three instruments:

Player	*Instruments*
1	Crash cymbal, bass drum, cowbell, high tam-tam
2	Gong, high tam-tam, low tam-tam, cowbell

EXAMPLE 11–5   Edgard Varèse: *Ionisation* (1931), mm. 75–81 *(© 1934 and 1967 by Colfranc Music Publishing Corporation—New York. Reproduced by courteous permission of E. C. Kerby Ltd., Toronto, General Agent.)*

3   Bongos, tenor drum, two bass drums

4   Snare drum, tenor drum

5   High siren, string drum

6   Low siren, slapstick, güiro

7   Three wood blocks (high, medium, and low registers)

8   Snare drum, high and low maracas

9   Thin snare drum, snare drum, suspended cymbals

10   Cymbals, sleigh bells, tubular chimes

11   Güiro, castanets, glockenspiel

12   Tambourine, two anvils, very deep tam-tam

13   Slapstick, triangle, sleigh bells, piano.

The passage quoted in Example 11–5 features the pitched instruments, including the piano, which we do not always think of as a percussion instrument. Notice the clusters on the bottom staff. The use of sirens (performers 5 and 6) was innovative at the time, but perhaps is more amusing than novel to today's audiences.

THE PIANO

The piano has been a particularly fertile field for those interested in experimenting with new sounds. Clusters, introduced in Chapter 3, were at first only a keyboard device; early examples included Henry Cowell's *The Tides of Manaunaun* (1912) and Charles Ives's Piano Sonata No. 2 (*Concord*) (1915), which calls for the use of a board to produce the cluster. Piano clusters are typically either diatonic (white keys), pentatonic (black keys), or chromatic. The clusters in Example 11–5 are chromatic clusters, played with the forearm.

A much more extreme alteration of the piano's timbre is accomplished by means of a *prepared piano*, in which objects are placed on and between the strings before the performance. Although predecessors date back at least to Ravel, Cage's *Bacchanale* (1938) is usually considered the first work for prepared piano. Cage's most famous composition for prepared piano is probably his *Sonatas and Interludes* (1948), a set of sixteen "sonatas," each in the traditional two-reprise form, with four interludes. A detailed set of instructions explains how bolts, screws, and pieces of hard rubber and plastic are to be used to prepare 45 of the 88 available notes. The resulting sounds are difficult to describe, some of them percussive, others tinny, still others sounding like the gongs of a gamelan orchestra (an early example of the oriental influence in Cage's music). The score itself gives little impression of the actual sound of these pieces, so there is no point in reproducing a musical example here, but the student is urged to listen to this intriguing work at the earliest opportunity.

Clusters and prepared notes are both played by the pianist at the keyboard, but a large array of other techniques call for the performer to reach inside the piano. These include plucking, striking, and scraping the strings using the fingers, fingernails, drumsticks, and so forth. Cowell was an innovator in this area as well, in pieces like *Aeolian Harp* (1923) and *The Banshee* (1925). Piano harmonics are also possible, as is hand muting. Yet another way to produce sounds from the piano is to have another instrument played into the piano while the damper pedal is depressed, causing the sympathetic vibration of some of the strings.

A unique approach to composing for the piano is taken by Conlon Nancarrow, who writes music for player piano (modified Ampico pianos, a sophisticated design) by punching holes in the paper rolls that control the instrument. Most of the effects that he obtains would be completely beyond the technique of any human pianist.

THE VOICE

The best-known vocal technique that originated in this century is *Sprechstimme*, a method that lies somewhere between speech and singing. Schoenberg first used it in *Pierrot Lunaire* (1912), an excerpt from which appears in Example 5–2 (p. 108). The small "x" on each stem of the vocal part is the symbol commonly employed to specify *Sprechstimme*. Notice that the voice part is labeled "Recitation."

Singers are also required to make any number of vocal "noises"— grunts, shouts, and so forth—and even to perform multiphonics. These are part of a more general tendency to treat the voice as another instrument, not only as a means of presenting a text. This was illustrated in Example 9–B–11 (p. 203), where the text is not some South Pacific dialect but instead is written in International Phonetic System notation.

INSTRUMENTATION AND ORCHESTRATION

Music of the nineteenth century tended to be composed for several standard ensembles: orchestra, string quartet, piano trio, and so forth. Though all of these combinations still exist, their dominance of the compositional scene has diminished. For one thing, it is commonplace today to add or omit instruments as demanded by the composer's conception of the way a piece should sound. The instruments added to an orchestra, for instance, might consist of anything from saxophones to wind machines to a toy piano. A number of new "standard" ensembles have attracted the attention of composers. One of these, the percussion ensemble, has already been discussed; others would include chamber orchestra, the concert band, and the woodwind ensemble. But in addition there are numerous works that call for an ad-hoc ensemble—one that is unique, or almost unique, to the particular composition. Examples would include Debussy's *Sonata for Flute, Viola, and Harp* (1916) and Crumb's *Madrigals*, Book I, for soprano, vibraphone, and contrabass (1965), among many, many others. There are even a number of works that leave the instrumentation unspecified, such as Stockhausen's *Sternklang* (Star-Sound) (1971), for five groups of performers, each one consisting of four instrumentalists and/or singers and a percussionist. Nevertheless, a fair proportion of twentieth-century works are for the symphony orchestra, and the next few paragraphs will outline some of the new approaches to orchestration.

An important development has been the expansion of the percussion section both in numbers of performers and, especially, in variety of instruments employed (see the section on percussion above). The more traditional orchestral instruments are expected to play in a much wider range than previously; the typical orchestral range has been expanded from about 5½ octaves to 7½ octaves and more.[5] The conventional spacing of a sonority, with wide intervals at the bottom and fairly even distribution in the middle and high registers, is now treated as only one of countless possibilities. The opening chord of Stravinsky's *Symphony of Psalms* is a famous example of unconventional spacing (see Example 11–6).

The use of multiple divisi in the strings (see for instance Example 11–4) illustrates the greater reliance on orchestral performers as potential

EXAMPLE 11–6   Stravinsky: *Symphony of Psalms* (1930), I, mm. 1–4 (piano reduction)
(Excerpted from the International Music Co. edition, New York, NY 10018.)

soloists, while the nineteenth-century preference for heterogenous doublings—that is, doublings involving two or more of the three main instrumental choirs—has been discarded in many works in favor of pure colors. Doubling frequently involves unconventional pairings or spacing, as in mm. 2–3 of Example 11–6, where the melody is played by bassoon and flute two octaves apart.

Octave doublings were, of course, a necessary part of conventional orchestration. One could hardly score a triad effectively for full orchestra without a number of octave doublings, and bass and melody lines were frequently doubled at the octave. But octave doublings were generally avoided in atonal and serial music, especially by Schoenberg and his followers, no matter what the medium, giving their orchestral music a distinctive sound. Perhaps a more far-reaching contribution by Schoenberg was his notion of *Klangfarbenmelodie*, or "tone-color melody," in which progressions of timbres would be equivalent in function to successions of pitches in a melody. Schoenberg used tone-color melody most systematically in the work from which Example 11–7 is excerpted. In this example a single chord is sustained throughout the four measures in two alternating timbres.

To some people, *Klangfarbenmelodie* has come to stand for simply "the principle of maximum variety of color,"[6] and as such is applied to

EXAMPLE 11–7 Schoenberg: *Five Pieces for Orchestra*, Op. 16 (1909, 1949), III, "Summer Morning by a Lake (Colors)," mm. 1–4 (reduced score) *(© 1952 by Henmar Press Inc. Used by permission of C. F. Peters Corporation.)*

music like that in Example 2–B–3 (p. 43). In the first six measures of that excerpt, the following solo timbres are heard:

Clarinet (low and middle registers)

Horn (low to moderately high registers)

Harp

Violin

Viola (pizzicato)

Cello (pizzicato and arco)

EXAMPLE 11–8   William Walton: Concerto for Viola and Orchestra (1929, 1962), I, mm. 1–7   (© 1930 Oxford University Press. Reproduced with permission.)

Perhaps a satisfactory definition of tone-color melody would be "the constant reorchestration of a line or sonority as it proceeds through time." In Example 11–8 the violas (not the solo viola), muted and (in mm. 4–7) bowing above the fingerboard, are doubled at various points by clarinet, bassoon, and bass clarinet, creating a subtle sort of timbral modulation that might well be characterized as *Klangfarbenmelodie*.

Spatial effects, such as separating the performers into two distinct groups, are not unique to the twentieth century, but they are an important feature of many twentieth-century works. This might involve multiple ensembles, as in Carter's *Symphony of Three Orchestras* (1977); offstage performers, such as the strings in Ives's *The Unanswered Question* (1906); or even performers located among the audience, as in Xenakis's *Polytope* (1967). Ideally, *Polytope* is performed as in Example 11–9, where the letters "A" through "D" represent the audience, the numerals "I" through "IV" represent the four small orchestras that perform the piece, and "X" represents the conductor. Space is equally important for small ensembles, and it is not uncommon for the score of a small ensemble to include a seating plan.

EXAMPLE 11–9   Xenakis: *Polytope* (1967), seating arrangement

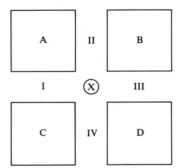

TRADITIONAL TEXTURES AND COMPOUND TEXTURES

Discussions of traditional musical textures generally sort them into three main categories:

1. Monophonic—a single line, perhaps doubled at the octave

2. Homophonic, meaning either

   a. Melody with accompaniment, or

   b. Chordal texture

3. Contrapuntal—relatively independent lines, either

    a. Imitative, or

    b. Free

    The traditional musical textures still exist, of course, and the vast majority of twentieth-century music probably can be analyzed texturally using those categories. Sometimes textures are complicated by harmonizing the individual lines, and we will refer to these as "compound textures." Debussy's music is especially rich in compound textures, although they certainly can be found elsewhere. One instance was seen in Example 3–B–1 (p. 72), where a three-part texture is thickened into eleven voices:

    Part One: Three voices on the immobile D–G–D in the highest register

    Part Two: Five voices in similar motion in the middle register

    Part Three: Three voices descending in parallel motion in the lowest register

    A more involved example is seen in Example 11–10, the final seventeen measures of one of Debussy's preludes. A three-part texture is found in mm. 48–53:

    (1), a B♭ ostinato/pedal point;

    (2), a glissando/ostinato in the middle register;

    (3), a melody in mm. 50–53 in the highest register.

EXAMPLE 11–10   Debussy: Preludes, Book I, "Sails" ("Voiles"), mm. 48–64

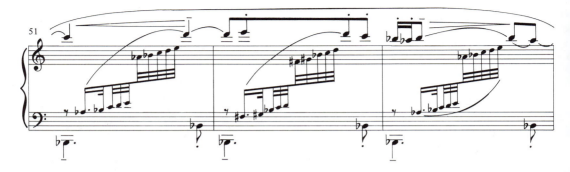

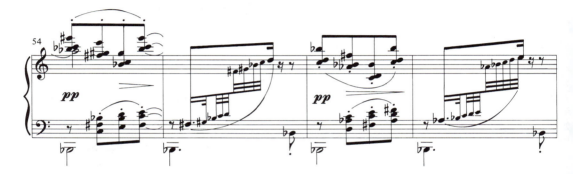

Très apaisé et très atténué jusqu'à la fin

The texture becomes compound in mm. 54–57:

(1) and (2), continuing;

(4), a figure, G♯–E–G♯–G♯, harmonized with secundal chords;

(5), a figure, C–E–F♯, harmonized with whole-tone chords.

In mm. 58–61,

(1) and (5), continuing;

(4), shortened to two chords;

(6), a melody harmonized in parallel major 3rds.

In mm. 62–64 only two elements remain: the glissando (2) and the remnants of the last melody (6).

POINTILLISM, STRATIFICATION, AND SOUND-MASS

Pointillism, stratification, and sound-mass are approaches to texture that have been developed in the twentieth century (although not without historical precedent). *Pointillism* gets its name from a technique used by some French painters in the nineteenth century that represented scenes by means of dots of color rather than lines. A pointillistic texture in music is one that features rests and wide leaps, a technique that isolates the sounds into "points." A good example can be seen in the piano accompaniment in Example 10–B–5 (p. 227). Pointillistic textures for an ensemble frequently also involve *Klangfarbenmelodie*, because the changes in timbre cause the points of sound to seem even further isolated from each other. The texture of Example 2–B–3, (p. 43), discussed earlier in connection with tone-color melody, is an example of a pointillistic texture combined with tone-color melody.

Stratification is a somewhat inexact term that is sometimes used for the juxtaposition of contrasting musical textures, or, more generally, of contrasting *sounds*. Though "strata" usually means layers on top of each other, the strata in this case are *next to* each other. Any abrupt change of texture or basic sound is an example of stratification, but this term is generally used in connection with pieces in which contrasts of texture or timbre are the primary elements in shaping the form of the piece (to be discussed later).

The term *sound-mass* is sometimes used for a chord in which the pitch content is irrelevant compared to the psychological and physical impact of the sound. The most characteristic examples of sound-mass (this term seems never to be used in its plural form) are large clusters, such as the ones in Example 3–24 (p. 64) or in the piano part in Example 11–5. But sound-mass can be created by other means as well—the brutal chords at the beginning of the "Dance of the Adolescents" in Stravinsky's *Rite of Spring* (1913) are actually polychords (E♭7 over F♭), but the effect created by the *fortissimo* successive down-bowed chords is that of sound-mass. Yet another kind of sound-mass can be created by extreme activity in a large ensemble, as in the hair-raising climax to Takemitsu's *Asterism*, (1968) where the effect is of every instrumentalist playing both loudly and randomly.

TEXTURE AS A FORM DETERMINANT

We have seen in earlier chapters that tonality has lost its power to control musical form and that in many works there are really no "themes" in the traditional sense. In the absence of tonal and thematic forces, other elements have to be employed to shape a composition—to give it form. In a number of twentieth-century compositions, the primary form-determining element is texture, usually with a good deal of assistance from dynamics, timbre, and register. Many such works are electronic, but others are written for conventional media.

One such work is Penderecki's *Threnody*. To this listener, the piece is in four sections, with a number of subsections:

Section	Begins at	Material
Part 1	0'0"	High entrances, *ff*, *dim*, with texture thinning; "busy" sounds , random effects.
Part 2	1'50"	Clusters *pp*, expanding, contracting, sliding, ending with stationary cluster; *ff* climax, followed by simultaneous ascent and descent.
Part 3	4'30"	Individual entrances build up to *ff* cluster; clusters center on one pitch, slow vibrato, *dim.*; silence.
Part 4	5'45"	Busy, random sounds (different from Part 1); high cluster superimposed, then crescendo to climax; *sub. pp*; silence; huge *ff* cluster ends the piece at 8'30".

Certainly there are different ways to hear this piece—more or fewer sections, and so forth—but probably every listener would agree that its shape is determined largely by texture and other elements that traditionally have had a secondary role in musical form. Incidentally, the final cluster covers the two octaves from C3 to C5 in quarter-tone intervals distributed among the 52 performers, obviously a prime example of sound-mass. The "busy" music from Part 1 appears above as Example 11–4.

SUMMARY

Musical timbre has been greatly altered by twentieth-century composers. The means of producing sounds with conventional instruments have been expanded to the extent that entire books are devoted to the new techniques for a single instrument. Ensemble timbre has been changed by these new techniques, as well as by the expanded role of the percussion section. Several new techniques of orchestral writing have been developed, among them *Klangfarbenmelodie*, or tone-color melody. Other important developments include the tendency to compose for ad-hoc combinations instead of the standard ensembles, and the creative use of space. Traditional textures—monophonic, homophonic, and contrapuntal—continue to be important in twentieth-century music. Other aspects of texture include compound textures, pointillism, stratification, and sound-mass. In many compositions texture has an important role in determining the form.

NOTES

1. An excellent survey, with references to a large number of scores, is provided by Gardner Read's *Contemporary Instrumental Techniques*.
2. Read, *Contemporary Instrumental Technique*, p. 185.
3. A more comprehensive list is provided in Reginald Smith Brindle's *Contemporary Percussion*.
4. Read, *Contemporary Instrumental Techniques*, pp. 183–84.
5. Henry Brant, "Orchestration," in John Vinton, ed., *Dictionary of Contemporary Music*, p. 543.
6. Reginald Smith Brindle, *Serial Composition*, p. 127.

EXERCISES

Part A: Fundamentals

1. What scale (missing its D♭) seems to be the basis of Example 11–6?

2. Provide the prime form of the five-note chord in Example 11–7.

3. What scale is being used in Example 11–10?

Part B: Analysis

1. Debussy: Preludes, Book II, "Dead Leaves" ("Feuilles mortes"), mm. 19–35. In your analysis, consider the excerpt to be in three phrases: (1) mm. 21–24, (2) mm. 25–30, and (3) mm. 31–35.

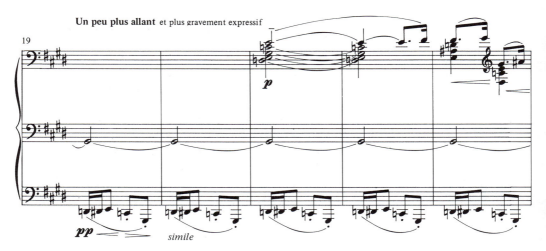

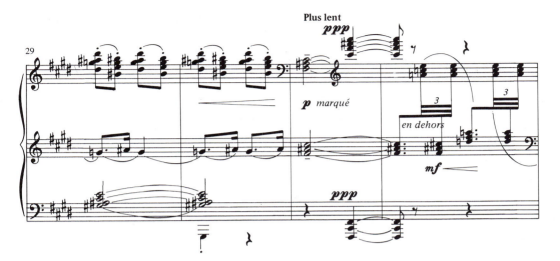

a. Analyze each phrase separately in terms of texture and compositional techniques. That is, separate and identify each element of the texture and discuss the compositional techniques involved with that element. Be sure to include voice leading in your discussion where appropriate.

b. What scale predominates in phrase 1, even if it doesn't account for every note? And in phrase 2?

c. What is the tonal center of each phrase? How is it established? What elements are in conflict with it?

d. An F♯ major triad is the basis of phrase 3. What is the relationship between that triad and the other two triads in that phrase?

2. Carry out a textural analysis of Example 7–1 (p. 147). Use an approach similar to that in Exercise 1A.

3. Listen several times to a recording of Ligeti's *Ramifications* (1969), for string orchestra. Then write out an analysis similar in format to the one of Penderecki's *Threnody* (p. 250).

4. The theme that is heard in mm. 1–2 of the "Fantasy" from Carter's *Eight Etudes and a Fantasy for Woodwind Quartet* (1950) returns in mm. 121–140, augmented and in a *Klangfarbenmelodie* setting. Devise a method to show through color-coding how the timbres vary in those final measures of the piece. The clarinet is in B♭.

Part C: Performance

Be prepared to demonstrate for the class a number of the new playing techniques that have been developed in this century for your instrument. You may find the following readings helpful in completing this assignment.

Part D: Further Reading

BARTOLOZZI, BRUNO.   *New Sounds for Woodwinds*.

BRANT, HENRY.   "Orchestration," in John Vinton, ed., *Dictionary of Contemporary Music*.

BRINDLE, REGINALD SMITH.   *Contemporary Percussion*.

————.   *The New Music*. See Chapter 15, "Colour—New Instrumental Usages," and Chapter 16, "Vocal Music—The New Choralism."

————.   *Serial Composition*. See Chapter 12, "Orchestration, Texture, and Tone Color."

BROOKS, WILLIAM.   "Instrumental and Vocal Resources," in John Vinton, ed., *Dictionary of Contemporary Music*.

BUNGER, RICHARD.   *The Well-Prepared Piano*.

COPE, DAVID H.   *New Directions in Music*. See the section titled "Sound Mass Evolution" in Chapter 3, and Chapter 4, "Instrument Exploration."

DELONE, RICHARD P.   "Timbre and Texture in Twentieth-Century Music," in Gary Wittlich, ed., *Aspects of Twentieth-Century Music*, pp. 66–207.

DEMPSTER, STUART.   *The Modern Trombone*.

ERICKSON, ROBERT.   *Sound Structure in Music*.

HEISS, JOHN C. "Some Multiple-Sonorities for Flute, Oboe, Clarinet, and Bassoon."

HOWELL, THOMAS. *The Avant-Garde Flute*.

KENNAN, KENT, AND DONALD GRANTHAM. *The Technique of Orchestration*. See Chapter 17, "Special Devices."

LANSKY, PAUL, AND MALCOLM GOLDSTEIN. "Texture," in John Vinton, ed., *Dictionary of Contemporary Music*.

READ, GARDNER. *Contemporary Instrumental Techniques*.

SALZEDO, CARLOS. *Modern Study of the Harp*.

SIMMS, BRYAN R. *Music of the Twentieth Century*. See Chapter 6, "Orchestration, Tone Color, and Texture."

TURETZKY, BERTRAM. *The Contemporary Contrabass*.

12

Timbre and Texture: Electronic

INTRODUCTION

The rise of electronic music is responsible for the most important development in musical timbre in the twentieth century. In the course of less than two decades, music progressed from a state of almost total dependence upon traditional acoustical instruments, some of which had not changed appreciably for centuries, to one that allowed the use of any sound that could be imagined or defined in acoustical terms. Though the effect of all of this on concert music has been considerable, it has been even greater on the various kinds of commercial music—from rock to film scores to advertising jingles.

The beginnings of electronic music go back at least to 1906, when Thaddeus Cahill installed his 200-ton Telharmonium, a precursor of the Hammond organ, in Telharmonic Hall in New York City; however, this and later experiments such as the Theremin and the Ondes Martenot made little impact. It was not until the first studies by Pierre Schaeffer and Pierre Henry in France in 1948–49 and the development of the tape recorder that the modern history of electronic music really got started. But before we begin our study, it will be helpful to introduce some terminology relating to musical acoustics.

SOME BASICS OF MUSICAL ACOUSTICS

What we identify as sound is in reality the reaction of the eardrum to varying air pressure. If the variations in air pressure come at regular intervals—that is, if they are *periodic*—and if the *frequency* of the variations is within a certain range, then we identify these variations as a *pitch*. The variations in air pressure occur in two phases, one of greater pressure than normal and the other of less pressure than normal. A convenient analogy is that of ripples in a pond after a pebble is dropped into it, the waves spreading outward from the source, lifting and then lowering any floating object in their path. A pressure wave is represented graphically in Example 12–1, where the normal air pressure is represented by the horizontal line, and the changes in air pressure are shown by the curved line. A complete *cycle* involves the movement from normal pressure through increased pressure to decreased pressure and back again to normal, as in a–b in Example 12–1. The greater the frequency is, measured in cycles per second (cps),[1] the higher the listener perceives the pitch to be. Humans can hear pitches roughly in the range from 20 cps to 16,000 cps, although this range, especially the top part, varies with the individual. As a point of reference, an orchestra tunes to A4 at 440 cps, more or less. The range of a grand piano is approximately from 27.5 cps to 4186 cps.

EXAMPLE 12–1   A Pressure Wave

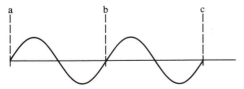

A second fundamental characteristic of a musical sound, after pitch, is its *loudness*. In acoustical terms, "loudness" is a psychological factor that is roughly equivalent to *amplitude*. The amplitude of the pressure wave in Example 12–1 is the distance from the horizontal line to the highpoint of the wave; the greater the amplitude, the louder the sound. Acousticians measure amplitude (or, to be exact, intensity) in terms of *decibels* (abbreviated dB). A decibel is the smallest change in intensity that humans can hear. The upward limit, or threshold of pain, is around 120dB.

A third characteristic of a musical sound is its *envelope*, which describes the way that the loudness, or amplitude, of a sound varies over time. For example, a drum rim shot has a very sudden beginning followed by an almost equally sudden diminuendo, while a note played on a flute might have a breathy, unfocused beginning followed by a crescendo. The envelope of a sound is represented graphically in Example 12–2, where the horizontal line represents silence and the angular line shows the changing amplitude of the sound through time.

The most complex characteristic of a musical sound is its timbre, or tone color. To discuss it, we must understand that most musical sounds consist of a fundamental pitch and a number of less audible higher pitches that occur at predictable intervals above the fundamental. The fundamental pitch is called the first *harmonic*, and the higher pitches are numbered successively as the second harmonic, third harmonic, and so on.[2] The frequency of each harmonic is a simple multiple of that of the fundamental pitch; that is, harmonic 2 is twice the frequency of the fundamental, harmonic 3 is three times the frequency of the fundamental, and so on. The harmonic series is crucial to the design of musical instruments, especially the winds. For example, the fingerings and slide positions of brass instruments are directly linked to the harmonic series. Example 12–3 illustrates the first eight members of the harmonic series beginning with A2.

The harmonic series over any other fundamental would contain the same sequence of intervals as those in Example 12–3: octave, perfect 5th, perfect 4th, major 3rd, and so on. Notice that each interval is smaller than the one before it. Except for the fundamental and its octave duplications, the frequencies of the harmonic series are not the same as those used in equal temperament, although some of them are very close:

Harmonic Series		Harmonic Frequency	Equal Temperament
(8)	A5	880	880
(7)	G5	770	784
(6)	E5	660	659.3
(5)	C♯5	550	554.4
(4)	A4	440	440
(3)	E4	330	329.6
(2)	A3	220	220
(1)	A2	110	110

EXAMPLE 12–2   An Envelope

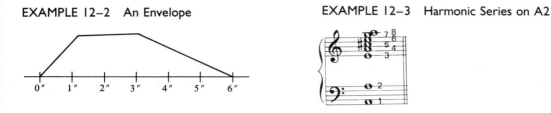

EXAMPLE 12–3   Harmonic Series on A2

The higher the fundamental, the fewer harmonics will fall within the range of our hearing. The fundamental at 110 cps would generate, in theory, dozens of harmonics within the 16,000-cps limit mentioned earlier, although most of them would be too weak in amplitude to be of consequence; on the other hand, the highest note on the piano, at 4186 cps, produces only three harmonics before exceeding the limit of our hearing. This has important implications in regard to timbre, because the relative amplitude of the various harmonics is largely responsible for the timbre of a musical sound. For example, a flute is strong in its first three harmonics, while the clarinet in the low register is very weak in the even-numbered harmonics. The pressure wave generated by most musical instruments is much more complex than that shown in Example 12–1, which illustrates a *sine wave*, a musical sound that contains no overtones. The pressure wave of most musical sounds, whether produced by traditional instruments or electronically, is a complicated shape that is the sum total of all of the harmonics present in the sound. For instance, if we combine the fundamental seen in Example 12–4a with only its second and third harmonics, we produce the more complex waveform seen in Example 12–4b.

EXAMPLE 12–4   A Sine Wave and a More Complex Waveform

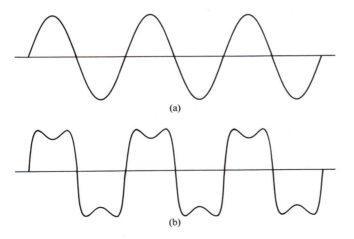

(a)

(b)

Though the harmonic series is crucial to musical timbre, it would be wrong to think that a musical sound is nothing but a simple combination of sine tones from the harmonic series. Studies of timbre have shown that the harmonics of a musical instrument have different envelopes and may even fluctuate unpredictably in pitch as a tone is sustained.

CONCRETE MUSIC

Most electronic music is assembled in some way by the composer and stored on recording tape. There are two primary sound sources available for electronic music. One of these is electronically synthesized sound, to be discussed in the next section. The other is simply all of the sounds available in the "natural" world, including musical instruments, voices, steam engines, dripping water, burning charcoal, or whatever the composer might wish to use. Electronic music using natural sounds as a sound source is referred to as *concrete music* (or *musique concrète*).

The sounds used in concrete music are usually altered in some way in the composition through the manipulation of the tape on which the sound has been recorded. The process typically involves several stages of recording, re-recording, and mixing. The alterations are basically carried out in five different ways, each of which can be combined with the others:

1. Change of tape speed
2. Change of tape direction
3. Tape loops
4. Cutting and splicing
5. Tape delay

Change of tape speed.   We are all familiar with the effect of starting a tape player or phonograph at the wrong speed: a speed greater than intended raises the pitch, a slower speed lowers it. Playing a 7½-ips tape at 3¾, exactly one-half the recorded speed, multiplies each frequency by one-half, lowering all the pitches by exactly one octave (refer back to the table in the previous section, and you will see that the ratio of every octave is 2/1). Playing a 33-rpm phonograph record at 45 rpm multiplies each frequency by 45/33, approximately 4/3, raising the pitch by a P4 (refer again to the table). When speed change is employed on a tape recorder that allows a wider range of speeds, a larger number of ratios can be produced, allowing more subtle graduations of pitch as well as glissandos. Change of speed also alters the timbre of a sound, because harmonics that were above the audible range in the original may become audible, or the reverse. An entertaining work that uses prerecorded sounds played at various speeds is Kenneth Gaburo's *Exit Music II: Fat Millie's Lament* (1965), briefly described in Chapter 7 (p. 146).[3]

Change of tape direction.   Playing a recorded sound backwards reverses its envelope, so that a sound that normally "decays," like a note played on the piano, will instead increase in amplitude. An early tape piece employing change of direction as well as speed is *Incantation* (1952), which was composed in tandem by Otto Luening and Vladimir Ussachevsky.

Tape loops.   A piece of tape on which a sound has been recorded can be cut out and the ends spliced together to make a loop. Obviously, the longer the sound, the longer the loop. When the loop is played on a tape player, the sound is repeated over and over, creating an ostinato. The tape loop in Steve Reich's *Come Out* (1966) is simply a recording of the words "come out to show them." Two copies of the loop were played on machines that run at slightly different speeds, the loops beginning together and moving slowly out of phase with each other; the result was recorded and made into two loops that were then played again on the same two machines, and so on, the process being repeated until an extremely dense texture developed.

Cutting and splicing.   By cutting and splicing, the composer can juxtapose sounds that are normally unrelated, or the envelopes of recorded sounds can be altered by cutting out and discarding the unwanted portions, a process that can disguise the source of the original sound more than one might expect. An example of a piece that uses this technique extensively is Cage's *Williams Mix* (1952), discussed briefly in Chapter 7 (p. 160). While most electronic compositions emerge from the composer's studio as tape recordings ready for performance, *Williams Mix* is a detailed set of instructions for splicing together six different categories of prerecorded sounds, and every "realization" of the piece will be unique.

Tape delay.   Echo effects can be achieved by playing a prerecorded sound on a tape recorder and simultaneously re-recording the sound on the same tape. Using either one or two tape recorders, the sound is channeled from the playback head back to a record head. At that point the sound is dubbed onto the tape at a lower amplitude, creating the echo effect. Obviously, the erase head has to be disabled so that the recording process does not erase whatever sounds already exist on the tape.

EXAMPLE 12–5 Tape Delay

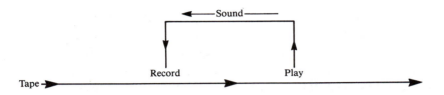

Of course, the farther apart the record and play heads, the greater the time between the original sound and its echo. A delay of about one second can be heard in the middle portion of Gaburo's *Exit Music II*.

ELECTRONICALLY SYNTHESIZED MUSIC

The first studio for electronically synthesized music was established in Cologne, West Germany, in 1951, only a few years after the first experiments with concrete music. For a time there was a bitter ideological struggle between the two camps, but most composers today feel free to employ any sounds, concrete or electronic, in their music. Many works, such as Stockhausen's *Song of the Youths* (*Gesang der Jünglinge*) (1956) and *Hymns* (*Hymnen*) (1967) employ both electronic and concrete sounds. It is safe to say, however, that the historical trend has been toward more electronic synthesis and less use of concrete sounds.

There are probably no two major electronic studios that are identical. Each one reflects the interests of the people who designed the studio and the state of the art at the time that the equipment was purchased, as well as budget constraints and space limitations. Some studios have a jerry-built appearance, with the various components scattered about on tables and in cabinets, while in others most of the equipment is gathered into self-contained units called *synthesizers*. The configuration of equipment in some studios is so distinctive that the connoisseur may be able to determine aurally that an electronic work was "realized" at that studio.

In general, most of the equipment found in an electronic studio falls into one of four categories. The following list is representative, but by no means exhaustive.

Sound-Producing Equipment	*Sound-Processing Equipment*
Oscillators	Mixers
Sine wave	Filters
Sawtooth wave	Equalizers
Square wave	Ring modulators
Triangular wave	Reverberation units
White-noise generators	

Controllers	*Sound Storage Equipment*
Envelope generators	Tape recorders
Sequencers	
Keyboards	

Each of these devices is briefly described in the following paragraphs.

An *oscillator* is an electronic device that produces a particular type of waveform at a frequency chosen by the composer. The oscillators used in electronic music produce *sine waves* (a fundamental pitch with no harmonics; see Example 12–1), *sawtooth waves* (a fundamental pitch plus all the members of its harmonic series; see Example 12–6a), *square waves* (a fundamental pitch plus the odd-numbered harmonics; see Example 12–6b),

EXAMPLE 12–6   Waveforms

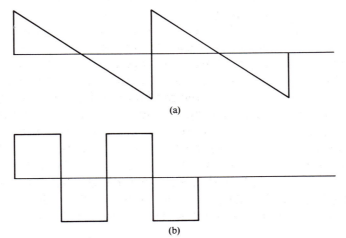

(a)

(b)

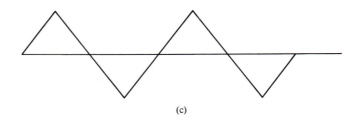

(c)

and *triangular waves* (same as a square wave, but with less amplitude in the upper harmonics; see Example 12–6c). White noise theoretically combines all audible frequencies in randomly varying amplitudes, resulting in a sound resembling hissing or radio static. The sounds produced by oscillators can be used in their pure form, or they can be altered in several ways. *Mixers* are used to combine sounds, whereas *reverberation units* "liven up" sounds by adding a variable amount of echo. The amplitude of some portion of the spectrum of a sound (for instance, that portion between 440 and 660 cps) can be reduced by the use of a *filter* or increased by means of an *equalizer*. A *ring modulator* produces as output the frequencies represented by the sums and the differences of the frequencies that are input to it. For example, sine waves at 400 cps and 560 cps would come out as 160 cps and 960 cps.

Events such as a change in frequency or amplitude can be controlled manually by various means, including knobs (or *potentiometers*) and the *keyboard*, which can be used as a tunable electronic-organ keyboard, among other things. Events can be controlled automatically by *voltage control*, an important aspect of electronic music since the development of the voltage-controlled synthesizer in the 1960s. One method of voltage control uses the pressure wave of one sound to control or "modulate" the amplitude or frequency of another. For example, a very low-frequency sine wave, say at 5 cps, could be used as the *modulating signal* to control changes in frequency of some other sound, perhaps a sawtooth wave at 440 cps, resulting in a smooth vibrato. A rectangular wave used as the modulating signal would result in a sound that alternates rapidly between two frequencies. If the frequency of the modulating signal in amplitude modulation or frequency modulation is high enough, the change in amplitudes or frequencies occurs so fast that it produces a new audible sound of its own, called a *sideband*, that may also be used compositionally. Another way to control the amplitude of a sound automatically is by the use of an *envelope generator*, a device that produces a signal that outlines the shape of an envelope specified by the composer. A *sequencer* is a voltage-control device that produces a series of voltages that are generally used to produce a series of frequencies. Often the series produced by the sequencer is used repetitively, resulting in a sound like that of a tape loop.

The *tape recorder* is an essential part of any electronic studio, for it is here that sounds are stored, either temporarily while a composition is under way, or permanently when the work is completed. Though cassette tape machines are sometimes used for producing copies in a convenient format, the professional-quality reel-to-reel tape recorder is the workhorse of the studio. These machines come in various configurations, generally two to eight "tracks" (paths on the tape on which sound is recorded) using tapes ¼" or ½" wide at speeds of 7½ ips or 15 ips. Good-quality machines allow "overdubbing" (recording over a sound without erasing it), and some allow speed variation in small increments between the usual tape speeds.

ANALOG AND DIGITAL SYNTHESIS

Electronic music synthesis has from the beginning made use of *analog* equipment like that described in the preceding section, but since the late 1970s there has been increasing interest in *digital* synthesizers. A basic difference between the two is that an analog device allows an infinite number of measurements within its range, whereas digital devices count in a limited number of steps. For example, the old-fashioned analog watch can theoretically display the time more accurately than a digital watch, because it is not limited to a fixed number of increments. The advantages of a digital system include its smaller size and the greater ease of "patching" the various components together. A more important advantage is its compatibility with digital computers, which has led to the development of the computer-driven digital synthesizer.

COMPUTERS AND ELECTRONIC MUSIC

Computers offer an alternative method of sound synthesis. Note that computer sound synthesis is not the same thing as computer composition, in which the computer makes compositional decisions (to be discussed in Chapter 14).

In the traditional method of using a computer for sound synthesis, the composer must specify for the computer the details of the desired sound—its frequency, harmonic structure, envelope, and so on—all of which can be made to change over time. The computer then calculates *samples* of the waveform, up to 50,000 samples for each second of music, and stores these samples as numbers. At some point, all of the stored numbers are sent at a predetermined rate from the computer to a *digital-to-analog converter*, which converts the numbers into voltages that can drive a loudspeaker or be recorded on tape as synthesized sound. The "turnaround time" from the specification of a sound to its actual production may range from overnight down to a matter of minutes, depending upon the facility.

Most programming languages for the synthesis of musical sounds are descended from a series of MUSIC programs (MUSIC 1, MUSIC 2, and so on) developed at the Bell Telephone Laboratories. Typically, the composer defines a number of "instruments" in terms that are similar to the techniques used on analog synthesizers. The instruments play a "score" that is also defined by the composer. Naturally, a long and complex composition requires the input of a large amount of data, but the data is precisely defined and can be retained or reworked at will. One example among many is Charles Dodge's *Changes* (1970), a work that makes extensive use of digital filtering.

Another important application of computers in music has been the study of the nature of sound, especially through digital sampling of musical sounds produced by traditional instruments. Some of these efforts have led to the synthesis of sounds that imitate musical instruments and the human voice, a new kind of concrete music. A fine example of vocal synthesis is Paul Lansky's *Six Fantasies on a Poem by Thomas Campion* (1979).

Though most serious work has been done on large "mainframe" computers or on medium-size computers that are designed especially for the purpose, a number of manufacturers now offer fairly sophisticated hardware (equipment) and software (computer programs) that allow any personal computer to be used for sound synthesis. More significant to serious composers has been the development of computer-driven digital synthesizers that can remember any desired "patching" and can store the composition in a purely digital form as it is being assembled. Some of these systems rival the traditional analog studio in terms of the sounds available, and they far surpass it where speed and convenience are concerned.

TAPE/LIVE MUSIC AND LIVE ELECTRONICS

The performance of an electronic composition in the concert hall is a somewhat eerie experience for the uninitiated. Because there is no parade of performers onto the stage, the audience has to be alerted to the fact that the piece is about to begin by dimming the lights. Then someone (who may be unseen) starts the tape player, and the audience listens, facing an empty stage. The applause at the conclusion of the piece is not for the performer, who is, after all, only a tape recorder, but instead for the composer, who is probably not there to hear it.

Whether or not audiences will ever warm to a concert format of this kind remains to be seen. Partly as a way to deal with this problem, but doubtless also for more pressing aesthetic reasons, many composers have written works that combine taped music with live performance on traditional instruments. Early examples include Edgard Varèse's *Deserts* (1954), for woodwinds, brass, percussion, and tape, and Stockhausen's *Contact* (*Kontakte*) (1960), for piano, percussion, and tape (an example of "moment form," discussed in Chapter 7). The tape portion of a mixed-media work may use only electronically synthesized sounds, but many, like Jacob Druckman's *Animus II* (1968), include concrete sounds derived from the conventional instruments used in the piece.

The term *live electronics* can refer to various techniques, from simple amplification of conventional instruments to the use of electronic instruments. George Crumb's *Black Angels* (1970) is an example of both of these, since it is intended ideally for an "electric string quartet" but may also be performed on the customary stringed instruments with contact microphones attached to the belly of the instruments. It is also possible to perform electronic music live with a synthesizer, whether analog or digital. In some works, like Stockhausen's *Mixture* (1964), the electronic equipment is only used to modify the sounds of conventional instruments, a kind of live concrete music, while in others, like Donald Erb's *Reconnaissance* (1967), the synthesizer is used as an instrument in its own right.

The greatest impact of electronics, from electrically amplified guitars to computer-driven synthesizers, has been in the various areas of commercial music. The development of electronic instruments for real-time ("live") performance over the past few decades has been phenomenal, and some idea of its impact can be gained by comparing the sales figures for traditional pianos and electronic keyboards:[4]

	Pianos	*Keyboards*
1983	155,268	392,000
1985	93,371	1,580,500

Though most live electronics are used by popular-style commercial groups, there are a number of artists, such as Laurie Anderson, who combine serious experimental techniques with a popular musical setting.

NOTATION OF ELECTRONIC MUSIC

There is no standard notation for electronic music,[5] and in fact most electronic pieces do not exist in notated form at all. The purpose of musical notation, after all, is to allow a composition to be performed, and this purpose is not relevant to most tape pieces that do not involve live performers. There are exceptions, of course, such as Cage's *Williams Mix* (discussed earlier in connection with concrete music), in which the "score" gives instructions for realizing the piece, and Stockhausen's *Electronic Study II* (1954), which shows frequency, envelope, and tape lengths in a graph form. (Timbre, the most characteristic element of electronic music, is not indicated in Stockhausen's score because only sine tones are used.)

When taped music is to be combined with live performers, some method of coordination has to be provided. One method is for one channel of the tape to provide cues to the performers through headsets, while another is to provide the performers with a score in which some kind of representation of the tape music is given. The composition from which Example 12–7 is excerpted is for cello and two-channel tape. At this point in the piece the taped music is heard for the first time, following a long introductory cello solo. The score instructs the person operating the tape player when to start and stop the tape, and it provides cues to help the cellist coordinate with the taped sounds, but it does not contain a complete transcription of the recorded music.

EXAMPLE 12–7   Mario Davidovsky: *Synchronisms No. 3* (1964)   *(Copyright © 1966 by Josef Marx. Used by permission of McGinnis & Marx Music Publishers.)*

SUMMARY

Disregarding some earlier "false starts," we can say that electronic music began in the late 1940s. In a few decades the medium has developed from concrete music to electronic synthesis, computer synthesis, and the computer-controlled digital synthesizer, and from a studio art to one that allows a variety of live-performance formats. The impact of electronics, from simple amplification to synthesizers, has been especially strong in commercial music. It is impossible to predict how far the electronic revolution will get with traditional concert audiences and ensembles, but builders of acoustical instruments know that they are in for some serious competition.

NOTES

1. Another name for cycles per second is *Hertz* (or *Hz*).
2. Those harmonics above the fundamental are also called *overtones*; thus, the first overtone is the second harmonic, the second overtone is the third harmonic, and so on.
3. A number of the examples in this section were suggested by Barry Schrader's *Introduction to Electro-Acoustic Music*, an excellent and highly recommended text.
4. *The New York Times*, November 16, 1986, p. H21.
5. This is not to say that no attempts have been made to develop such a notation. See, for example, Louise Gariépy and Jean Décarie, "A System of Notation for Electro-Acoustic Music: A Proposition," in *Interface*.

EXERCISES

Part A: Tape Recorder Techniques

The following techniques can be used with any reel-to-reel tape recorder; they should be tried both separately and in combination. They are probably most successful when done as class projects. The first step is to record at different speeds a number of sounds, musical and otherwise, to be used as source material.

1. *Speed Change*. Play back the recorded sounds at different speeds, both faster and slower, by means of the speed setting on the tape recorder. More subtle changes of speed may be achieved by putting light hand pressure on the left-hand reel.

2. *Change of tape direction*. Turning the tape over and running it backwards will not give the desired effect on most machines, because the original tracks no longer come into contact with the playback head. But it is simple to reverse tape direction, without even removing the tape from the machine, by rethreading the tape as shown below (suggested by Hubert Howe, *Electronic Music Synthesis*, p. 62).

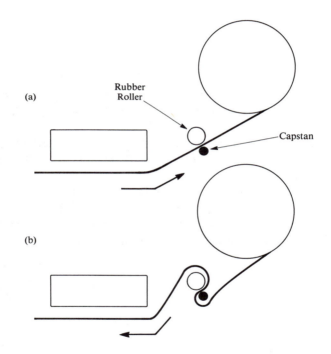

3. *Tape loops*. Cut a portion of the tape to the desired length and splice the ends into a loop. Thread it through the tape player and then to two reels mounted on pencils held by assistants.

4. *Cutting and splicing*. Try cutting out random pieces from a recorded sound and splicing the remainder together. Or cut out the attack portion of a sound, if you can find it on the tape, to observe the effect.

5. *Tape delay*. This technique may not be available on your machine; check the owner's manual. If not, an interesting type of real-time tape delay can be obtained by using two machines. Thread the tape from the left reel of one machine through the heads of both machines and to the right reel of the second machine. Set the first machine to record, plug a microphone into it, and set the second machine to play. Start both machines simultaneously, and speak or sing into the microphone. By careful adjustment of volume settings and speaker placement, you should be able to get a very effective tape delay from the second machine.

Part B: Studio Visit

A visit to an electronic studio with the help of a competent guide is a valuable experience for which there is no substitute. If this is impossible, find a musician in the area who owns a computer-driven synthesizer and would be happy to demonstrate it.

Part C: Listening

The following works are listed in the order in which they were mentioned in the chapter. Listen to as many of them as you can, or listen to other electronic works of your own choosing.

Kenneth Gaburo: *Exit Music II: Fat Millie's Lament*
Otto Luening and Vladimir Ussachevsky: *Incantation*
Steve Reich: *Come Out*
John Cage: *Williams Mix*
Karlheinz Stockhausen: *Song of the Youths*
Karlheinz Stockhausen: *Hymns*
Charles Dodge: *Changes*
Paul Lansky: *Six Fantasies on a Poem by Thomas Campion*
Edgard Varèse: *Deserts*
Karlheinz Stockhausen: *Contact*
Jacob Druckman: *Animus II*
George Crumb: *Black Angels*
Karlheinz Stockhausen: *Mixture*
Donald Erb: *Reconnaissance*
Karlheinz Stockhausen: *Electronic Study II*
Mario Davidovsky: *Synchronisms No. 3*

Part D: Further Reading

BATEMAN, WAYNE. *Introduction to Computer Music.*

BEAUCHAMP, JAMES. "Electronic Music: Apparatus and Technology," in John Vinton, ed., *Dictionary of Contemporary Music.*

BRINDLE, REGINALD SMITH. *The New Music.* See Chapter 10, "Concrete Music," and Chapter 11, "Electronic Music."

COGAN, ROBERT, AND POZZI ESCOT. *Sonic Design.* See Chapter 4, "The Color of Sound."

COPE, DAVID H. *New Directions in Music.* See Chapter 5, "Electronic Music," and Chapter 6, "Computer Music."

DALLIN, LEON. *Techniques of Twentieth Century Composition.* See Chapter 19, "Electronic and Other New Music."

DAVIES, HUGH. "Electronic Music: History and Development," in John Vinton, ed., *Dictionary of Contemporary Music*, pp. 212–16.

DODGE, CHARLES, AND THOMAS A. JERSE. *Computer Music.*

DWYER, TERENCE. *Composing with Tape Recorders.*

FENNELLY, BRIAN. "Electronic Music: Notation," in John Vinton, ed., *Dictionary of Contemporary Music*, pp. 216–20.

HOWE, HUBERT S. *Electronic Music Synthesis.*

LUENING, OTTO. "Origins," in John H. Appleton and Ronald C. Perera, eds., *The Development and Practice of Electronic Music*, pp. 1–21.

SCHRADER, BARRY. *Introduction to Electro-Acoustic Music.*

SIMMS, BRYAN R. *Music of the Twentieth Century.* See Chapter 14, "Electronic Music."

13

Serialism After 1945

INTRODUCTION

The end of World War II in 1945 was followed by two major developments in music. One of these was the beginnings of electronic music, the subject of Chapter 12. The other development, the subject of this chapter, was the dissemination of the serial technique and the extension of its principles into all facets of musical composition.

Although Schoenberg composed his first twelve-tone work in 1921, serialism did not appeal at once to a large number of composers outside of his immediate circle. But when World War II ended, interest in serialism spread rapidly, and the technique was taken up with enthusiasm by the younger generation of composers as well as by established composers as diverse as Copland and Stravinsky. It may be that serialism represented to some composers a rationality that was welcome after the irrational horrors of the war, and the fact that Hitler's regime had tried to suppress serialism certainly did nothing to harm its postwar reputation. In the United States, considerably less affected by the war, interest in twelve-tone music was due in part to Schoenberg's tenure from 1936 on as a professor at the University of California at Los Angeles.

But many of the new adherents to serialism felt that Schoenberg had not taken the technique far enough. Instead of restricting serialism to the domain of pitch class, these composers felt that other aspects of composition should also be controlled by some kind of precompositional plan. This approach has been given various labels, among them "total serialization," "total control," "generalized serialism," and "integral serialism."

INTEGRAL SERIALISM

In classical serial technique, the composer constructs the pitch series before beginning the actual composition. The compositional process is thereby restricted to the extent that, once having begun the presentation of some form of the row, the notes of the row must be used in order; however, everything else is left up to the creativity and skill of the composer. Anyone who has ever composed a twelve-tone piece knows that it is far from a mechanical or automatic procedure.

Some of the areas in which the composer has complete freedom are:

Rhythm
Dynamics
Register
Articulation
Row Form

It is these areas that the proponents of integral serialism looked at most closely, (though others, such as timbre, were not ignored). Many examples of integral serialism apply serial techniques to only a few of these aspects, whereas others are so thoroughly preplanned that they truly are automatic, in the sense that all of the composer's decisions were made before the actual notation of the piece was begun. In the next several paragraphs we will examine approaches to integral serialism in three very different works by composers from the United States, France, and Italy.

MILTON BABBITT: THREE COMPOSITIONS FOR PIANO (1947) No. 1

In this composition, evidently the very first to employ integral serialism, Babbitt "serialized" the dynamics by associating a particular dynamic level with each row form:

$$P = mp \ (pp \text{ in mm. } 49–56)$$
$$R = mf \ (p)$$
$$I = f \ (mp)$$
$$RI = p \ (ppp)$$

There is obviously no true dynamic series here, no parallel to the series of twelve pitch classes; nevertheless, the dynamic levels are controlled pre-compositionally, which is the only requirement for integral serialism. Turn back to Example 6–3 (p. 125) to see an excerpt from this work. You can tell from the dynamic levels in the excerpt that the row forms used are:

	m. 9	m. 10	m. 11	m. 12
Top staff:		R	I	I
Bottom staff:	P	RI	RI	

The rhythm in this composition is organized around the number series 5–1–4–2, which sums to 12. This series of numbers is always associated in some way with the P form of the pitch set. To invert the number series, Babbitt subtracts each number from 6:

$$
\begin{array}{cccc}
6 & 6 & 6 & 6 \\
-5 & -1 & -4 & -2 \\
\hline
1 & 5 & 2 & 4
\end{array}
$$

Six is chosen here because it is the only value that can be used if the resulting differences are going to sum to 12 (and they must, in order to be associated with the inversion of the twelve-tone pitch series).

The resulting durational set is:

$$P = 5 \ 1 \ 4 \ 2 \qquad R = 2 \ 4 \ 1 \ 5$$
$$I = 1 \ 5 \ 2 \ 4 \qquad RI = 4 \ 2 \ 5 \ 1$$

Each member of the durational set is always associated with its corresponding row form. The durational set is expressed in a variety of ways (rests,

EXAMPLE 13–1   Babbitt: *Three Compositions for Piano* (1947), No. 1, mm. 49–52
(© copyright 1957 by Boelke-Bomart, Inc., Hillsdale, NY.)

phrase marks, and so on). In Example 13–1 groups of notes are formed by making the last note of a group longer than the others and/or following the last note by a rest. The series being stated in the excerpt are:

	mm. 49–50	*mm. 51–52*
Top staff:	P (5–1–4–2)	RI (4–2–5–1)
Bottom staff:	RI (4–2–5–1)	I (1–5–2–4)

Notice that the rhythms of the two RI forms in the excerpt are similar, but not identical.

   The rhythm series is expressed in Example 6–3 (p. 125) in different ways. In the left hand in mm. 9–10, the P and RI rhythm series is stated by means of phrase marks and accents. The I form in the right hand, m. 12, is presented the same way. The other measures in the excerpt are organized rhythmically by using the sixteenth-note as the unit of measure. For example, in m. 10 the right hand states 2–4–1–5 by durations of two sixteenths (one eighth), four sixteenths (two eighths tied), one sixteenth, and five sixteenths (a sixteenth tied to a quarter).

Register appears to be left open, except in the voicing of trichords. When Babbitt segments the pitch series into vertical trichords, as in mm. 10–11 of Example 6–3, (p. 125), he voices the trichords in relation to the row in this way:

	1–3	4–6	7–9	10–12
P =	Up	Down	Up	Down
I =	Down	Up	Down	Up
R =	Up	Up	Down	Down
RI =	Down	Down	Up	Up

That is, the members of a prime form of the row would be voiced in trichords as:

```
3   4   9   10
2   5   8   11
1   6   7   12
```

The three row forms in Example 6–3 that are used trichordally are:

m. 10, r.h.: R–0   (E G♯ A) (F♯ B   G) (D♭ C   D) (F E♭ B♭)

m. 11, r.h.: I–1   (B F♯ E) (G   A   G♯) (D B♭ E♭) (C D♭ F)

m. 11, l.h.: RI–1 (F D♭ C) (E♭ B♭ D) (G♯ A   G) (E F♯ B)

PIERRE BOULEZ: STRUCTURES Ia (1952)

European composers, unaware of Babbitt's work in the United States, developed a different approach to integral serialism. In some works each note has its own duration, dynamic level, and articulation, all precompositionally assigned. The multiplicity of dynamic levels was especially troublesome for performers, but the rhythms were also difficult because they were generally ametric.

Structures Ia uses as its primary material the following pitch series (borrowed by Boulez from *Mode de valeurs et d'intensités* (1949), composed by his teacher, Messiaen):

E♭	D	A	A♭	G	F♯	E	C♯	C	B♭	F	B
1	2	3	4	5	6	7	8	9	10	11	12

As we shall see, the pitch series is made to govern duration, dynamic level, articulation, and row choice.

The first step is to make a matrix of prime forms of the series. The second row of the matrix begins with the second note of the original series, the third row begins with the third note, and so on:

Eb	D	A	Ab	G	F♯	E	C♯	C	Bb	F	B
D	C♯	G♯	G	F♯	F	Eb	C	B	A	E	Bb
A	Ab	Eb	D	C♯	C	Bb	G	F♯	E	B	F
Ab	G	D	etc.								

Notice that this is not the kind of twelve-note matrix discussed in Chapter 10.

Next, each note name is replaced with the order number that the note had in the original series. That is, every Eb is replaced with 1, every D with 2, every A with 3, and so on:

1	2	3	4	5	6	7	8	9	10	11	12
2	8	4	5	6	11	1	9	12	3	7	10
3	4	1	2	8	9	10	5	6	7	12	11
4	5	2	8	9	12	3	6	11	1	10	7
5	6	8	9	12	10	4	11	7	2	3	1
6	11	9	12	10	3	5	7	1	8	4	2
7	1	10	3	4	5	11	2	8	12	6	9
8	9	5	6	11	7	2	12	10	4	1	3
9	12	6	11	7	1	8	10	3	5	2	4
10	3	7	1	2	8	12	4	5	11	9	6
11	7	12	10	3	4	6	1	2	9	5	8
12	10	11	7	1	2	9	3	4	6	8	5

A similar matrix of inversions must then be constructed:

Eb	E	A	Bb	B	C	D	F	F♯	G♯	C♯	G
E	F	Bb	B	C	C♯	D♯	F♯	G	A	D	G♯
A	Bb	Eb	E	F	F♯	G♯	B	C	D	G	C♯
Bb	B	E	etc.								

And again the matrix is converted into order numbers from P-0:

1	7	3	10	12	9	2	11	6	4	8	5
7	11	10	12	9	8	1	6	5	3	2	4
3	10	1	7	11	6	4	12	9	2	5	8
10	12	7	11	6	5	3	9	8	1	4	2
12	9	11	6	5	4	10	8	2	7	3	1
9	8	6	5	4	3	12	2	1	11	10	7
2	1	4	3	10	12	8	7	11	5	9	6
11	6	12	9	8	2	7	5	4	10	1	3
6	5	9	8	2	1	11	4	3	12	7	10
4	3	2	1	7	11	5	10	12	8	6	9
8	2	5	4	3	10	9	1	7	6	12	11
5	4	8	2	1	7	6	3	10	9	11	12

Structures Ia is a work for two pianos, and the two pianos between them state all 48 forms of the row: Piano I states the twelve P forms and the twelve RI forms, and Piano II states the twelve I forms and the twelve R forms. The transposition levels for the row forms are selected by using the order numbers in the two matrices. For example, the twelve P forms in Piano I are governed by the first row of the inversion matrix (1,7,3, etc.); thus, the prime beginning with order number 1 would be first, the prime beginning with order number 7 would be second, and so on. (Note that these are not the same as P-1 and P-7.) In Example 13–2, Piano I states the prime beginning with order number 1, while Piano II states the inversion beginning with order number 1.

The duration of each note is also dictated by the two matrices. All twelve rows of each matrix are worked through both forwards and backwards to provide durations for the 576 notes in the piece (12 notes × 48 row forms). The order numbers are used as multiples of 32nd-notes, so that the order number 1 represents one 32nd-note, 2 represents a sixteenth-note, 3 a dotted sixteenth-note, and so on. The duration series in Example 13–2 are:

Piano I: 12 11 9   10 3   6   7   1   2   8   4   5

Piano II: 5   8   6   4   3   9   2   1   7   11 10 12

EXAMPLE 13–2   Boulez: *Structures Ia* **(1952), mm. 1–7**   *(Copyright 1955 by Universal Edition (London) Ltd., London. All rights reserved. Used by permission of European American Music Distributors Corporation, sole U.S. agent for Universal Edition London.)*

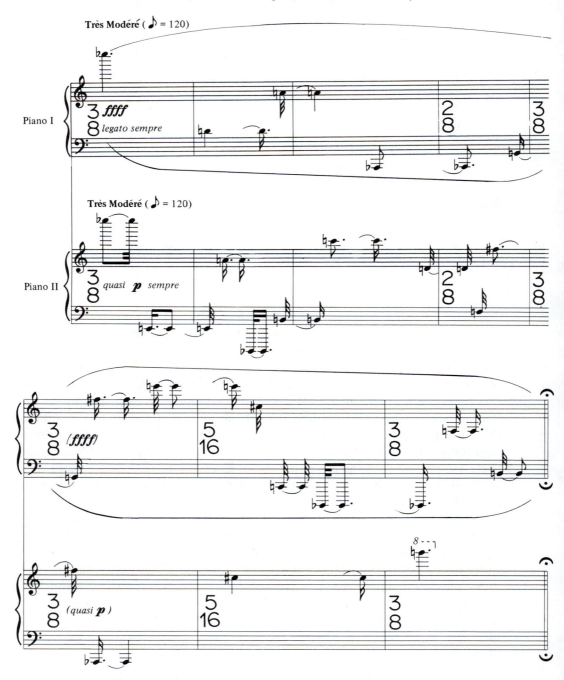

If you compare these duration series with the number matrices, you will see that Piano I is taken from the last row of the I matrix, whereas Piano II is taken from the last row of the P matrix, both in retrograde order. Boulez's rhythmic structure, with 48 rhythmic patterns, is obviously more complicated than Babbitt's, with only four.

Dynamics and articulation are serialized by making a list of twelve dynamic levels (*pppp* to *ffff*) and ten "modes of attack." A single dynamic level and a single articulation are used with each row form, the particular one to be used being again dictated by the number matrices. In this case, instead of rows, diagonals of the matrices are used, some for the dynamics and others for articulation. Because the order numbers 4 and 10 do not appear in the articulation diagonals, the fourth and tenth modes of attack are not needed. In Example 13–2, Piano I uses the twelfth dynamic level and the twelfth mode of attack, while Piano II uses the fifth dynamic level and the fifth mode of attack.

Once all of these procedure were established, the actual notation of the composition could begin; however, by now there were few decisions left to be made. One of them was the choice of time signatures, which do not seem to follow any particular pattern; another was the choice of register. Octave register appears to be controlled only to the extent that a pitch class occurring in two row forms simultaneously must be used in the same register.

LUIGI NONO: IL CANTO SOSPESO (1956), II

The pitch material of this composition derives from a series that is usually characterized as a "wedge" row (Example 13–3a); it can also be viewed as a hexachord followed by its retrograde at the tritone (Example 13–3b). In view of the structure of the duration set, the second interpretation is probably more appropriate. Only P-0 is used in this movement.

EXAMPLE 13–3   Series from Nona's *Il canto sospeso*

The duration set is a palindrome[1] based upon a Fibonacci series. This series, discussed in Chapter 7 in connection with musical form and the golden mean (see p. 158), is an infinite one in which each number (after the first two) is the sum of the previous two numbers:

1   2   3   5   8   13   21   34   etc.

Nono uses the first six numbers and their retrograde for his duration set:

1   2   3   5   8   13   13   8   5   3   2   1

In mm. 108–42 of this movement (the movement begins with m. 108), these values are distributed as needed among four rhythmic strands. Each strand uses its assigned values as multiples of some basic duration:

Strand A: eighth-note
Strand B: triplet eighth-note
Strand C: sixteenth-note
Strand D: quintuplet sixteenth-note

All four strands begin simultaneously and proceed at their own rates without pause, except that the four strands are distributed among eight voice parts, which allows for breathing. Example 13–4, which shows the first presentation of the rhythmic series, may help to clarify how this works. All four strands start simultaneously at the beginning of the excerpt, with the first four durational values—1, 2, 3, and 5—distributed from the top down. As the duration of each strand is exhausted, the next durational value is assigned to it: 8 for Strand A; 13 for Strands B and C; 8, 5, and 3 for Strand D; 2 for Strand C; and 1 for Strand D.

Pitch classes from P-0 are also distributed in order among the four strands as needed. In Example 13–4, Strand A would get order numbers 1 and 5, B would receive 2 and 6, C would receive 3, 7, and 11, and D would use 4, 8, 9, 10, and 12.

In the score, Example 13–4 appears as in Example 13–5. The strands are distributed as follows:

Strand A: Alto 2
Strand B: Soprano 2 – Basso 1
Strand C: Soprano 1 – Soprano 1 + Tenor 2 – Tenor 2
Strand D: Alto 1 – Basso 2 – Soprano 1

EXAMPLE 13–4   Nono: *Il canto sospeso*, II, mm. 108–10 (rhythm only)

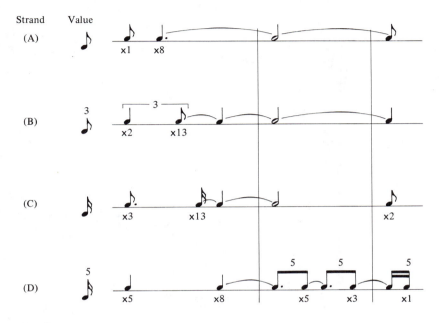

The first note in m. 3, Basso 2, is evidently an error and should be a sixteenth-note quintuplet.[2]

Because the pitch and duration sets are of equal length, if the composition were continued in this manner each member of the row would always be assigned to the same number from the duration series. To avoid this, the duration set is rotated for each statement of the row:

Statement 1:   1   2   3   5   8   13   13   8   5   3   2   1

Statement 2:   2   3   5   8   13   13   8   5   3   2   1   1

Statement 3:   3   5   8   13   13   8   5   3   2   1   1   2

etc.

In the coda (mm. 142–57) each strand presents the entire duration series independently. The entrances are staggered, with Strand A beginning, followed by Strands B, C, and D. This allows all four strands to reach their maximum level of activity simultaneously for the climax of the movement in m. 150.

EXAMPLE 13–5 Nono: *Il canto sospeso, II, mm. 108–10*

INTEGRAL SERIALISM IN PERSPECTIVE

The three works that have been surveyed here demonstrate just three of many possible approaches to integral serialism. None of them serialize register or timbre, but all three serialize rhythm, and it is interesting to compare them in that regard. Babbitt's rhythmic series is apparently not derived from his pitch series at all, which might seem a weakness since there is no single organizing force at work. There is a connection between Nono's pitch series and his rhythmic series, in that both are symmetrically designed, but there is not a direct one-to-one correspondence between the two. Boulez probably comes closest to the ideal of having a pitch series control all elements of a work, but the listener could never recognize the relationship between a pitch series and a duration series derived from *order numbers* of transpositions and transposed inversions of the pitch series.

Babbitt later devised other methods that linked the durations more closely with the original pitch series. One method derives the duration set from P-0 by numbering the notes of P-0 chromatically, using the first note as 0:

P–0:	G	Bb	F#	B	G#	A	Eb	F	C	E	D	C#
	0	3	11	4	1	2	8	10	5	9	7	6

By substituting 12 for the 0 that begins the row, a durational set is established. The numbers in the set can serve as multiples of any constant value. In Example 13–6 the constant value is the eighth-note. Alternatively, the same series can be interpreted as *time points* within a measure. That is, the series 0, 3, 11, 4, etc., can be interpreted as the 0th eighth-note in a measure, the third eighth-note in a measure, the eleventh eighth-note in a

EXAMPLE 13–6   A Durational Series

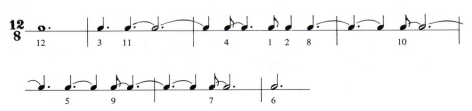

EXAMPLE 13–7   A Time-Point Series

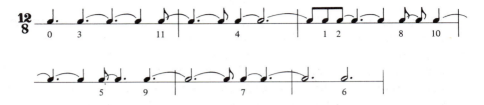

measure, the fourth eighth-note in a measure, and so on, as in Example 13–7. The twelve eighth-notes in each measure are numbered 0 through 11 instead of 1 through 12, in order to correspond with the range of values in the duration series.

The durations in Example 13–7 closely reflect the intervals between the adjacent notes of the series. To illustrate this, count the number of ascending half-steps between each note and the next one:

P–0: G   Bb F♯ B G♯ A Eb F C E D C♯ (G)

        3   8   5   9   1   6   2   7   4   10 11 (6)

These numbers, it turns out, are the same as the durations in Example 13–7. That is, the first note is three eighth-notes in duration, the second is eleven eighth-notes, and so on.

Although Examples 13–6 and 13–7 were derived from the same pitch series, each is unique, and each could be subjected to transposition, inversion, and retrograde operations.

The most difficult problem faced by the integral serialists was the lack of enthusiasm on the part of the musical public. The compositional method was ultimately irrelevant to the listener, since none of the relationships were audible. In fact, some of the most tightly controlled works give the listener the impression that they are completely random and disorganized (*Structures Ia* is a good example of this).

OTHER ASPECTS OF SERIALISM

Our two chapters on serialism have not by any means exhausted the subject. A really thorough discussion of this topic (and one is sorely needed) would require many chapters. We should not leave the subject, however, without briefly mentioning a few other aspects of serialism.

Though most serial works use a pitch series of twelve tones, there are some that use more or fewer than twelve. Stravinsky used the following five-note set in his *In Memoriam Dylan Thomas* (1954):

E   E♭   C   C♯   D

Berio used a thirteen-note set in *Nones* (1954). Notice that this set is symmetrical around its central note, A:

C   E♭   B   A♭   F   E   A   D   C♯   B♭   G   E♭   F♯

And Example 6–12 (p. 135), while not taken from a strictly serial composition, does employ a sixteen-note pitch series.

Rotation of sets or of portions of sets is another possibility that composers have explored. Stravinsky used two methods of hexachordal rotation for *Abraham and Isaac* (1963).[3] In the first, the pitch classes are rotated in a circular fashion, right to left:

G   G♯   A♯   C   C♯   A
G♯   A♯   C   C♯   A   G
A♯   C   C♯   A   G   G♯
C   C♯   A   G   G♯   A♯
C♯   A   G   G♯   A♯   C
A   G   G♯   A♯   C   C♯

The second method of rotation works just like the first, but all are transposed to begin with the same note:

G   G♯   A♯   C   C♯   A
G   A   B   C   G♯   F♯
G   A   A♯   F♯   E   F
G   G♯   E   D   D♯   F
G   D♯   C♯   D   E   F♯
G   F   F♯   G♯   A♯   B

Less-systematic reordering of rows also occurs. George Rochberg's *Twelve Bagatelles* (1952) use a single row in only a few transpositions, but the row is frequently reordered. Example 13–8 employs the following row forms:

RI–7:	B	C	F	D	F♯	B♭	E	E♭	A	C♯	G	A♭
I–7:	A♭	G	C♯	A	E♭	E	B♭	F♯	D	F	C	B
	1	2	3	4	5	6	7	8	9	10	11	12

EXAMPLE 13–8 *Twelve Bagatelles* (1952), No. 8, mm. 1–8. *(© 1955 Theodore Presser Company. Used by permission of the publisher.)*

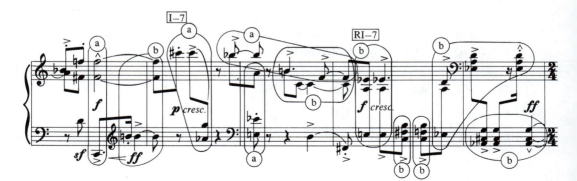

Whereas the rows in mm. 1–4 are presented in the correct order, those in mm. 5–8 are not; the final RI-7 is particularly reordered. Rochberg's purpose may have been to emphasize two particular arrangements of an [0,1,6] set type, labeled here as "a" and "b."

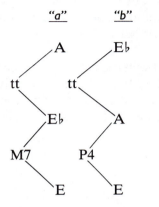

Occurrences of these two arrangements (or their inversions) are shown in the example. Notice particularly how many of them occur in mm. 5–8, where the rows are reordered.

Serialism has also been employed in electronic and microtonal music, an example of the latter being Ben Johnston's String Quartet No. 2 (1964).

MUSIC AFTER SERIALISM

While no doubt there are composers who are still writing serial music, its real strength as a movement died out in the 1960s. Composers turned to other things—to timbre and texture, to improvisation, to minimalism, even to tonality. A great deal of atonal music continues to be written, but it is rarely serial and more often is in a free atonal idiom (see Chapter 9). There are several reasons for the decline of serialism. One is the insistence upon originality that has robbed the twentieth century of any chance of developing a "style" in the way that there are Baroque and Classical styles. Also, the demands that integral serialism made on listener and performer proved intolerable to both. In the words of one writer and composer who was active throughout this period:

And so integral serialism quickly reached an impasse, through its own limitations and the burdens it laid on performers. But its importance, in both aesthetic and historical contexts, must not be denied, for it forged a completely new musical language, as different from anything that had gone before (except Webern) as chalk from cheese, and paved the way to a new, more spontaneous music which is still the most potent means of emotive expression today.[4]

The same writer goes on to summarize the movement from free atonality in the early 1900s to serialism in the 1920s, then to integral serialism in the 1950s, and finally back to free atonality in the 1960s: "The cycle was then complete and serialism had come and gone, but leaving decisive and lasting traces of its sojourn."[5]

SUMMARY

Integral serialism refers to the precompositional control not only of pitch, as in classical serialism, but of other elements of a composition as well. Rhythm, dynamics, articulation, register, row form, and timbre have all been subjected to precompositional ordering. In some cases these orderings are independent of each other, but often the composer attempts to relate all of the musical materials to a single series.

Other aspects of serialism discussed in this chapter included the use of tone rows with fewer or more than twelve pitch classes, the use of rotation, and the reordering of rows.

Though serialism has declined as a compositional technique, its influence on later styles has been substantial.

NOTES

1. A palindrome is a structure that reads the same backwards as it does forwards. Examples are the word "noon" and Messiaen's nonretrogradable rhythms (see p. 134).
2. There are apparently at least two other errors, in mm. 125 and 135, both being occasions when the last note of the row is articulated slightly after the first note of the next statement. The second of these makes little difference, but "correcting" m. 125 significantly alters mm. 125–42.
3. George Perle and Paul Lansky, "Twelve-Note Composition," in *The New Grove Dictionary of Music and Musicians.*
4. Reginald Smith Brindle, *The New Music*, p. 52.
5. Ibid., p. 53.

EXERCISES

Part A: Fundamentals

1. Suppose that P-0 of some row begins on B♭ and ends on D. Fill in the missing information below.

	Row form	First note	Last note
a.	P-0	D	B♭
b.	P-__	__	A♭
c.	R-0	__	__
d.	R-__	__	F
e.	I-0	__	__
f.	I-__	C	__
g.	RI-0	__	__
h.	RI-__	E♭	__

2. Identify any rows discussed in this chapter that are all-interval rows.

3. Identify any rows discussed in this chapter that are derived sets, and explain your answer.

4. Is combinatoriality employed in Example 13–1? Explain how you can tell that it is or is not.

5. Same question for Example 13–2.

Part B: Analysis

1. Boulez: *Structures Ia* (1982), mm. 8–15 (see p. 293). This excerpt is a continuation of Example 13–2. When doing the following exercises, consider both excerpts, as well as the discussion of *Structures Ia* in the text.

   a. Identify the P forms in Piano I, and explain how they are derived from the matrices.

   b. Do the same for the I forms in Piano II.

   c. Study the durations used in Piano I, and explain how they are derived from the matrices. A rest should be counted as part of the duration of the note that precedes it.

d. Do the same for Piano II.

e. Try to determine what the dynamic "scale" must be, if $1 = pppp$ and $12 = ffff$. Hint: Boulez inserts *quasi p* between *p* and *mp* and *quasi f* between *mf* and *f*.

f. Use the dynamic scale to determine which matrix diagonals are being used for Piano I and Piano II. Note that the dynamics in Example 13–B–1 count twice for each piano because they apply to two row forms.

2. Analyze Stravinsky's use of his five-note row in the "Dirge-Canons (Prelude)" from *In Memoriam Dylan Thomas* (discussed on p. 287). In addition to labeling the row forms, comment on the relative consonance and dissonance of the vertical sonorities used.

Part C: Composition

1. Compose an excerpt that will be similar to Nono's *Il canto sospeso* (discussed earlier). Instead of four strands use three—eighth-note, triplet eighth-note, and sixteenth-note—or choose three durations of your own. Notate each strand on a separate staff. Use Nono's pitch set, but instead of using Nono's twelve-element duration series, use this eleven-element series: 1, 2, 3, 5, 8, 13, 8, 5, 3, 2, 1. Continue through at least three statements of the durational series (33 notes). If possible, this should be composed for instruments in your class. Make the rhythms as easy to read as you can, and include an analysis.

Part D: Further Reading

BRINDLE, REGINALD SMITH. *The New Music*. See Chapter 5, "Integral Serialism," and Chapter 6, "Numbers."

———. *Serial Composition*. See Chapter 14, "Permutations and Other Variants of a Series," and the section titled "Integral Serialism" in Chapter 15.

DALLIN, LEON. *Techniques of Twentieth Century Composition*. See Chapter 15, "Total Organization."

GRIFFITHS, PAUL. *Modern Music*. See Chapter 2, "New York, 1948–50," Chapter 3, "Darmstadt/Paris, 1951–52," and pp. 155–64 of Chapter 9, "American Serialism → Computer Music."

GRIFFITHS, PAUL. "Serialism," in Stanley Sadie, ed., *The New Grove Dictionary of Music and Musicians*.

(Boulez: *Structures Ia* (1982), mm. 8–15.)

Simms, Bryan R. *Music of the Twentieth Century*. See pp. 84–90, 108–12, 348–52.

Wittlich, Gary. "Sets and Ordering Procedures in Twentieth-Century Music," in Wittlich, ed., *Aspects of Twentieth-Century Music*. See pp. 430–44.

14

The Roles of Chance and Choice in Twentieth-Century Music

INTRODUCTION

There has been a general tendency in Western music to restrict the performer's options ever more closely, and at the same time an increasing dedication to honoring the composer's intentions at the expense of the performer's creativity. Compare Bach's *Well-Tempered Clavier* (1722, 1742), which lacks any indications of tempo, dynamics, or articulation, with Debussy's Preludes (1910, 1913), which is full of detailed and descriptive instructions, and compare them both with the examples of integral serialism in which every note has its own dynamic marking and articulation. Though elements of chance are present in any live musical performance (after all, there is always the possibility of a mistake), the emphasis has usually been on more control, not on improvisation.

Nevertheless, an important force in music in the second half of the twentieth century has moved in just the opposite direction, toward less control by the composer and more creative responsibility for the performer. As we shall see, this new responsibility can range from making an insignificant decision to shaping all aspects of the piece. In either case, the composer deliberately leaves something unspecified, up to chance or to the whim of the performer. Two terms used for music of this sort are *indeterminacy* and *aleatory*. Though some authors attempt to make a distinction between these two terms, we will not do so in this text.

A less significant but related movement has made use of chance in the compositional process itself. If it is a good thing for the composer to be less involved in the way a piece is to be performed, then it might follow that the composer should also be less involved in the way that it is composed, and this can be accomplished by introducing elements of chance into the compositional process.

These two approaches—chance in composition and choice in performance—form the two related branches of *experimental music*, a term that is appropriate for any music in which the final product is deliberately kept beyond the control of the composer.

CHANCE IN COMPOSITION

In order to allow chance to play a part in composition, the composer must decide what aspects of the work are to be decided by chance and what the range of probabilities of each aspect should be. For example, we could compose a piece for piano without dynamics and then apply the dynamics randomly by flipping coins or rolling dice. We would still have to decide on the range of the dynamics (perhaps *ppp* to *fff*) and how often they were to change. In general, however, composers who make use of chance apply it much more broadly than this.

The most influential composer to make extensive use of chance in composition is an American, John Cage, who was mentioned in Chapter 8 in connection with Oriental philosophy (see p. 178). In a number of his chance compositions, Cage made use of procedures drawn from the *I-Ching*, a Chinese treatise on probabilities, making each decision by tossing a coin six times and looking up the result on a table of "hexagrams" that represent symbolically the 64 possible outcomes (that is, 2 to the 6th power) for six coin tosses.

Imaginary Landscapes No. 4 (1951) provides an early example of Cage's use of chance and an example of his originality as well. Presumably Cage decided without the help of chance the instrumentation of this piece (twelve radios) and the number of performers (two for each radio). The *I-Ching* was employed to help determine the changing dynamic levels and wavelengths to which each radio would be set. All of this is notated on a twelve-stave score employing both traditional musical symbols and numbers. Even though the score is precisely notated, chance has a role in the performance as well, because the signals that the radios pick up are unpredictable and will vary with each performance. The *I-Ching* was also used by Cage for *Williams Mix* (see pp. 160 and 261), as well as in other works.

Composers have employed other random decision-making techniques as well, of course. Cage used imperfections in paper to determine the placement of notes in *Music for Piano* (1952–56) and astronomical maps for *Atlas Eclipticalis* (1962). Perhaps the most outlandish use of chance is *The Thousand Symphonies* (1968) by Dick Higgins, in which the "score" was produced by firing a machine gun at manuscript paper.

Computers have been used to some extent in chance composition, since they can be programmed to produce an apparently random series of numbers within a specified range and to use those numbers in decision-making processes. The speed of a computer makes practical the use of much more complex probabilistic procedures. Conditional probabilities, for example, can vary according to one or more conditions that have been decided on previously. As a very simple example, suppose we want to generate a melody that will conform to the following rules:

1. Use only the notes C, E, and G.
2. Allow no repeated notes.
3. Use fewer G's than C's or E's.
4. Distribute the C's and E's evenly.

The following table would tend to produce such a melody, although we still must specify its length and the first note. To use the table, find the most recent note on the left border. Then use the percentages shown in that row to generate some note on the top border. For instance, if C is the most recent note generated, then the next note will probably be E (75%) but might be G (25%).

	C	E	G
G	50%	50%	0%
E	75%	0%	25%
C	0%	75%	25%

Conditional probabilities can be nested to any depth, with the result that the selection of a particular event may depend upon the results of the last several decisions.

Lejaren Hiller is a composer whose name is often associated with computer composition.[1] Together with Leonard Isaacson, he composed the first serious computer piece, the *Illiac Suite for String Quartet*, in 1957. Though the *Illiac Suite* was somewhat tentative creatively, the *Computer Cantata* (1963), by Hiller and Robert Baker, is a more substantial composition and explores conditional probabilities systematically. Other composers associated with this technique include Iannis Xenakis, who calls his computer music "stochastic music," Larry Austin, whose *Canadian Coastlines* (1981) is a complex eight-part canon for instruments and tape, and Barry Vercoe, whose *Synapse for Viola and Computer-Synthesized Tape* is a serial work in which many of the details were decided on by a computer.

CHOICE IN PERFORMANCE

Aleatory in performance can range all the way from the most insignificant detail to the entire shape of the piece. On the one hand are works in which the indeterminate elements may be so unimportant that any two performances of the piece will be very similar; on the other hand are pieces that are totally improvised and will vary greatly from one performance to the next. The elements of composition that may be left up to the performer include the following:

Medium (instrumentation)

Expression (dynamics, etc.)

Duration (rhythm and tempo)

Pitch

Form

In practice, these categories often appear in combination, but it will be useful to discuss them briefly individually, after which we will consider some examples from the literature.

Leaving the performing medium unspecified is not a practice unique to the twentieth century—Bach's *Art of Fugue* (1750) is a famous eighteenth-century example—but it is a practice that had been largely abandoned for some time. Nevertheless, a number of twentieth-century works leave open either the performing medium or the number of performers, or both.

Expression, including everything from dynamics and articulation to the most subtle nuance, has been of increasing concern to most composers. Even from Mozart to Beethoven we see development in this area, and much more from Beethoven to Debussy. However, composers interested in allowing the performer to have more freedom frequently omit expression marks, although the usual practice is not to do so unless other aspects of the piece are also indeterminate.

Indeterminacy in duration can be handled in a number of ways. Tempos can be "as fast as possible" or "as slow as possible." Rhythm can be left open by providing noteheads on the staff while leaving the durations completely up to the performer. The composer can exercise more control by the use of *proportional notation*, in which the spacing of the notes on the page indicates their approximate durations, as in Example 6–9 (p. 131).

A simple example of pitch indeterminacy is the instruction "as high as possible." More extended examples often show the general contour, while leaving the precise pitches up to the performer. An instance of this was encountered in Example 6–10 on p. 132. Here the flutes are given apparently random contours to follow repetitively for eighteen seconds, after which all are to begin at a fairly low pitch and work their way upward. A composer may choose not to provide even a contour, in which case the choice of pitch and register is entirely up to the performer.

The usual method of leaving the form of a work unspecified, short of total improvisation, is to allow the performer or conductor to choose the order in which the sections of a piece will be performed, and even whether they will be performed at all. This approach to form is sometimes called *open form* or *mobile form*.

SOME EXAMPLES OF PERFORMER INDETERMINACY

Stockhausen's *Piano Piece XI* (*Klavierstück XI*) (1956) was one of the first European works to employ open form. The score, a single page roughly 21 × 37 inches, consists of nineteen precisely notated segments of varying lengths, the proportions being governed by a Fibonacci series.[2] The segments are played in any order, and the performer is instructed to choose the order randomly without intentionally linking one to another. If a segment is played a second time, instructions in parentheses such as *8va* may allow some variation. When a segment is "arrived at for the third time," the piece is over, even though some segments may not have been played at all. Each segment is followed by symbols that specify tempo, dynamics, and mode of attack, and these are to be applied to the *next* segment in each case (the performer chooses the tempo, dynamics, and mode of attack for the first segment that is performed).

Cornelius Cardew's *Octet '61 for Jasper Johns* (1961) is a free-form composition "not necessarily for piano." The score consists of sixty "signs" that are to be interpreted cyclically—that is, sign 60 is followed by sign 1. The performer may begin anywhere and end anywhere, and the signs may be taken in reverse order if desired. An additional wild-card sign is provided for use "anywhere and as often as desired." The first six signs are shown in Example 14–1. Notice that sign 1 includes the Arabic numerals 6 and 7, sign 3 contains 3 and 5, and sign 6 contains 1, 6, and 7. Cardew provides hints for interpreting some of the symbols used in the signs, but the instructions emphasize creativity and interpretation rather than conformity. As an illustration of one of the many ways of interpreting signs 1–6, Cardew provides the illustration seen in Example 14–2. His key to the illustration follows the example.

EXAMPLE 14–1 Cardew: *Octet '61 for Jasper Johns* (1961), signs 1–6 *(Used by permission of C. F. Peters Corporation, on behalf of Hinrichsen Edition, Ltd., London. © 1962 by Hinrichsen Edition, Ltd.)*

EXAMPLE 14–2 Cardew: *Octet '61 for Jasper Johns* (1961), illustration and key from instructions to score *(Used by permission of C. F. Peters Corporation, on behalf of Hinrichsen Edition, Ltd., London. © 1962 by Hinrichsen Edition, Ltd.)*

1. Seven taken literally as a configuration in musical space. Six Cs, one added to each of the first six signs.
2. Add E flats.

3. Three As. Five A flats. Three sustained notes *forte*: the others *piano* or *pianissimo*. Five-note cluster-type chord.

4. Two chords *piano* following the dot-dash rhythm of the Gs in 3.

5. Slide from E down towards B.

6. Six different registers for D (colour pitch). Seven described as in 1. One described as subsequent cluster. One C at given pitch—longer duration.

Stockhausen's *Piano Piece X* (*Klavierstück X*) (1961) calls for a tempo "as fast as possible." Macro-durations are indicated above the staff, as in Example 14–3. Here the durations above the staff are a quarter-note, a double whole-note tied to an eighth note, an eighth-note, and so on. The pitches on the staff are to be played within the given duration, with ascending and descending beams indicating *accelerando* and *ritardando*. The long slurs that join some stems (for instance, the F♯4–G4 in the right hand near the beginning) call for the first note to be sustained until the second one is reached. The visual attractiveness of *Piano Piece X* is part of its appeal, and the same is true of many works composed in the second half of the century. Perhaps more than in any other period, it is helpful for the contemporary composer to be competent at drafting.

Morton Feldman's *The Straits of Magellan* (1962), for seven instruments, is a good example of controlled ensemble improvisation. Each box in Example 14–4 represents a unit of the basic tempo, M.M. 88. An empty box stands for silence. The other boxes are to be realized by improvisation, except that the symbol in each box restricts what the performer can do:

Arabic numeral: Play that many notes in succession, except for the pianist, who should play them as a chord.

Roman numeral: Play that many notes as a chord.

F: Flutter-tongue one tone.

T: Double-tongue one tone.

Diamond: Play as a harmonic.

The dynamics are specified as "very low throughout," and "all sounds are to be played with a minimum of attack."

The third movement of Lukas Foss's *Baroque Variations* (1967) is titled "On a Bach Prelude (Phorion)" and is based on the Prelude to Bach's *Partita in E Major* for solo violin (an example of quotation music—see Chapter 8). This orchestral work requires a number of choices on the part

EXAMPLE 14–3 Stockhausen: *Piano Piece X* (1961), first system

Karlheinz Stockhausen

Klavierstück X

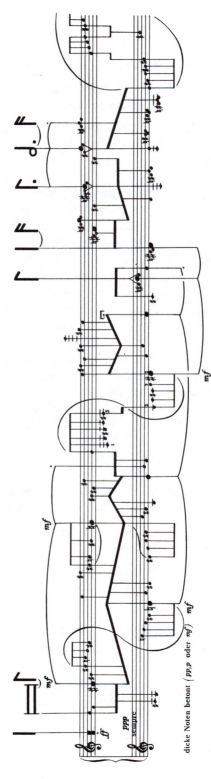

dicke Noten betont (*pp, p* oder *mf*)

EXAMPLE 14–4   Feldman: *The Straits of Magellan* (1962), first 20 boxes on p. 1   *(© 1962 by C. F. Peters Corporation. Used by permission.)*

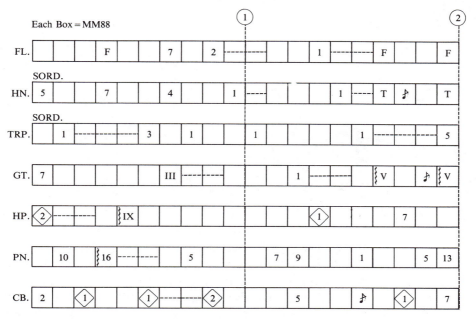

of both the conductor and the performers. For example, at rehearsal no. 2 in the score, a section that "should last circa 2 minutes," the conductor chooses from four groups of instrumentalists, cueing first one, then another, with only general instructions in the score concerning which groups to favor and which to neglect. At 3, five soloists play passages they have selected independently from the "Bach sheet" provided with the score, while at 5 the woodwinds are provided with noteheads and the instruction to "place anywhere within bar, unevenly. Vary placement." Similar techniques are used throughout the movement, with nearly all of the pitch material being derived from the Bach work.

Foss's *Thirteen Ways of Looking at a Blackbird* (1978) uses a number of interesting techniques, including tape delay and pitch indeterminacy. The tenth song begins with a thirty-second improvised duet for flute and percussion, the percussionist playing on the strings of a piano with tape-covered triangle beaters. Example 14–5 shows the composer's instructions for this duet along with a sample beginning. Note especially the instruction to "Use all twelve notes." The effect desired here, as in most improvisations, is one of free atonality, not serialism, and certainly not diatonicism.

EXAMPLE 14–5   Foss: *Thirteen Ways of Looking at a Blackbird* (1978), X, instructions and
first system   *(Copyright © 1979 by Pembroke Music Co., Inc. Reprinted by permission.)*

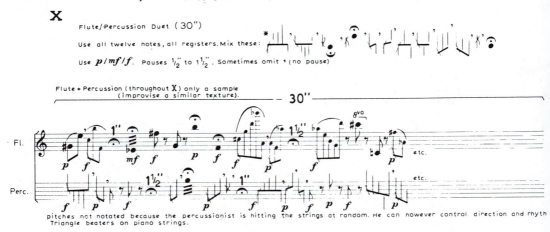

The single movement of Witold Lutoslawski's Symphony No. 3 (1983)
contains a number of *ad libitum* passages, most of them involving a kind of
uncontrolled imitation. In Example 14–6 the conductor provides cues at
nine points (see the arrows above the score) but otherwise does not con-
duct. The winds play their repeated patterns at a fast tempo, essentially in
an uncoordinated fashion, until the conductor cues a change of pattern (the
last arrow) or begins a conducted section. Notice that each group (piccolo/
flutes, oboes, and horns) has its own pitch material and that the patterns
within each choir are somewhat similar, resulting in uncontrolled imitation
within each group. In this excerpt, all of the instruments except for the
piccolo sound as written, and an accidental applies only to the note it
precedes.

GRAPHIC SCORES AND TEXT SCORES

A graphic score is one in which conventional musical notation has been
abandoned in favor of geometric shapes and designs that suggest more or
less clearly how the music is to be performed. The Feldman excerpt (Example 14–4) is an example of one approach to graphic notation. Whereas
Feldman provides fairly specific guidance for his performers, Martin Bart-
lett provides much less for the unspecified ensemble that is to perform the
second movement of *Lines from Chuang-Tzu* (1973). In this movement,
shown in its entirety in Example 14–7, dynamics are indicated by the size of
the dots. Nothing else is specified.

EXAMPLE 14–6   Lutoslawski: Symphony No. 3 (1903), pp. 1–2 (winds only)

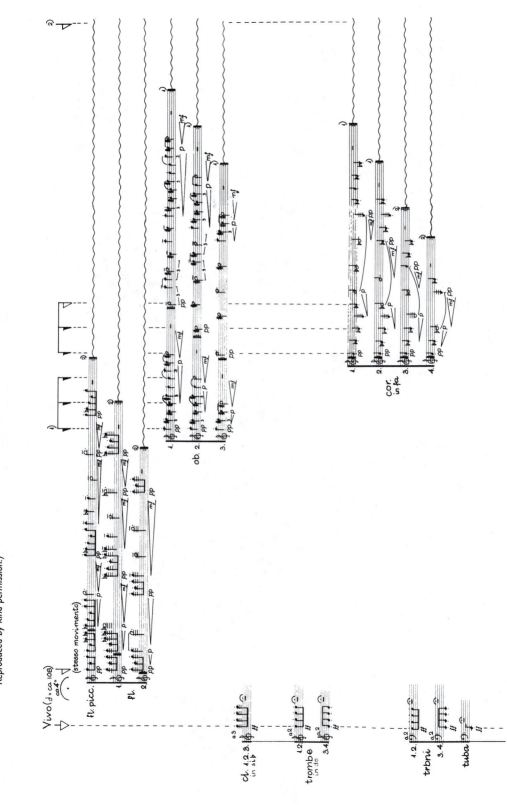

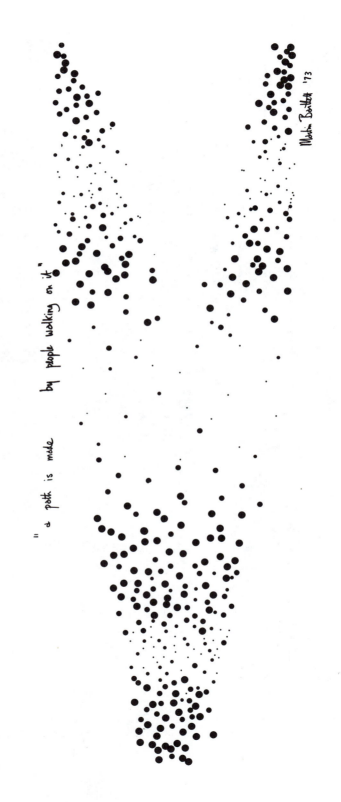

EXAMPLE 14–8   Mortimore: *Very Circular Pieces* (1970), "Circular Piece."   *(Reprinted from SOURCE: Music of the Avant Garde, Issue 10, 1971, with permission from Composer/Performer Edition, 2109 Woodbrook, Denton, TX 76205.)*

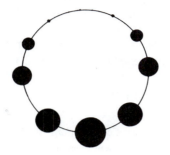

Even less information is given by Robin Mortimore for *Very Circular Pieces* (1970). In the movement shown in Example 14–8, "Repeat" is the only performance instruction.

A text score is one that consists only of words. The text usually provides instructions for an improvisation, but it may do little more than set a mood. Two examples will suffice as models. Christian Wolff's "Play," from the *Prose Collection* (1969), is fairly specific in its instructions. The beginning is shown in Example 14–9.

EXAMPLE 14–9:   Wolff: *Prose Collection*, "Play," first 46 words   *(Copyright © G. Schirmer, Inc. International copyright secured. All rights reserved. Used by permission.)*

Play, make sounds, in short bursts,
Clear in outline for the most part;
quiet; two or three times more towards
as loud as possible, but as soon as you
cannot hear yourself or another player
stop directly. Allow various spaces
between playing (2, 5 seconds, indefinite). . . .

The second example, Stockhausen's *For Times to Come* (1970), is a composition for an unspecified ensemble, and it illustrates what Stockhausen calls "intuitive music."

EXAMPLE 14–10:   Stockhausen: *For Times to Come* (1970), "Waves"   *(Reprinted with permission of Stockhausen-Verlag, 5067 Kuerten, West Germany.)*

Overtake the others
Hold the lead
Allow yourself to be overtaken

Less often

MUSIC ON THE FRINGE

In the 1960s and 1970s especially, a number of composers wrote pieces that seem to many musicians to push the limits of what can be called "music." Traditional definitions of music often include references to organized sound and to the expression of ideas and emotions, but some works challenge these notions. One example is the last movement of Dick Higgins's *Constellations for the Theater (Number X)* (1965), a text score given in its entirety as Example 14–11.

EXAMPLE 14–11   Higgins: *Constellations for the Theatre (Number X) (1965)*, "A Winter Carol"   From Constellations and Contributions by Dick Higgins. (Copyright © 1961 by Richard C. Higgins. All rights reserved. Reprinted by permission.)

> Any number of people may perform this composition. They do so by agreeing in advance on a duration for the composition, then by going out to listen in the falling snow.

This is not the only work to concentrate the attention of the audience on the natural sounds that exist in the environment. Pauline Oliveros's *Bonn Feier* (1976) is an environmental theatre piece that uses an entire city or university as its performance stage. All of the normal activities that take place in the environment are part of the performance, but there are also a large number of specialized performers—actors, groups of musicians, picketers carrying blank signs, and so on. In addition, there are a number of "costumed guardians" who stand near the sources of everyday environmental sounds (motors, practice rooms, traffic) and point them out to people who pass by. The piece ends with a "final ritual" in which the performers move in a circle around a bonfire chanting "Feier" (the German word for a celebration or festival) "until each person can no longer participate."[3]

Other works seem at first to be hopelessly absurd, but the underlying purpose may still be serious. A movement of Mortimore's *Very Circular Pieces* (1970) contains the performance instruction "Play until 2000 A.D." What are we to do with this? Does it mean the piece is not to be performed at all? Or are we to keep it in our minds until the year 2000? Or is the purpose to encourage us to meditate on the coming millennium? And what about Paul Ignace's *Symphonie Fantastique No. 2,* a duplication of the Berlioz work sprung upon an unsuspecting concert audience, many of whom had heard the Berlioz the previous night? Is the purpose here humor, surprise, or, as the composer suggests, to get people to listen to the music in a new way?[4]

The list of musics "on the fringe" goes on and on. There is, for example, "biofeedback music," in which the performers control the sounds by means of changing the alpha-wave output from their brains. More sinister is a category that David Cope calls "danger music."[5] Some of it suggests self-directed violence, as in Takehisa Kosugi's *Music for a Revolution*, which begins, "Scoop out one of your eyes five, years from now,"[6] while others, such as Philip Corner's *One Antipersonnel-Type CBU Bomb Will Be Thrown into the Audience*, are more threatening to the audience.

Lively accounts of these and other "fringe" movements can be found in the books by Cope and Michael Nyman listed at the end of this chapter.

SUMMARY

Experimental music, in which the composer consciously abdicates control over the compositional process or the performance, or both, has been an important element of music in the second half of the twentieth century. Chance in composition has involved the use of a number of decision-making techniques, including the *I-Ching*, while the computer has made practicable aleatoric compositions that are much more complex. The element of chance (or, from the performer's viewpoint, choice) has been even more influential in the performance of music than in composition. The improvised portions of a score may be insignificant, or improvisation may be the major element of interest in the work. New notations have been devised for indeterminate music, including proportional and graphic notation; text scores dispense with notation entirely. Finally, a number of "fringe" movements have ranged from the absurd to the violent, calling into question our notion of what music really is.

NOTES

1. Do not make the all-too-common error of confusing computer sound synthesis (see Chapter 12) with computer composition. Either or both may be employed in a particular composition.
2. Robin Maconie, *The Works of Karlheinz Stockhausen*, p. 101.
3. Oliveros, *Bonn Feier* (Smith Publications, 1977).
4. Cope, *New Directions in Music*, pp. 303–4.
5. Cope, *New Directions*, p. 306.
6. Michael Nyman, *Experimental Music*, p. 68.

EXERCISES

Part A: Analysis

1. Study the pitch material in each of the three choirs in Example 14–6, remembering that the score is written at concert pitch and that an accidental applies only to the note it precedes.
    a. What is similar about the pitch material in the three choirs?
    b. Analyze the pitch-class set types found in each choir.
    c. Do the pitch classes used in the winds complete an aggregate?
    d. How does the pitch material in the three choirs relate to the E's that open the movement?

2. Look up the word "music" in at least two dictionaries, and copy out the definitions. (Use standard dictionaries—"music" is not defined in *The New Harvard Dictionary of Music*.) Then relate those definitions to the kinds of works discussed in this chapter. Do some of the works lie outside the definitions, and if so, should the definitions be changed? Are the definitions even too restrictive for more conservative twentieth-century music? Can you suggest a better definition for "music," or a term for the kinds of pieces that you feel are not really music?

Part B: Composition and Performance

1. Compose and rehearse an improvisatory piece for ensemble. Try to restrict the choices of the performers so that the piece will have the same basic shape each time it is performed. Explain how your controls will satisfy the assignment. Then perform it twice for the class.

2. Compose a graphic score to be performed by a soloist (unspecified medium), with few instructions. Explain (to your instructor) how you decided on the arrangement of the graphic symbols and how they might be interpreted. Have it performed by a volunteer from your class.

3. Compose a short piece for some instrument in your class in which some of the compositional decisions are made by random choice (flipping coins, etc.), and explain how you composed it. Make two versions of the piece, and have both performed for the class.

Part C: Further Reading

BATEMAN, WAYNE. *Introduction to Computer Music.* See Chapter 11, "Composition with the Computer."

BRINDLE, REGINALD SMITH. *The New Music.* See Chapter 8, "Indeterminacy, Chance, and Aleatory Music"; Chapter 9, "Improvisation—Graphic Scores—Text Scores"; and Chapter 12, "Cage and Other Americans."

CHILDS, BARNEY. "Indeterminacy," in John Vinton, ed., *Dictionary of Contemporary Music.*

COPE, DAVID H. *New Directions in Music.* See Chapter 8, "Improvisation"; Chapter 9, "Indeterminacy"; and Chapter 10, "The New Experimentalism."

DALLIN, LEON. *Techniques of Twentieth Century Composition.* See Chapter 18, "Indeterminate Procedures."

DODGE, CHARLES, AND THOMAS A. JERSE. *Computer Music.* See Chapter 8, "Composition with Computers."

GRIFFITHS, PAUL. "Aleatory," in Stanley Sadie, ed., *The New Grove Dictionary of Music and Musicians.*

————. *Modern Music.* See Chapter 7, "Chance and Choice," and Chapter 10, "Indeterminacy—Changing the System."

KARKOSCHKA, ERHARD. *Notation in New Music.*

KOSTELANETZ, RICHARD. ED. *John Cage.*

NYMAN, MICHAEL. *Experimental Music.* See Chapter 3, "Inauguration 1950–60: Feldman, Brown, Wolff, Cage"; Chapter 4, "Seeing, Hearing: Flexus"; Chapter 5, "Electronic Systems"; and Chapter 6, "Indeterminacy 1960–70: Ichiyanagi, Ashley, Wolff, Cardew, Scratch Orchestra."

SIMMS, BRYAN. *Music of the Twentieth Century.* See Chapter 13, "Indeterminacy."

STONE, KURT. *Music Notation in the Twentieth Century.*

15 | Minimalism and Neoromanticism

INTRODUCTION

Minimalism and neoromanticism, two important trends in more recent music, are the subject of this chapter. Whereas American music has long been viewed by Europeans and Americans alike as an offshoot of the European musical tradition, minimalism and neoromanticism both developed first in the United States and only later were adopted by European composers. Another aspect shared by these two styles is that they are both tonal, with few exceptions, and, as we will see, the harmonic styles that they employ are often remarkably traditional.

MINIMALISM

Minimal music, also called *process music*, *phase music*, *pulse music*, *systemic music*, and *repetitive music*, may have had its roots in some of the works that Cage, Wolff, and Feldman composed in the 1950s, but the first important example of what has become known as minimalism was Terry Riley's *In C* (1964). This composition, still well known after a quarter-century, exemplifies most of the characteristics of the minimalist style, and we will discuss it in some detail.

In C is a composition of unspecified duration to be performed by an unspecified ensemble. The score consists of 53 figures—most of them quite short—that are to be performed in order. Each motive is repeated as often as the individual performer desires, except that the performer has an obligation to contribute to the overall ensemble effect. This means that the performers more or less randomly follow each other through the score, sometimes leading the rest of the ensemble, at other times lagging behind, so that several motives may be heard simultaneously, even though gradual progress is being made toward ending the piece. This process, sometimes called "phasing," resembles that of a traditional canon, which is why *In C* was discussed in Chapter 7 under the heading "Canon and Fugue" (see p. 156).

The pitch material of the figures is extremely limited, very different from the complex motivic material of the avant-garde composers of the same period. They begin by establishing C major (see figures 1–2 in Example 15–1). A half-cadence on the dominant is reached at figure 15 (see figures 14–15), followed by an E minor section in figures 18–28 (see figure 22). After a return to C in 29–34 (see figure 29), a tonally ambiguous climax

EXAMPLE 15–1   Riley: *In C* (1964), Figures 1, 2, 14, 15, 22, 29, 35, 52, 53   *(Used by permission of the composer.)*

is reached at 35 (see figure 35). The remainder of the piece seems to return to C for a while but ends in G minor (see figures 52–53). Superimposed over this modulating canon is a constant pulse, or ostinato, provided by a pianist playing the two highest C's on the instrument in steady eighth-notes.

In all, the work employs only nine of the twelve pitch classes, and the nine are introduced gradually:

Figure	New Pitch Class
1	C, E
2	F
4	G
9	B
14	F♯
22	A
35	B♭
45	D

Because it occurs so rarely, the introduction of a new pitch class, or of a new register, becomes a major event in the piece. Even without mentally cataloguing the pitch material used up to that point, the listener is immediately affected, even shocked, by the appearance of a previously unheard pitch.

Many of the characteristics of minimalism have been encountered in our discussion of *In C*. These characteristics would include the following:

Restricted pitch and rhythm materials
Tonal (or neotonal) language
Diatonicism
Use of repetition
Phasing
Drones or ostinatos
Steady pulse
Static harmony
Indeterminacy
Long duration

Many of these aspects are also found in some kinds of Eastern music, as is the meditative quality characteristic of many minimalist works. Riley, Steve

Reich, and Philip Glass, the three Americans most closely associated with minimalism, all studied Eastern music, Glass's study of the improvisations of Ravi Shankar being especially important to the development of his mature style.[1]

Reich's *Come Out* (1966) was mentioned in Chapter 12 in reference to the tape loops that were used to construct the piece (see p. 261). *Come Out* concentrates on the phasing aspect of minimalism, taking it much further than *In C* does, and it incidentally illustrates the interest that some twentieth-century composers have had in mixing their music with politics. In this case, a victim of police violence during the 1964 Harlem riots wanted to prove that he was injured so that he would be taken to the hospital. He explains, "I had to, like, open the bruise up and let some of the bruise blood come out to show them." The words "come out to show them" were transferred to two loops and played simultaneously, but since no two tape players operate at precisely the same speed, the words move gradually out of phase. A recording of that process was in turn converted into two loops, and so on, building up the texture of the work to a dense and complex level.[2]

Notice that the phasing process in *Come Out* is different from that used in *In C*, because in *Come Out* the part that takes the lead keeps it and pulls ever farther ahead of the follower. Reich used the same approach for live performers in *Piano Phase* (1967). In this work the two pianists repeat in unison the pattern seen in Example 15–2, but soon Piano II increases the tempo slightly until the two instruments are one sixteenth-note apart. This process is repeated until Piano II completes the "loop" and rejoins Piano I in unison.

EXAMPLE 15–2   Reich: *Piano Phase* (1967), m. 1   *(© copyright 1980 by Universal Edition (London) Ltd., London. All rights reserved. Used by permission of European American Music Distributors Corporation, sole U.S. and Canadian agent for Universal Edition London.)*

Gradually moving out of phase as in *Piano Phase* is difficult for performers to accomplish. Reich employs a simpler solution in *Clapping Music* (1972). Here the two performers clap the first measure in unison twelve times. They then move on to the second measure, in which the pattern in the Clap 2 part has been shifted one eighth-note to the left. After twelve times through this measure, the performers move on to the next, where Clap 2 is shifted one more eighth-note, and so on, until they are once more in unison.

A variation on the phasing technique was introduced by Reich in *Drumming* (1971) and *Six Pianos* (1973) (rescored as *Six Marimbas* in 1986). *Six Pianos* begins with four of the pianists playing a repeated rhythmic pattern in unison (rhythmic unison, not pitch unison). The two "out-of-phase" pianists, in unison with each other, gradually introduce a rhythmic pattern that, when completed, turns out to be the same as the original one, but two beats out of phase with it. Similar techniques are used in Reich's *Sextet* (1985). An important difference between this technique and the earlier phase pieces is that in this case the relationship between the two out-of-phase parts does not change through time.

Though phasing is important in many of Reich's pieces, this is not true of all minimalist music.[3] Frederic Rzewski's *Coming Together* (1972), for example, another work with political overtones, is for a narrator accompanied by a single musical line, so phasing is impossible. Glass's *Strung Out* (1967) is for a single amplified violin, which begins by stating the central motive of the piece, seen in Example 15–3. Like *In C*, it gradually introduces pitches, in this case all diatonic to C major, until the climax of the piece is reached about 10'30" into the performance, after which the entire piece is repeated. Though the gradual introduction of pitches is important, the listener's attention is also drawn to the variation of the original motive, as well as to the two startling changes of bow technique (at about 2'50" and 6'25").

EXAMPLE 15–3   Glass: *Strung Out* (1967), opening five notes   *(© 1984 Theodore Presser Company. Used by permission of the publisher.)*

Nor is phasing a factor in Glass's ensemble works. Instead, the focus is on repetition, pulse, and triadic harmony. His music is insistently tonal, with harmonic progressions that range from banal to surprising. An example on the banal side is *Modern Love Waltz* (1977), where the harmony alternates throughout between an A major triad or an A dominant 7th chord and a B♭ dominant 7th chord.

The usual approach that Glass takes in his more recent music is to establish a tempo through a pulsating background chord, over which various accompanimental figurations are laid. Changes of harmony follow, without disturbing the pulse or the accompanimental figures. After some time, an abrupt shift of tonal center, while maintaining the original pulse, announces a new section with new accompanimental figures. Melody in the traditional sense is absent. Glass frequently uses a singer in his works, but the vocalist usually has no text and instead is treated as an instrument.

Glass has achieved substantial popular success, enabling him to embark on larger projects. These include the operas *Einstein on the Beach* (1975), *Satyagraha* (1980), *The Photographer* (1983), *the CIVIL warS* (1984) and *Akhnaten* (1985), and the movie score for *Koyaanisqatsi* (1982), as well as collaborations with various dance companies.

The influence of the minimalists has been considerable. In the United States this can be seen in the music of Laurie Anderson, a "performance artist" whose work lies somewhere between the traditionally popular and traditionally serious, and in rock music in groups such as Tirez Tirez. A number of younger composers like John Adams (*Shaker Loops* [1978], *Nixon in China* [1987]) have adapted the style to their own requirements, and minimalism has also been important in dance choreography. In Europe, minimalism has had an influence on the music of a large number of composers and experimental rock groups.[4] Unfortunately, the student of this music will find that much of it is available only in recorded form, so the analytical process must be predominantly aural.

NEOROMANTICISM

In Chapter 8 we discussed the use of musical quotations in twentieth-century music, especially in music composed in the mid-1960s and later. In most cases these fragments were quoted out of context, superimposed on an atonal, avant-garde background, or swallowed up in a collage of other quotations in a stream-of-consciousness style. In the music of George Rochberg, this quotation technique led eventually to a "real and personal rapprochement with the past"[5] in the form of a traditional tonal style with a distinctive Romantic flavor, a style that is often referred to as neoromanticism.

Rochberg's first neoromantic work was his String Quartet No. 3 (1972). The beginning of the first movement[6] is devoted to the kind of dissonant and disjunct figure that one might expect at the outset of an atonal work (Example 15–4). A more lyrical, yet still dissonant, figure interrupts at m. 27, but the dissonant opening motive returns in m. 40. Another lyrical section, related to the one at m. 27, begins at m. 64, and

EXAMPLE 15–4   Rochberg: String Quartet No. 3 (1972), I, m. 1   *(Copyright © 1973, 1976 by Galaxy Music Corp., New York. Used with permission.)*

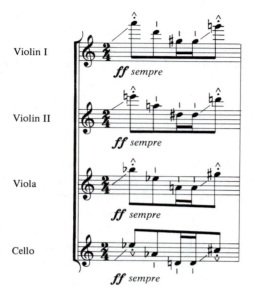

EXAMPLE 15–5   Rochberg: String Quartet No. 3 (1972), I, mm. 81–102   *(Copyright © 1973, 1976 by Galaxy Music Corp., New York. Used with permission.)*

NB: Vlns. 1-2 still rubato; loose

contains elements of polytonality and the whole-tone scale. This leads to the passage shown in Example 15–5. In that excerpt, at m. 87 a B major triad appears beneath the whole-tone/polytonal material. This is followed in mm. 90–102 by a conventional harmonic progression in the key of B major, although we are reminded from time to time of the whole-tone/bitonal material. This B major progression, though not a quotation, is handled in a manner that strongly suggests nineteenth-century music, yet it seems somehow to have a beauty and meaning that it would not possess if it appeared in a nineteenth-century composition. Its purity and the directness of its communication are striking when they are juxtaposed against the typically dissonant and symmetrical twentieth-century structures.

Not all of Rochberg's music since 1972 is neoromantic (his String Quartet No. 7 [1979], for example, is not at all in that style), but much of it is. Often Rochberg will include both tonal and atonal movements in the same work, rather than mixing the two together in a single movement as in Example 15–5. The first movement of his String Quartet No. 6 (1978) is atonal, but the second movement is a tonal scherzo and trio, and the third is a set of continuous variations on the tune from Pachelbel's Canon in D. Every movement but the fourth in his String Quartet No. 5 (1978) is in the neoromantic style; the third movement is a scherzo and trio in a familiar nineteenth-century idiom (see Example 15–6), although the careful observer might quibble with a few details, such as the parallel 5ths in m. 6.

EXAMPLE 15–6   Rochberg: String Quartet No. 5 (1978), III, mm. 1–8   *(Copyright © 1973, 1976 by Galaxy Music Corp., New York. Used with permission.)*

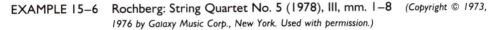

EXAMPLE 15–7   Penderecki: Symphony No. 2 (1980), mm. 1–8 (*© B. Schott's Soehne, Mainz, 1980. All rights reserved. Used by permission of European American Music Distributors Corporation, sole U.S. agent for B. Schott's Soehne.*)

Though Rochberg is the composer whose name is most closely associated with neoromanticism, he is not the only representative of the style. The series of works composed by David Del Tredici on Lewis Carroll's *Alice* stories are an important example. The best-known European associated with neoromanticism is Krzysztof Penderecki. His Symphony No. 2 (1980), for example, though chromatic, is clearly in F♯ minor. The beginning of this work, shown in Example 15–7, seems to suggest that key, but it soon shifts to F minor. Especially striking and Romantic in flavor is the progression B minor–F minor in mm. 6–7.

Some of the music of Frederic Rzewski might be considered neoromantic, although the motivation in his case often seems to be political instead of musical, an example being his piano variations on *The People United Will Never Be Defeated!* (1975). Finally, there is always the possibility that composers may decide to treat the Romantic era with irony and humor, just as the Baroque and Classical periods were treated by the neoclassical composers (see Chapter 8). This may be the case with pieces like Ladislav Kupkovič's *Requiem for My Suicide* (1982), a piano piece that might be described as a poor imitation of Chopin.

SUMMARY AND CONCLUSION

While the post-serial avant-garde tradition has not died out, it has certainly met with serious opposition in the forms of indeterminacy, minimalism, and neoromanticism. Indeterminacy, the subject of Chapter 14, was a reaction against the total control that is the basis for integral serialism. Minimalism opposes the atonal ideals of the incessant recycling of pitch material, of constant variation, and, of course, of atonality itself. Neoromanticism does these things too, but it represents also a complicated relationship between today's composer (and listener) and the music of the past.

And so twentieth-century music continues as it has always been—a maddening but fascinating collage of approaches and materials, a period without a style. It may be, of course, that the difference between composers and techniques that seem so blatant to us will seem to be only matters of detail to later generations, and that the music of the twentieth century will have a characteristic "sound" that will be easily identified, much as the sound of Haydn and Mozart represents a certain portion of the eighteenth century. But those who struggle to understand twentieth-century music are generally more impressed by its contrasts than by its consistencies.

One can't help but wonder about Brahms, who died in 1897 (when this writer's grandparents were teenagers): What would he think of what has happened to music, and could he have predicted in 1890 what music might be like in our time? Surely none of us can imagine what music will be like at the end of the twenty-first century, when the grandchildren of today's college students will themselves be grandparents, and the newest of today's music will represent a bygone era. It is enough, perhaps, if we can greet each turn in the musical road with an open mind, a receptive ear, and a sense of what has come before.

NOTES

1. John Rockwell, *All American Music*, p. 111.
2. Barry Schrader, *Introduction to Electro-Acoustic Music*, pp. 19–20.
3. Some writers prefer to treat phase music as a separate category from minimalism, since minimalist music does not always employ phasing, but they share many of the same characteristics and are often created by the same composers.
4. A representative list is given in Wim Mertens, *American Minimal Music*, p. 11, to which might be added the names of Simon Bainbridge (British) and Wolfgang Rihm (German).
5. Rochberg, in the liner notes for Nonesuch album H-71283, *George Rochberg: String Quartet No. 3*.
6. An analysis of the first 100 measures of this movement appears in Jay Reese, "Rochberg the Progressive," in *Perspectives of New Music*.

EXERCISES

Part A: Analysis

1. Listen to a recording of Riley's *In C* (1964). Excerpts from this work are given in Example 15–1. Try to notate the other figures that make up the work.

2. Listen to a recording of Glass's *Strung Out* (1967). The opening is given in Example 15–2. Using a watch with a second hand, identify the introduction of new pitches (not pitch classes) as well as other significant events in the piece, such as changes in articulation. The piece is played twice without pause on the only available recording.

3. Analyze the harmonies and nonchord tones of the B major progression in Example 15–5.

4. Do the same for Example 15–6 (entire excerpt). You will find two chords that are almost traditional augmented-6th chords, but not quite.

5. Listen to the entire third movement of Rochberg's String Quartet No. 5. Diagram the form. Identify as many tonal areas and important cadences as you can (the movement begins in A minor).

6. Listen to the entire third movement of Rochberg's String Quartet No. 6. Write down the two lines that constitute the four-measure theme (the key is D major). Then try to follow the theme through the subsequent variations. After several variations (how many?), the theme is augmented into an eight-measure form for one variation—this happens again later. In other variations, the original lines of the theme are almost totally obscured, but the basic four-bar structure is still audible in most cases. Rochberg occasionally ends a variation on I instead of V, and in two variations he inverts the descending contour of the original melody. Try to identify and characterize each variation.

Part B: Composition

1. Compose *In F*, an imitation of Riley's *In C*, for instruments and/or vocalists in your class. See the discussion of *In C* in the text.

2. Compose a phase piece in imitation of Reich's *Clapping Music* for some combination of performers in your class. See the discussion of this work in the text.

3. Try to compose a neoromantic excerpt in imitation of the first movement of Rochberg's String Quartet No. 3. This is a difficult assignment, because the tonal music should not sound silly or mawkish when it enters. Write this for some combination of performers in your class.

Part C: Further Reading

COPE, DAVID H. *New Directions in Music*. See "Minimal and Concept Music" (pp. 309–14), "The New Tonality" (pp. 324–26), and the analysis of Rzewski's *Coming Together* (pp. 327–30).

GRIFFITHS, PAUL. *Modern Music*. See "Minimal Music" (pp. 176–81).

MERTENS, WIM. *American Minimal Music*.

NYMAN, MICHAEL. *Experimental Music*. See Chapter 7, "Minimal Music, Determinacy, and the New Tonality."

REESE, JAY. "Rochberg the Progressive."

SCHWARZ, K. ROBERT. "Steve Reich: Music as a Gradual Process."

SIMMS, BRYAN R. *Music of the Twentieth Century*. See Chapter 16, "Recent Music in Europe and America."

Bibliography

ALDWELL, EDWARD, AND CARL SCHACHTER. *Harmony and Voice Leading*. New York: Harcourt Brace Jovanovich, 1979.

APPLETON, JOHN H., AND RONALD C. PERERA, EDS. *The Development and Practice of Electronic Music*. Englewood Cliffs, NJ: Prentice-Hall, 1975.

AUSTIN, WILLIAM W. *Music in the 20th Century*. New York: W. W. Norton, 1966.

BARTOLOZZI, BRUNO. *New Sounds for Woodwind*, Translated and edited by Reginald Smith Brindle. London: Oxford University Press, 1967.

BATEMAN, WAYNE. *Introduction to Computer Music*. New York: John Wiley, 1980.

BENWARD, BRUCE. *Music in Theory and Practice*. 3rd ed. Dubuque, IA: Wm. C. Brown, 1986.

BERRY, WALLACE. *Form in Music*. 2nd ed. Englewood Cliffs, NJ: Prentice-Hall, 1986.

_____. *Structural Functions in Music*. Mineola, NY: Dover, 1987.

BRINDLE, REGINALD SMITH. *Contemporary Percussion*. London: Oxford University Press, 1970.

_____. *Musical Composition*. London: Oxford University Press, 1986.

_____. *The New Music*. London: Oxford University Press, 1975.

_____. *Serial Composition*. London: Oxford University Press, 1966.

BUNGER, RICHARD. *The Well-Prepared Piano*. Colorado Springs, CO: Colorado College Music Press, 1973.

CARR, IAN. *Miles Davis*. New York: William Morrow, 1982.

CHOU, WEN-CHUNG. "Asian Concepts and Twentieth-Century Western Composers," *Musical Quarterly* 57:2 (April 1971), pp. 211–29.

CHRIST, WILLIAM, AND OTHERS. *Materials and Structure of Music*. 2nd ed. Englewood Cliffs, NJ: Prentice-Hall, 1973.

COGAN, ROBERT, AND POZZI ESCOT. *Sonic Design*. Englewood Cliffs, NJ: Prentice-Hall, 1976.

COPE, DAVID H. *New Directions in Music*. 4th ed. Dubuque, IA: Wm. C. Brown, 1984.

CRAFT, ROBERT. *Stravinsky: Chronicle of a Friendship, 1948–71*. New York: Alfred A. Knopf, 1972.

DALLIN, LEON. *Techniques of Twentieth Century Composition*. 3rd ed. Dubuque, IA: Wm. C. Brown, 1974.

DEMPSTER, STUART. *The Modern Trombone*. Berkeley, CA: University of California Press, 1979.

DESTWOLINSKY, GAIL. *Form and Content in Instrumental Music*. Dubuque, IA: Wm. C. Brown, 1977.

DODGE, CHARLES, AND THOMAS A. JERSE. *Computer Music*. New York: Schirmer Books, 1985.

DWYER, TERENCE. *Composing with Tape Recorders*. London: Oxford University Press, 1971.

ERICKSON, ROBERT. *Sound Structure in Music*. Berkeley, CA: University of California Press, 1975.

FINK, ROBERT, AND ROBERT RICCI. *The Language of Twentieth Century Music*. New York: Schirmer Books, 1975.

FORTE, ALLEN. *The Structure of Atonal Music*. New Haven, CT: Yale University Press, 1973.

GARIÉPY, LOUISE AND JEAN DÉCARIE. "A System of Notation for Electro-Acoustic Music: A Proposition." *Interface* 13:1 (March 1984), pp. 1–74.

GRIFFITHS, PAUL. *Modern Music*. London: J. M. Dent & Sons, 1981.

GRIMES, EV. "Ev Grimes Interviews John Cage." *Music Educators Journal* 73:3 (November 1986), pp. 47–49ff.

GROUT, DONALD JAY. *A History of Western Music*. 3rd ed. New York: W. W. Norton, 1980.

HARDER, PAUL O. *Bridge to 20th Century Music*. Boston: Allyn and Bacon, 1973.

HEISS, JOHN C. "Some Multiple-Sonorities for Flute, Oboe, Clarinet, and Bassoon." *Perspectives of New Music* 7:1 (Fall–Winter 1968), pp. 136–42.

HICKS, MICHAEL. "Text, Music, and Meaning in the Third Movement of Luciano Berio's *Sinfonia*." *Perspectives in New Music* 20 (1981–82), pp. 199–224.

HINDEMITH, PAUL. *Craft of Musical Composition*. London: Schott, 1968.

HOWAT, ROY. "Bartók, Lendvai, and the Principles of Proportional Analysis." *Music Analysis* 2:1 (March 1983), pp. 69–95.

HOWE, HUBERT S. *Electronic Music Synthesis*. New York: W. W. Norton, 1975.

HOWELL, THOMAS. *The Avant-Garde Flute*. Berkeley: University of California Press, 1974.

KARKOSCHKA, ERHARD. *Notation in New Music*. Translated by Ruth Koenig. New York: Praeger, 1972.

KENNAN, KENT, AND DONALD GRANTHAM. *The Technique of Orchestration*. 3rd ed. Englewood Cliffs, NJ: Prentice-Hall, 1983.

KOSTELANETZ, RICHARD, ED. *John Cage*. New York: Praeger, 1970.

KOSTKA, STEFAN AND DOROTHY PAYNE. *Tonal Harmony with an Introduction to Twentieth-Century Music*. 2nd ed. New York: Alfred A. Knopf, 1989.

KRAMER, JONATHAN D. "The Fibonacci Series in Twentieth Century Music." *Journal of Music Theory* 17:1 (Spring 1973), pp. 111–48.

————. "Moment Form in Twentieth Century Music." *Musical Quarterly* 64:2 (April 1978), pp. 177–94.

KŘENEK, ERNST. *Studies in Counterpoint*. New York: G. Schirmer, 1940.

LENDVAI, ERNÖ. *Béla Bartók: An Analysis of His Music*. London: Kahn & Averill, 1971.

MACONIE, ROBIN. *The Works of Karlheinz Stockhausen*. London: Oxford University Press, 1976.

MAEGAARD, JAN. "A Study in the Chronology of op. 23–26 by Arnold Schoenberg." *Dansk aarbog for musikforskning* (1962), pp. 93–115.

MERTENS, WIM. *American Minimal Music*. New York: Alexander Broude, 1983.

MESSIAEN, OLIVIER. *The Technique of My Musical Language*. Paris: Alphonse Leduc, 1944.

NYMAN, MICHAEL. *Experimental Music*. New York: Schirmer Books, 1974.

OSMOND-SMITH, DAVID. *Playing on Words*. London: Royal Music Association, 1985.

PARTCH, HARRY. *Genesis of a Music*. 2nd ed. New York: Da Capo, 1974.

PERLE, GEORGE. *Serial Composition and Atonality*. 5th ed. Berkeley: University of California Press, 1981.

PERSICHETTI, VINCENT. *Twentieth-Century Harmony*. New York: W. W. Norton, 1961.

PISTON, WALTER. *Harmony*. 5th ed. Revised by Mark DeVoto. New York: W. W. Norton, 1987.

PROCTOR, GREGORY. "Technical Bases of Nineteenth-Century Chromatic Harmony: A study in Chromaticism." Ph.D. Diss., Princeton University, 1978.

RAHN, JOHN. *Basic Atonal Theory*. New York: Longman, 1980.

READ, GARDNER. *Contemporary Instrumental Techniques*. New York: Schirmer Books, 1976.

REESE, JAY. "Rochberg the Progressive." *Perspectives of New Music* 19 (1980–81), pp. 394–407.

REID, SARAH. "Tonality's Changing Role: A Survey of Non-Concentric Instrumental Works of the Nineteenth Century." Ph.D. Diss., University of Texas, 1980.

RINGO, JAMES. "The Lure of the Orient." *American Composers Alliance Bulletin* 7:2 (1958), pp. 8–12.

ROCKWELL, JOHN. *All American Music*. New York: Alfred A. Knopf, 1983.

SADIE, STANLEY, ED. *The New Grove Dictionary of Music and Musicians*. London: Macmillan, 1980.

SALZEDO, CARLOS. *Modern Study of the Harp*. New York: G. Schirmer, 1921.

SAMSON, JIM. *Music in Transition*. New York: W. W. Norton, 1977.

SCHMALFELDT, JANET. *Berg's Wozzeck*. New Haven, CT: Yale University Press, 1983.

SCHOENBERG, ARNOLD. *Style and Idea*. Berkeley, CA: University of California Press, 1984.

SCHRADER, BARRY. *Introduction to Electro-Acoustic Music*. Englewood Cliffs, NJ: Prentice-Hall, 1982.

SCHWARZ, K. ROBERT. "Steve Reich: Music as a Gradual Process." *Perspectives of New Music* 19 (1980–81), pp. 373–92; 20 (1981–82), pp. 225–86.

SHIR-CLIFF, JUSTINE, AND OTHERS. *Chromatic Harmony*. New York: The Free Press, 1965.

SIMMS, BRYAN R. *Music of the Twentieth Century*. New York: Schirmer Books, 1986.

SMITHER, HOWARD E. "The Rhythmic Analysis of Twentieth-Century Music." *Journal of Music Theory* 8:1 (Spring 1964), pp. 54–88.

STONE, KURT. *Music Notation in the Twentieth Century*. New York: W. W. Norton, 1980.

STRAVINSKY, IGOR. *Poetics of Music*. Cambridge, MA: Harvard University Press, 1947.

TURETZKY, BERTRAM. *The Contemporary Contrabass*. Berkeley, CA: University of California Press, 1974.

ULEHLA, LUDMILA. *Contemporary Harmony*. New York: The Free Press, 1966.

VAN DEN TOORN, PIETER C. *The Music of Igor Stravinsky*. New Haven, CT: Yale University Press, 1983.

VINCENT, JOHN. *The Diatonic Modes in Modern Music*. New York: Mills Music, 1951.

VINTON, JOHN, ED. *Dictionary of Contemporary Music*. New York: E. P. Dutton, 1974.

WEBERN, ANTON. *The Path to the New Music*. Edited by Willi Reich; translated by Leo Black. Bryn Mawr, PA: Theodore Presser, 1963.

WINOLD, ALLEN. *Harmony: Patterns and Principles*. Englewood Cliffs, NJ: Prentice-Hall, 1986.

WITTLICH, GARY, ED. *Aspects of Twentieth-Century Music*. Englewood Cliffs, NJ: Prentice-Hall, 1975.

WUORINEN, CHARLES. *Simple Composition*. New York: Longman, 1979.

YASSER, JOSEPH. *A Theory of Evolving Tonality*. New York: American Library of Musicology, 1932.

Index

Pages numbered in **boldface** contain musical examples.